Build Your Brain Power
The Art of Smart Thinking

Simon Wootton and
Terry Horne

D0994889

While every effort has been made to ensure that the contents of this book are as accurate and up to date as possible, neither the publisher nor the author(s) can be held responsible for any consequence arising from the use of information contained herein.

Build Your
Brain Power
The Art of Smart
Thinking

Simon Wootton and
Terry Horne

First published in Great Britain in 2015 by Hodder Education. An Hachette UK company.

Based on material previously published as *Train Your Brain*.

This edition published in 2015 by John Murray Learning

Copyright © Simon Wootton and Terry Horne 2015

British Library Cataloguing in Publication Data: a catalogue record for this title is available from the British Library.

Library of Congress Catalog Card Number: on file.

ISBN 9781473611801

e ISBN 9781473611818

1

Cover image © iStock

Typeset by Cenveo® Publisher Services.

Printed and bound in Great Britain by CPI Group (UK) Ltd., Croydon, CR0 4YY.

John Murray Learning policy is to use papers that are natural, renewable and recyclable products and made from wood grown in sustainable forests. The logging and manufacturing processes are expected to conform to the environmental regulations of the country of origin.

Hodder & Stoughton Ltd
Carmelite House
50 Victoria Embankment
London EC4Y 0DZ
www.hodder.co.uk

Also available in ebook

Acknowledgements

We are indebted to so many brain researchers (biologists, biochemists, neurologists, neuroscientists, dietitians, social workers and cognitive psychologists) and so many research centres specializing in brain research, that it is iniquitous to name only some individuals and some centres. That said we especially acknowledge that much of our material was first researched with, or by, Roger Armstrong at Lancashire Business School, University of Central Lancashire; Peter Checkland, University of Lancaster; Tony Doherty, Director of the Centre for Social Enterprise, University of London; P. J. Howard at the Centre for Cognitive Studies in Carolina, USA; Dr Kawashima in Japan and Cordelia Fine in Australia; Charles Handy, Rita Carter, Richard Nelson-Jones, Julian Baggini, Anne Thomson, Deborah Sumner, Tracy Bowell, John Haigh, John O'Keefe, John Stein and Brian Butterworth in the UK and James Fixx and his friends in MENSA USA.

This book has been a long journey with many companions, usually for part of the way. Part-way companions have included our many research students, undergraduates and postgraduates. We thank them for their legacy of findings and good questions.

We are grateful to each other for the very different skills that we bring to our common writing table. Without Simon's background as a biochemist and a manager it would have been harder to track Susan Greenfield's emerging model of the 'chemical brain' and to drive the project forward. Without the breadth of Terry's experience as a manager, writer, poet, educationist and philosopher, it would have been harder to develop the concepts of applied thinking and the programmes that can train your brain to use it.

Moreover, none of this would have been written accessibly if it were not for the tact and writing skills of our editor, Victoria Roddam. Unflappable and unfazed by our academic preoccupations, she resolutely returned our manuscripts until they were right for her readers. We are grateful for her guiding hand behind it all.

We thank finally our families: Fakhrun Nisa and Danya Horne; and Gillian, Ellis, James and Holly Wootton, for their sacrifices and support in this, our joint endeavour.

Contents

Meet the authors

Welcome to *Build Your Brain Power*!

We both started our adult lives as chemists: Terry specialized in the chemistry of complex organic molecules and Simon specialized in biochemistry. Later, while working for pharmaceutical companies like Pfizer and Eli Lilly, Simon was very involved with pharmaceutical drugs that effectively changed the chemistry of the brain, in order to help manage moods, or alleviate depression. At this point our career paths diverged. Simon moved into health services, both private and NHS, while Terry became interested in managers and how they thought about solving problems, taking decisions and making plans.

Happily, some years later, our career paths converged. Simon returned to university and, based on his research, together we wrote *Strategic Thinking*, one of Kogan Page's bestselling books on strategy. *Strategic Thinking* has been translated into Chinese, Spanish and Russian, and is on its third edition. With another research student, Tony Doherty, there followed *Managing Public Services – Implementing Changes: A Thoughtful Approach to the Practice of Management*, a bestselling book for Routledge, which is now in its third edition.

In the meantime, the number of students going to university had risen from 1 in 10 school leavers, to 4 in 10 school leavers. Many of these additional students had neither the thinking skills, nor the cognitive capacity to study properly for a degree. How could thinking skills and cognitive capacity be developed?

We put our heads together – literally – and began to think about the brain as if it were a chemical factory. In this we had support from Professor Susan Greenfield, one of the world's leading neuroscientists. Together, we produced what Susan Greenfield has since described as 'the world's most advanced models of the way the brain thinks.'

There are two important implications of our models of the way the brain thinks. Firstly, Simon knew that the chemical reactions which carry your thoughts through your brain can be made to go faster and further by changing the general chemical conditions in your brain; he also knew that you can learn to control those chemical conditions by choosing what you eat, what you do and how you feel. We had discovered that your effective intelligence was determined by your choices, and not just by your genes.

Secondly, Terry was fascinated by Susan Greenfield's idea of neuromodulation. This was the realization that once one of your thoughts had caused a particular neural pathway to be run, this changed the residual chemicals left along the neural pathway. Those chemicals then made it easier for that neural pathway to be run again. We had discovered that the very act of thinking strengthens your ability to think. It is now possible to design thinking activities which connect up different parts of your brain and which can then strengthen those connections.

The brain training books which Simon and Terry have written for managers, students, adults and the over 50s, are the result of a happy convergence of biochemistry and cognitive science.

Build Your Brain Power
Simon Wootton and Terry Horne

Foreword

We are living in a time of exciting yet frightening technological change. Our daily lives are being transformed in ways that would have been inconceivable even five or ten years ago. Suddenly a variety of new developments, be they in information technology, nanotechnology or biotechnology, seem to be converging and coming at once. These innovations are touching every corner of our lives, but perhaps the change which is the most relevant of all is that we are living longer and healthier lives. Sadly, this scenario does not entirely bring completely happy news. First, the fast pace of new technologies and how they change are making demands on our well-being as well as on our cognitive capacities in ways that would never have applied to previous generations. Stress (and with it the myriad problems of general health) is rampant in our current society in a way that was never spoken of even during the devastating world wars of the twentieth century. Moreover, the demands that employees may feel are made upon them may well precipitate an increase in psychiatric disorders. Indeed, the World Health Organization lists depression, which could soon be affecting as many as one in four, as the most serious disease this century.

Not only must our brains adapt to this new world, but the longer lives we are living mean that diseases of older people will come to the fore. Since medical progress is making such spectacular advances in the traditional spheres ranging from cancer and orthopaedics to transplant surgery, it is not surprising that the final frontier is indeed the brain. Alzheimer's disease worldwide is on the increase with 44 million people now suffering from the disease, and the total set to soar to 76 million by 2030. Intellectual giants such as Iris Murdoch and Bernard Levin, felled by this devastating disease, stand as a stark reminder to us all. The good news is that Alzheimer's disease is not a natural consequence of ageing: we know that although the incidence of the disease is increasing in proportion with the number of old people, it remains a specific problem. That of course does not stop the rest of us from being concerned about the deterioration of our brains, just as we might be worried about inefficient and less obliging muscles and joints as we age.

Over the last ten or twenty years, neuroscientists have learned much about the development and ageing of the brain. We now know that although you are born with pretty much all the brain cells you'll ever have, it is the growth of the connections between the brain cells that accounts for the growth of the brain after birth. So even if you are a clone, or an identical twin, you will have a unique configuration of brain cell connections where experience has, almost literally, left its mark on your brain. Perhaps the most famous incidence of this so-called 'neuronal plasticity' was reported some time ago with London taxi drivers. London taxi drivers are famed for having to undergo a rigorous exam of 'the knowledge' where they are compelled to learn, without recourse to a manual, all the street names and one-way systems of London. There is thus a huge burden on their working memory. Interestingly enough, in brain scans, this somewhat unusual daily burden on memory is actually reflected in the enlargement of the brain territory in an area related to memory, the hippocampus. Another more everyday example has been shown with a piano-playing experiment in which, even after five days, a group practising five-finger exercises had enhanced brain territory in the areas relating to finger movements, compared with no enhancements in a control group who simply had to stare at the piano for the same length of time. Even more interesting is that a third group, who merely imagined they were practising the exercises, showed a similar enhancement to those who were actually going through the motions! It is clear then that thinking also leaves its mark on the brain. There is no such distinction between 'mental' and 'physical'.

Moreover, we know that the more the brain is stimulated, as with the piano players and the taxi drivers, the more the brain cell connections will prosper, flourish and remain strong. Even in rats, a stimulating environment can lead to the growth of the branches from cells, which by increasing the surface area, increases the potential of those brain cells to form more connections. Clearly then our much prized 'cognitive and mental abilities' are now being traced to their physical bases in the brain.

The more we can understand about how to stimulate the brain in a way that promotes and sustains these connections, then clearly the more beneficial it will be – like exercise for the body in sustaining muscle strength. This book is a marvellous overview of the latest findings and observations that should enable us to do just that. Not only is it an up-to-date review of the latest thinking in science concerning diet, environment, stress and all the other factors that feature in modern life but, exceptionally, this is the first book to the best of my knowledge that gives practical advice on how to exploit those findings and apply them to your own life. There are easy to assimilate summaries, and the material to be covered is made clear at the beginning of each chapter. In addition, there are exercises and helpful appendices, all making for an enjoyable and comprehensive read. This book will exercise your brain in two ways: on the one hand by your following the exercises and advice that it gives; on the other hand even just reading it should make you pause and reflect on just how wonderful your brain and mind are, and how they are worth preserving.

Professor Susan Greenfield

First thoughts

Brain science and brain development in adults

COGNITIVE SCIENCE AND THE FRACTURED SKULL

During the last century, world wars and motorbikes cracked many skulls and, as a result, brain science made rapid progress! The effects of these head injuries were studied by biologists, mathematicians, physicists, chemists, psychologists, pharmacologists, sociologists and philosophers. Their collective studies gave birth to what we now call 'cognitive science'.

As cognitive science grew, so did ideas about the way the brain could enable you to think reflectively, creatively and critically. Your brain gives you the ability to respond differently at different ages and stages of your life. It is the basis of your freedom to choose.

The consequences can be far reaching. '*I think therefore I am*', might become '*I can think differently, therefore I can be different.*' You are not entirely a prisoner of your genes.

From the 1960s onwards, cognitive scientists were able to provide scientific support for important human values, like personal freedom, personal choice, personal responsibility and personal development, at a time when such ideas were under attack from post-modernist thinkers. Cognitive science helped ideas like self-reliance and self-development to take root in education and to fuel political change. Cognitive science helps you to challenge the idea that your life is determined by the economic or social circumstances of your birth.

Almost 2,500 years ago, Socrates was already urging you to use your brain to question your life. He said, '*the unexamined life is not worth living*'. Cognitive science now holds out the possibility not only of examining your life, but of changing it, if you wish.

The mind–matter debate: does it really matter?

One idea that was popular in the 1970s and 1980s was that it was useful to view the brain as computer hardware and the mind as computer software. The idea is beguiling. There are many useful parallels. For example, when you turn off a computer, the software cannot work. Your brain needs a reliable supply of energy or it will suffer rather like your computer suffers. A computer needs background software, for example, the software that periodically clears 'garbage' and consolidates memory files. Your brain is the same – it has autonomic activities that operate when you are asleep. Likewise, just because a computer is turned on, it doesn't mean that all the software programs are running. Some programs need to be requested explicitly. In the brain, this 'requesting' is called 'metacognitive thinking'. It involves the part of the brain called the 'frontal cerebral cortex'. Many of the exercises in this book will help you to develop the frontal cortex of your brain, so that you can learn to direct your own thinking.

So enchanting is the computer metaphor that it still holds sway, despite being seriously challenged by Professor Susan Greenfield in her book, *The Human Brain*, which was published in 1997. She described how traditionally viewed products of the mind, like ideas or images, could cause chemical changes in the brain. Importantly for this book, cognitive science has demonstrated that mental exercises can change the chemical structures that underpin your memory and your intelligence.

Remember this

In the 1980s the process by which thinking took place in the brain seemed to be electrical. This led to analogies between computers and the brain. Although many of these analogies were helpful, they did tend to reinforce the idea that our capacity for thought was limited by the hardware we had inherited. The discovery that the process of thinking was chemical helped to free us from these limitations.

Brain research and brain scanning: lessons and limitations

Since the 1990s, ideas on brain training have benefited greatly from the ability to watch images of brains while their owners are thinking about different types of decisions, problems and plans. CAT (computerized axial tomography) scanners use computers to combine X-ray 'slices' of the brain and can be used to map the structures of the brain. PET (positron emission tomography) scanners, which follow traces of radioactive isotopes introduced into the brain fluid, are better for monitoring brain activity. The uses of these two types of scanner are limited, because overdoses of X-rays or radioactivity would be harmful. Much safer is the use of MRI scanners. MRI (magnetic resonance imaging) scanners use radiowaves to excite proteins in the brain. Changes in surrounding magnetic fields can then be used to monitor blood flows in different parts of the brain, in real time.

Health warning

The new technologies and tools of the cognitive scientist are impressive, but you should not suspend the healthy scepticism that our training in critical thinking will encourage. Brain scans, for example, show what is happening when people think. This is a correlation. Yet a correlation is not necessarily a cause, or a consequence. Remember also that the person under the scanner is not you. Throughout this book, we suggest plans of action that are clearly implied by the reasonable conclusions we have inferred from normally reliable sources. However, these tests were not carried out on you. As an individual you are unique. The action plans we offer may have been trialled by our students, but it is for you to decide how well they work for you.

Thinking and the brain: logical computer or chemical factory?

From the 1970s onwards, we have been trying to imagine what happens inside a person's brain, when they try to think. We, and others, were trying to help students, teachers, managers, therapists, social workers and public sector workers to learn to think more effectively about the kinds of decisions they needed to take, the kinds of problems they needed to solve, and the kinds of plans they needed to make.

At first, we were helped by the then prevailing model of brain-as-computer. However, we kept finding aspects of the ways our students were thinking that the computer model failed to explain. In 1997, Susan Greenfield's model of the brain as a chemical factory liberated us from the straitjacket of our computer model. Suddenly we could better understand the successes and the difficulties we were having with our students. Her neurochemical approach gave us ways to understand what we already knew.

At last, we could understand why, for many students, learning almost anything seemed to increase their capacity to learn, irrespective of the subject matter. For other students, lots of repetitions of relatively simple thinking tasks seemed to produce marked improvements in their capacity to think. This supported our emerging view that thinking was a skill, or rather a combination of ten or so contributory skills (see Figure 0.1).

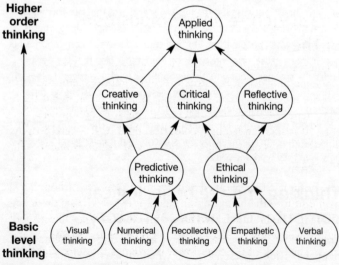

Figure 0.1 Applied thinking – a combination of ten thinking skills.
Source: Horne & Wootton, 2003.

Although logic remains the backbone of good thinking, it is a necessary but not sufficient condition for thinking well. Parts of the brain, other than the frontal cerebral cortex, seem to have a role to play if thinking is to be first-class applied thinking.

In *The Human Brain* (Greenfield, 1997), we found that, for example, the parts of your brain that control visual images, and the parts of your brain that empathize with the likely thoughts and feelings of other people, can work in concert with other parts of the brain that hold different facets of your memory. All these parts of the brain can help the frontal lobe of the cortex to take a more logical decision, or make a more rational plan. We discovered that otherwise matched groups of students who were encouraged to draw, sketch or map problem situations, could think more quickly and more accurately, and produce neater, more elegant solutions, than groups of students who were not directed to do so. Susan Greenfield's work gave us the confidence to extend our ideas on combination thinking, and to devise brain training exercises that involve the simultaneous use of different parts of the brain.

The structure and composition of the brain

If you want to build your brain power, it can be helpful to find out something about the structure and composition of the brain you are seeking to train. Inside your skull, your brain has the consistency of a sloppy undercooked egg. It has no moving parts. It is surrounded by a colourless fluid (CSF – cerebrospinal fluid), which is circulating constantly. CSF contains mainly salt and sugar.

The brain itself is wrinkled and creamy in colour. Although it would fit into the palm of your hand, it is as heavy as three bags of sugar. The brain has two halves and looks rather like a small cauliflower whose stalk tapers to become the top of your spinal cord. The back of the cauliflower overhangs the stalk slightly. The overhang is called the 'cerebellum'. The main part is called the 'cerebrum'.

If you turn the brain over, you will see distinct regions that occur in pairs; the underside of the brain appears to be symmetrical about a central line running from the front to the back of the brain. That's the shape. What about the size, and does it really matter? Scientific studies across several animal species, including humans, challenge the notion that brain size alone is a measure of intelligence for example. Rather, scientists now argue, it is a brain's underlying organization and activity at its synapses (the communication junctions between neurons through which nerve impulses pass) that dictate intelligence, memory and other brain abilities.

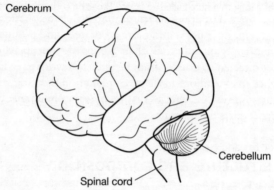

Figure 0.2 The brain.

Different jobs for different bits of the brain

Your cerebral cortex is divided into about 50 different areas, many of which have a definite specialized function. In some parts of the cortex, towards the back for instance (the posterior parietal cortex), the distinction between the areas is more blurred. The posterior parietal cortex handles many sensations – sound, sight, touch and movement.

The frontal lobes of mature learners become active when they are asked to empathize, make predictions or tackle problems that involve planning, complex decisions or creative thinking. Teenagers, or young adults under 25, often struggle with these kinds of thinking tasks. Often the development of the frontal area of their cerebral cortex lags behind the 'bushing' of their back brain, which is preoccupied with sensation and stimulation. Until the development of the frontal lobes catches up, young people are usually reluctant to volunteer verbal information and they can appear to be anti-social and to have 'heads like sieves' when it comes to remembering things.

Neurons – the building blocks of the brain

Neurons have a squat, blob-like body, called a 'soma', about 0.04 mm across. The soma sprouts tiny branches called 'dendrites'. Commonly, neurons appear elongated, with dendrites at either end, sometimes on the end of a long thin fibre called an 'axon'. The axon is commonly two to three times longer than the body of the neuron, though spinal neurons can trail axons a metre long. So, squat somas with stubby dendrite branches and long thin tails: these are your neurons, the building blocks of your intelligence, your personality, your hopes, your fears and your expectations.

The role of the soma is to ensure the survival of the neuron, but what about the dendrites and axons, what do they do?

▶ Dendrites and axons

The dendrites are receiving stations for chemical messages sent out by neighbouring neurons. The chemical messages converge down the dendrites into the neuron body. If the signals are strong enough, the neuron will generate an electrical charge that will be conducted down the axon, towards the dendrites of neighbouring neurons.

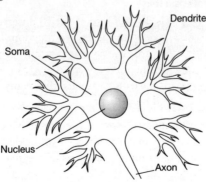

Figure 0.3 The soma.

The charges are carried by either positively-charged sodium, potassium or calcium cations, or by negatively-charged chloride anions. The charged anions and cations cannot normally pass through the fatty inter-layers of the neuron wall. However, an accumulation of negative charges on the inside of the wall of the neuron will attract, rather like a magnet, ions and proteins of opposite charge to the outside of the neuron wall, thereby generating a potential difference, or voltage, across the cell wall. When this voltage reaches about 80 millivolts (mV), channels open through the neuron walls to allow positively-charged ions (usually sodium) to enter the neuron to neutralize the negative charges on the inside of the neuron. When the charge inside the neuron becomes about 20 mV positive, then potassium ions, positively charged, are allowed through the wall of the neuron until a negatively-charged state is restored inside the neuron. All of this happens in a thousandth of a second.

Synapses: how to bridge that gap

What happens when the electrically-charged chemicals hit the gap between the end of the axon and the dendrite of a neighbouring neuron?

Until the 1950s, it was not possible to see into the synaptic gap – to see how the chemicals jumped across. With the advent of electron microscopes, which have magnification factors of over 10,000, chemicals were detected in the synaptic gap. Among the chemicals detected were many differently shaped molecules of acetylcholine derivatives. These acetylcholine derivatives belong to a general class of brain chemicals known as 'neurotransmitters'.

The more frequently that electrically-charged chemicals were seen arriving at the end of the axon, the more frequently acetylcholine neurotransmitters were seen to be launching themselves into the water in the synaptic gap. The small size of the neurotransmitters enabled them to diffuse very quickly across the salty water that surrounded the axons and dendrites. They crossed the gap in less than a millisecond, but how did they know which dendrite to choose?

Each neurotransmitter swimming across the gap is like a jigsaw piece, looking for a dendrite with a receptor molecule of exactly the right shape to make a perfect fit. Once the neurotransmitter finds and locks onto a correctly fitting receptor, this signals to the channel in the wall of the second neuron to admit a charged chemical. An accumulation of charged chemicals moves down the dendrites of the second neuron into the cell body, and out along the axon of the second neuron, to the edge of the next synaptic gap, where it stares across the water at a third neuron. This is going on inside your chemical brain 24 hours a day, a million times a second!

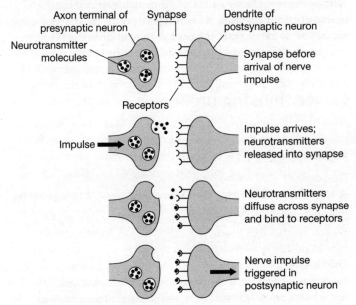

Figure 0.4 Transmitting nerve impulses.

The direction and speed of transmission of the electrical charges is determined by the direction and condition of the axons. If the axon is already connected to a dendrite of another neuron, then that predetermines the direction taken by the charge. If the axon is surrounded by a thick sheath of healthy myelin insulation, the transmission will be fast and accurate. Because we often wish to minimize the delay between one thought and the next, or between thought and action, chemical charges hustle down axons at more than 400 kph, provided the myelin insulation of the axon is in good enough condition.

Other thinking organs

We tend to think of our internal organs as specialists, highly refined machines that work all the time at specific tasks. The one exception is the brain which can make many decisions and manage our behaviour with incredible speed and efficiency.

Research now shows that the brain doesn't have a monopoly on this. The heart and stomach, for example, are fully equipped to do some thinking of their own. And sometimes they're giving the brain orders instead of taking them.

THE HEART

Work has revealed that the heart has a complex intrinsic nervous system that is sufficiently sophisticated to qualify as a 'little brain' in its own right. The heart's brain is an intricate network of several types of neurons, neurotransmitters, proteins and support cells similar to those found in the brain proper. Its elaborate circuitry enables it to act independently of the cranial brain – to learn, remember, and even feel and sense. The heart's nervous system contains around 40,000 neurons, called sensory neurons. Information from the heart – including feeling sensations – is sent to the brain through several nerves. These nerve pathways enter the brain at the area of the medulla, and cascade up into the higher centres of the brain, where they may influence perception, decision making and other cognitive processes.

THE STOMACH

The stomach does a lot more than produce acid for your last meal. It also fires off signals to the brain via its own extensive network of neurons. There are 100 million neurons in this 'brain'. This far outnumbers the neuron supply in the spinal cord or the rest of the nervous system outside of the brain.

Although not involved in conscious thought or decision making, the stomach brain enables the gut to make its own decisions regarding the behaviour of the digestive system. And the stomach has plenty to tell the brain as well. Research shows that about 90 per cent of the fibres in the vagus nerve – the main nerve for the gut – carry information from the gut to the brain. It turns out that 'butterflies' and that 'sinking feeling' in the stomach have a neurological basis. Neurons lining the stomach are filled with neurotransmitters, chemicals that help nerve cells communicate with one another. One key neurotransmitter is serotonin, which plays a major role in mood regulation. While serotonin is also found in the brain, 95 per cent of the body's supply is in the stomach. This abundance explains why drugs like Prozac, known as selective serotonin reuptake inhibitors (SSRIs), help elevate mood by increasing serotonin levels but may also cause stomach disturbances.

THE AMAZING BRAIN

It is the quantity (and quality) of neuron connections, not the number of neurons, that appears to determine your mental potential and your mental performance. This changes our view on the way the adult brain develops. Work by Siegler at Carnegie Mellon University (USA), in the late 1990s, on embryos, babies, pre-school infants, teenagers, adults and seniors, indicates that brain development is ongoing throughout adult life and that you need not accept the definite cut-offs that were once expected in the development of adult intelligence and in the applied thinking skills that contribute to it.

When we were young... and learning

The surfeit of synapses makes new learning easy for teenagers and young adults, but the lag in the development of the frontal cortex means that this area of a young person's brain must be engaged explicitly before critical thinking and reflective learning can fully exploit the learning potential promised by the young person.

Every year, the young adult brain can lose up to seven in a thousand of its neurons, causing the young adult brain to shrink and lose weight. In fact, neuron loss can be more than compensated for by learning things, almost anything, because learning increases the density of the synaptic connections in the neurons that remain. Also, by applying what you have learned or thought about, you can increase the thickness of the myelin insulation around the axons of the surviving neurons. This thicker myelin insulation results in quicker and clearer electrical transmission through the brain and more secure storage of information, with less risk of it being corrupted. Thicker myelination improves the recall of memories and the speed and accuracy of thinking. The brain training activities in this book are designed to promote both an increase in synaptic connections and a thickening of the myelin insulation in your brain.

UNREASONED AND UNREASONABLE BEHAVIOUR

The brain growth spurt that began when you were a teenager started at the back of your brain, heightening your awareness and sensitivity to sounds, lights, tastes and touch. Because the spurt in the middle of your brain came later, you might not have felt in control of your emotional reactions and impulses. Also, you might have felt awkward or clumsy in some movements. It was probably the lag in the development of your frontal cortex that was, or continues to be, your biggest disability. The frontal cortex is involved in reasoning, planning, predicting and decision making. Small wonder the behaviour of many young adults often seems unreasonable and lacking in direction and to have little regard for risk and consequence.

The young adult brain

It will come as a surprise to many exasperated parents and motor insurance companies that there is such a thing! Yet the young adult brain is often confused. Your brain experienced explosive dendrite growth when you were a teenager, and when you were a young adult your brain was bombarded by the stimulation of physical, emotional and social changes. As a young adult, your response to this excess capacity and stimulation was probably volatile. In 2004, brain imager Jay Giedd realized that this explosive growth in the young adult brain normally continues until the age of 25, much longer than had previously been thought. Giedd found that the development of the prefrontal cortex, the part of the brain that deals with decision making, tends to lag behind the development of the rest of the brain. No wonder young adults struggle with reasoning, planning and making decisions, unless they are given specific metacognitive teaching and support!

THE ADULT BRAIN

Normally, after the age of about 17, your brain will start to show a net loss of neurons. Your loss can be as high as seven to ten neurons a year out of every thousand you have, especially if you drink alcohol, or use certain other drugs (see Chapter 1). Don't panic! You can preserve and even improve your IQ, and the intelligence of your behaviour, as an adult. This is because many of the thinking skills that contribute to intelligent behaviour improve naturally as you get older, as long as you learn to use them explicitly when you need them. This kind of thinking is called 'applied thinking' and it is a precursor to more intelligent behaviour (see Chapter 4).

It is a mistaken belief that memory necessarily deteriorates with age. In fact, your ability to recall early knowledge and experiences may get better. This is because recall benefits from repetition and the older you are the more likely you are to have repeated the recall. On the other hand, what is likely to deteriorate as an adult is the speed at which you can form new memories. New information processing often does slow down. The brain training exercises in this book can help you avoid this. There are activities that can help to reverse any decline in processing speed and new memory formation that you may have already suffered (see Chapter 3). You can also learn to use predictive thinking skills, so that you can make an earlier start on thinking tasks that might otherwise be impaired by slower processing (see Chapter 8).

▶ Causes of damage and decline in the adult brain

It is fortunate that brain training can repair damage, because your adult brain is susceptible to damage from:

- ▶ alcohol (see Chapter 1)

- ▶ poor diet and food additives in processed food (see Chapter 1)

- ▶ lack of exercise (see Chapter 1)

- ▶ grief, low mood or pessimism (see Chapter 2)

- ▶ raised blood pressure and stress (see Chapter 5)

- ▶ all manner of environmental threats (see Chapter 5)

- ▶ lack of conversational relationships (see Chapter 10)

Overall, mental performance doesn't necessarily decline with age if you stay healthy. Certain illnesses and diseases can directly lower mental performance, but just getting older doesn't necessarily do so. People who do not use their brains productively as they get older tend to drag down the average scores for older adults and so obscure the high scores of those older people who use their brains actively.

Edward Coffey, of the Henry Ford Foundation, reported that even adults aged from 65 to 90, who used their brains actively, continued to perform well with no signs of loss of memory or reason, despite their MRI scans showing shrinkage in the size of their brains. In 2002, Quartz reported on a famous study of 4000 nuns. This study was commenced by David Snowdon in Kentucky, USA, in 1986. The study is particularly interesting because all the nuns have similar lifestyles but some continue to teach and to be mentally active and some don't. The nuns who continue to be mentally active are currently living, on average, four years longer, and their brain autopsies show, on average, 40 per cent more synapses and thicker myelin insulation on their axons.

Applied thinking appears to help you keep your brain healthier and to keep you living longer. Thinking adds years to your life and life into your years. So think on!

THE ADVANTAGES OF A CHEMICAL BRAIN

Chemicals react to different extents, and at different speeds, depending on the chemical environment in which the reaction takes place. You have the ability to change the chemical environment in which your brain is trying to do its chemical work. As a result, you can affect the extent and speed of the chemical reactions in your brain, and so improve its performance. You can change the chemical environment in your brain through diet, sleep, ergonomics and stress reduction, and by doing mental and physical exercises.

A chemical model of the brain can help you to understand how the frequent practice of separate and combined applied thinking skills, even at a relatively undemanding level, can progressively improve the speed and accuracy of your thinking, because each repetitive pass through a neuron increases the thickness of its myelin insulation.

Remember this: The chemicals in your cortex

The speed of chemical reactions, and the extent to which they are completed, can be affected by the presence and concentration of other chemicals in the vicinity. You can control the presence and concentration of the chemicals in your brain through what you eat, how you feel and what you do.

If a problem recurs, a chemical model of the thinking process leaves open the exciting possibility that you won't always come up with the same response, or solution. Because the neurons that are involved the first time are changed by that involvement, the chances are increased of a novel response should the same problem or input be presented a second time. This has important implications for the development of creative thinking (see Chapter 9). Not only do we think and learn, but the way we think and learn gets better in the process. In a chemical brain, the slightly threatening advice, '*Use it or lose it*', can be replaced by, '*Use it as much as you can, it can only get better*'.

However, it does seem to matter what you use it for, and how you use it. More chemical connections are generated by activities involving memory, calculation, problem solving, decision making, prediction and presentation than by physical activities alone.

Finally, a chemical brain holds out the prospect of improving mental functions during adulthood, rather than inevitable decline. Your brain weight will not decline significantly before you are 90 years of age and, on average, 80 per cent of your brain weight will still be left even at 90. That is more than enough neurons as long as they are well connected. And 80 per cent is an average. If you train your brain, your brain weight is likely to be above the average, like the nuns who are continuing to learn and teach.

Brain chemistry has shown that Alzheimer's and Parkinson's are diseases – illnesses. Illnesses may produce premature ageing, but they are not a necessary consequence of getting older. That is not to say that your neurons will not change at all during your old age. They will. Consequently, you may perform less well on time-constrained problem solving and on tasks that require rapid memorization of new information but, as is shown in *Keep Your Brain Sharp* (Horne and Wootton, 2010), these disadvantages can be more than compensated for by exploiting the many aspects of mental functioning that improve with age, like verbal reasoning, reflective learning, prediction and creativity. In the end, what matters most is not the weight of your brain, but the extent and quality of its interconnectedness, and this is helped by social learning, thoughtful conversation, meaningful relationships and broad experience. This book contains sections on each of these.

Focus points

✳ The brain is wrinkled, creamy in colour and surrounded by cerebrospinal fluid.

✳ The brain was once viewed as a computer.

✳ Brain scans enable scientists to watch images of your brain while you think about decisions, problems and plans.

✳ Your brain is like a chemical factory – you have a neurochemical brain.

✳ The brain has no structural moving parts.

✳ Different parts of your brain perform different roles.

✳ Neurons – brain cells – have dendrites and axons.

✳ Thinking involves chemical reactions along the axons of the neurons.

✳ How many interconnections you have between the different parts of your brain affects your intelligence.

✳ How frequently the interconnections have been used, determines how quickly and accurately they work.

Dig deeper

Giedd, J., 'What Makes Teens Tick', *Time* (10 May, 2004), p. 63.

Greenfield, S. A., *The Human Brain: A Guided Tour* (London: Weidenfeld & Nicolson, 1997).

Huizink, A., 'Prenatal stress and risk for psychopathology', *Psychological Bulletin* (January 2004).

Howard, P. J., *The Owner's Manual for the Brain: Everyday Applications from Mind and Brain Research* (3rd edn, Austin, Texas: Bard Press, 2006).

Quartz, S. R., and Sejnowski, T. J., *Liars, Lovers and Heroes* (New York: HarperCollins, 2002).

Schaie, K., *Intellectual Development in Adulthood: The Seattle Longitudinal Study* (Cambridge: Cambridge University Press, 1996).

Hadhazy A., *How the Guts Second brain influences Mood and Well Being*. Scientific Americans Feb 12, 2010

Next steps

* Keep learning.
* Keep your mind active.
* Learn new things, e.g. a new piano piece.
* Keep up ordinary activities, e.g. going for a walk, but on an unfamiliar route.
* Embrace a new hobby.

All of the above will keep the electricity flowing along your neurons a little better, a little longer.

PART ONE
AT HOME

1

Powering up your brain

In this chapter you will learn:

▶ *to eat the food your brain needs, when it needs it*

▶ *to minimize damage to your brain from alcohol, tea, coffee, cannabis, cola, ticks and cigarettes*

▶ *to use sleep, exercise, smart drugs, dark chocolate and sex to rejuvenate your brain.*

▶ *about our 'other brains'*

The state of your brain is as much a lifestyle choice, as a genetic inheritance.

Terry Horne, 2003

Introduction

Your brain can change in response to the way you exercise and the way you breathe. It can also change in response to what you eat, drink and smoke. It is changed by what you do and don't do. Your brain, it appears, can change its structure in response to your lifestyle. Your brain is able to adapt in this way because, according to the previous Chief Executive Officer (CEO) of the UK Medical Research Council ,Colin Blakemore, your brain is not only a chemical factory, it is an extremely busy chemical factory. Your brain needs energy for more than 1 million chemical reactions every second!

Your brain can be changed by what you do with it – hence we have designed exercises for you to do and puzzles and problems for you to solve. However, your brain is not only changed by what you do with it, it is also changed by what you do to it. Here, in Chapter 1, we look at what you do to your brain when you feed it, and what you can do to revive it. We will look at diet, exercise, sleep, sex and the effect of dark chocolate.

The need for vitamins and minerals

At least ten different B vitamins can affect the neurotransmitters in your brain. The B vitamins help in the formation of new neurotransmitters. Anderson found that people had difficulty in thinking and concentrating when their vitamin B1 levels were low.

VITAMINS: TO SUPPLEMENT OR NOT?
Any beneficial effects from vitamins C, B1 and B5, and the minerals boron, zinc and selenium, are better obtained through a long-term adjustment to the diet than through taking supplements. You can usefully increase the proportion of berries such as blackcurrants, redcurrants, bilberries, strawberries and especially blueberries in your diet. Also try increasing the proportion of spinach, green cabbage, broccoli and watercress.

Do not take iron tablets (unless your doctor advises you to do so due to, say, anaemia). Although in general your body will tell you what's good for you, when in doubt, you should consult your doctor.

Remember this: Better than popping pills

Many of the chemical reactions involved in thinking are sensitive to traces of certain minerals and vitamins. Chronic deficiencies of these minerals and vitamins can seriously impair performance. Taking action on what you routinely eat and drink is a more effective remedy for deficiency than taking tablets or vitamin supplements.

Food for thought

* Under normal circumstances, the brain uses mainly glucose for energy. With the aid of oxygen, B vitamins and minerals, the glucose is oxidized to produce water, carbon dioxide and energy – enough to fuel a million chemical reactions a second!
* Neurons, and the sheaths surrounding their axons, need to be kept in good condition and phosphatidyl choline is essential for that maintenance. But to work, Maguire discovered that phosphatidyl choline needs certain B vitamins.
* Folic acid and selenium have been found to boost cognitive functioning. Folic acid is found in dark leafy green vegetables. Selenium is a mineral found in seafood, wholegrain breads, nuts and meat.
* Connors reported that boron, iron and zinc improve mental activity. The mineral boron is found in broccoli, pears, peaches, grapes, nuts and dried beans. Zinc can be found in fish, beans and whole grains. The vitamin C in citrus fruits and salads enhances the absorption of iron. Iron helps to form ferroxyhaemoglobin, which is used to carry oxygen in the blood, through the body, to the brain.
* In humans, neurotransmitters like dopamine and norepinephrine are essential for mental alertness and acuity, and for high speed calculation, evaluation, and critical thinking. Eating protein increases the supply of neurotransmitters. The implication is that we should eat more protein if we wish to be mentally alert and quick-thinking. (Some of the lowest rates of dyslexia in the world are found in Japan, which has the highest per capita consumption of fish.)

THE DANGERS OF FAT-FREE DIETS!

By all means eliminate solid, saturated transfats from your diet. Transfats have no unsaturated bonds in them and so it is very hard for your body to break them down and get rid of them. They tend to hang around in your body, eventually clogging up your arteries and destroying your waistline. Transfats deprive your muscles and your brain of the oxygen they need to work effectively. They also interfere with two unsaturated fats, omega-3 and omega-6 that your brain really needs. Without unsaturated fats in your diet, your brain can't produce acetylcholine and without this, your brain cells will become 'stiff' and brittle. You will suffer memory loss and your thinking speed and accuracy will deteriorate. Such a fat-free diet will not only kill your brain cells, it may also kill you! De Angelis found that low-fat diets increased death rates from depression, suicide and accidents. Of course, obesity and heart disease also threaten your life and so it is understandable that you might want to diet to reduce your weight, but a very low-fat diet is not a safe way to do it.

Breakfast clubs and other myths

While it is true that children at school will find it hard to concentrate, think (and therefore learn) if they feel hungry, it matters crucially what it is that you insist they eat for breakfast. School breakfast clubs often offer toast (and jam) – often white toasted bread at that. This will rapidly metabolize into glucose and produce insulin-driven pangs of hunger well before lunch. Even milk and cereal (especially if sugary) will burn up within two hours. To work, breakfast clubs must serve protein and complex carbohydrates.

Remember this: 'When' is as important as 'what'

From the point of view of mental performance, even more important than what you eat seems to be when you eat it. Speed and accuracy of thinking are favoured by eating protein and complex hydrocarbons for breakfast and lunch and leaving simple carbohydrates, like sugary cakes, puddings and biscuits (if you must), until later in the day.

Try it now: Your daily bread

On days when you are involved in mainly mental, not physical, activity, try to eat complex carbohydrates, like fruit, salad and raw vegetables, and proteins, like fish or poultry, during the daytime. Keep grain carbohydrates, like bread and cereal, and fats, like avocado, cheese, milk, liver and red meat, until after work in the evening. Homemade ice cream before bed (but never before driving) will help you to sleep (see Chapter 2).

For enhanced thinking speed and accuracy: If you can face protein first thing, start with it. Try eggs – boiled, scrambled, poached or, especially good, a Spanish omelette. Any kind of fish, especially smoked oily fishes, like kipper, mackerel or salmon are an excellent addition. The Dutch, the Scandinavians and some Germans serve up wonderful platters of cold meat for breakfast. Try stewed fruit, berries, blackcurrants, nuts or seeds. Have fresh fruit if possible. Avoid bread and cereals if you can – keep until evening, otherwise favour wholegrains.

Morning: Try fresh fruit, fruit juice or mixed dried fruit that has been soaked overnight in cold tea or orange juice. Drink plenty of water.

Daytime: Try any protein, especially oily fish like mackerel, herring, salmon or sardines with cooked dark green vegetables like spinach and cabbage, or with salad and raw vegetables, like carrots or celery. *Eat the protein first.* If you need dessert, try fruit salad or just fresh fruit. Avoid biscuits, bread, pasta, pizza or pastry. Drink as much cold or bottled water as you can. If you must, follow the meal with tea, preferably green or herbal, not coffee.

Evening: Wholemeal bread and cereals eaten in the evening will help you to relax and sleep. So will fats, especially dairy if combined with fresh fruit. Cooking with rapeseed oil or linseed oil provides omega-3 fatty acids. Flax, hemp, sesame and pumpkin oils help maintain the important balance between omega-3 and omega-6. The wholemeal bread will provide selenium. Pasta will provide energy for physical exercise the next day. This is the time of day when puddings will do least harm to your thinking. Try fresh fruit crumbles made with bran and oat toppings, or homemade ice cream made from yoghurt and fresh fruit.

A brain salad

This brainy salad recipe was adapted from an original by Allegra McEvedy.

Serves 2

200g broccoli, cut into bite-sized florets

120g peas, fresh or frozen

100g cucumber, cut into small, slim batons

100g good quality feta cheese, crumbled

20g toasted seeds (sesame, sunflower, flax and pumpkin)

50g avocado, cut into pieces

30g quinoa

Small handful of fresh mint, roughly chopped

Dressing: 2 dessert spoons lemon juice plus 4 dessert spoons extra virgin olive oil.

Cover the quinoa with cold water, about an inch above the quinoa, then let it gently simmer until the water has gone – about 15 minutes. Spread it on a tray to cool.

Put an inch of hot water into a saucepan with a pinch of salt and cover. Once boiling, drop in broccoli and peas and put the lid back on. Drain after three minutes. Run the veg under cold water to take the heat out. This keeps them green.

Now build your salad in layers, starting with the first ingredient on the list and ending up with the dressing, just before you eat.

The effects of diet and exercise

DIETING, SNACKING AND GRAZING

The British Association for the Advancement of Science reports that whether or not people who diet frequently lose weight, they certainly lose mental performance. Jenkins took people with normal eating habits and divided them into two groups: one group ate the traditional three meals a day; the other consumed identical food, but 'grazed it' over 17 snacks per day. The 'grazers' maintained a more stable insulin level and had lower cortisol levels (see Chapter 5). Research undertaken on students either 'grazing' or not eating at all during a thinking test showed that those permitted to snack on raw vegetables achieved higher scores than a matched group who were not allowed to snack.

Snacking and grazing

Thinking consumes energy and needs fuel. Where possible, try to have evenly spaced snacks rather than a few large meals. Large meals are often preceded by reduced ability to concentrate and followed by periods of drowsiness. However, do not snack on sweets, biscuits or refined, fatty or salty carbohydrates. Snack on proteins such as yoghurts, unsalted cheese, nuts or seeds. Salads are good but not as convenient, unless pre-prepared from finely chopped leaves, like lettuce, rocket, cabbage, fresh spinach or watercress and well mixed with, say, salmon, tuna, smoked fish, nuts, beans or poultry. Raw vegetables, like carrots, are easy to nibble. Fresh fruits like apples and pears are socially acceptable snacks at any time.

SWEETS AND ANAEROBIC EXERCISE

People who become anxious frequently often crave the tranquilizing effect of the serotonin that is formed from the tryptophan released into their blood when they eat carbohydrates. Perhaps that is why people who are over-anxious often crave sweet things. Sweet things are usually sweet because they contain refined sugar. For the anxious person, this has the advantage that refined sugar is very rapidly absorbed by the body, so the calming effect is almost immediate. A serious downside, however, is that you can get an over-production of insulin. Excess insulin provokes hunger pains and makes mental concentration very difficult. It also produces craving for more sweet food and so the cycle gets worse. Body weight as well as mental functioning can then suffer.

With extra body weight, brain oxygenation through exercise becomes less attractive, thereby adding to the prejudicial image of overweight people as slothful mentally, as well as physically. Overweight people can be at a serious disadvantage even when competing for jobs where mental (as opposed to physical) agility is being sought.

If your diet contains too much processed or refined carbohydrate, like sugar, then the insulin-producing systems in your body may become diseased or exhausted. The risk is that you will suffer type 2 diabetes, and with it the risk of heart disease, damaged eyesight and other neuropathic complications.

Remember this: Sugar produces sweet dreams

Simple carbohydrates increase the serotonin in your brain and make you less mentally alert, even sleepy. If eaten a few hours before bedtime, your sleep may be deeper and more restful and this will improve your performance on thinking tasks the following day.

Going through the wall

Use endurance anaerobic exercise to manage anxiety (see Chapter 2) and stress (see Chapter 5), or just to lose weight. You will get the calming effect of increased serotonin because tryptophan is bumped off your body's fatty acids as you burn off your body fat. In this way, you can manage your stress and lose weight at the same time.

How to have bigger brainwaves

Bagley found that for some mental activities, like imagining, inventing, envisaging, or creative thinking, it can be helpful to slow down the electrical brainwave patterns. He used an electroencephalograph (EEG), to compare electrical wave patterns in the brains of people carrying out different kinds of thinking tasks. People solving problems rationally, logically or mathematically were likely to have EEG cycles running between 20 and 23 cycles per second. Subjects coming up with new, innovative, creative ideas for solving problems were more likely to have EEG cycles running between 11 and 17 cycles per second, i.e. much slower, bigger brainwaves. These slower, bigger brainwaves, which are associated with more creative thinking, can be produced by endurance exercise, meditation or breathing deeply.

Remember this: Perspiration and inspiration

By using exercises which relax your muscles, or yoga postures and visual fantasies that slow and deepen your breathing, it is possible to lengthen the electrical EEG waves recorded in your brain. These bigger brainwaves are associated with an increased probability that you will have a 'brainwave' as a creative or inventive inspiration.

THE POSITIVE EFFECT OF RELAXATION ON THINKING

Gelb found that the tested cognition and memory of people taught how to relax was 25 per cent higher than in a control group. He found similar gains when posture was improved prior to thinking tasks. According to McWilliams, massage and yoga can increase relaxation and control the frequency of the electrical brainwaves in your head. This is because excessive stress (see Chapter 5) and anxiety (see Chapter 2) impair thinking, and relaxation lowers the cortisol associated with both. However, if you are not excessively stressed or anxious, the effect on your mental performance will be adverse; 25 per cent of students require stimulation and mild anxiety provocation (for example, deadlines, presentations, public questioning) to get them 'into the zone' of readiness to think!

Try it now: Breathe in inspiration

You can do these exercises in a seated position. Just push your chair clear of your desk or table. For creative and imaginative thinking, force every last bit of breath out of your body, especially by squeezing the muscles of the stomach and buttocks. Hold this state as long as you can and then allow the breath to rush in and appear to fill all the cavities of your body, from your abdomen up to the upper regions of your chest. Raise your shoulders to suck in the last breath. Hold as long as you comfortably can. Repeat three times. Use a finger to lightly close one nostril and breathe normally. Jot down every new idea that occurs to you – however crazy these ideas may seem. Now change from the slow deep breathing rhythm that is needed for creative thinking to the quicker, shallower upper chest breathing that favours critical thinking. To do this, stand with knees relaxed, your feet about as far apart as your shoulders, and imagine you are squeezing a rug on the floor between your feet. Hold your arms straight out in front of you and slide your palms back and forth over each other as fast as you can without a break, while counting backwards from 100. Do not ease off. Try to accelerate for the last 50 counts. When you reach zero, straighten your knees and drop your head as near to the floor as you can. Use one hand to tap up the opposite side of your body, from your ankles to your head, as you slowly straighten up. Bend down again and repeat with the other hand tapping the other side of your body. Your electrical brainwave cycle will now be much quicker. You will be better prepared for a quick 'thinking-on-your-feet' evaluation of the creative ideas you just produced when you were breathing deeply and slowly through one nostril.

THE EFFECTS OF AEROBIC EXERCISE

Dienstbier reports that aerobic exercise enhances thinking performance. Brain activity is fuelled by oxygen and aerobic exercise increases the supply of oxygen to the brain. Herman divided people into three groups: group one was given vigorous aerobic exercise; group two was given moderate anaerobic exercise; and group three was given a placebo activity not involving exercise at all. The two exercise groups consistently showed significantly higher scores on reasoning and thinking tests than the non-exercisers. The exercise regimes were rotated around the groups and the most enhanced reasoning and thinking scores continued to be achieved in the group that was exercising aerobically. According to Bagley, anaerobic exercise is better for enhancing creative thinking, although it will improve critical and reflective thinking as well, if your overall thinking is temporarily impaired by anxiety (see Chapter 2) or stress (see Chapter 5).

Remember this: Fresh air, fresh thinking, fresh ideas

Your mental activity and mental energy are fuelled by oxidizing the carbohydrates in your food. Oxygen is carried to your brain in your blood and the rate at which it is supplied depends, among other things, on the resting metabolic rate at which your heart pumps your blood. This can be raised by periodic (3–5 times per week) aerobic exercise and by regular daily exercise like brisk walking and use of the stairs.

Try it now: Movement and the mind

How to sit and stand

Avoid lifts and escalators. Seek out stairs. Do not lie if you can sit, or sit if you can stand, or stand if you can walk, or walk if you can run, or drive if you can cycle. When sitting on a chair, push your buttocks into the back of the chair. Do not cross your legs. Place feet firmly apart on the floor, about the same distance apart as your shoulders. Imagine you are trying to crumple a rug between them. The same applies when standing, but relax your knees. Once an hour, rub the palms of your hands together as vigorously as circumstances allow. Keep rubbing while you count backwards from 100 to zero.

When standing, sitting or lying down, try to imagine that your navel is a large nut connected by a bolt through to your backbone. Imagine the bolt slowly tightening as you breathe in. Keep your navel bolted to your backbone.

Memorable yoga

To improve your mental concentration and memory, try removing your shoes and standing tall with your feet together. Breathe in deeply and transfer your weight onto your right foot, placing the sole of your left foot as high up the inner thigh of your right leg as you comfortably can, with the toes of your left foot pointing down your right leg to the floor.

Press your left foot against the right leg and with the right leg push back against the left foot. If you can, raise your arms upwards on either side of your head and press the palms of your hands together. Focus the eyes on something just above head height and breathe deeply in and out, counting backwards from eight. Repeat with your left leg.

Try it now: Tactile stimulation – put your head in your hands

Give time to hobbies that involve physical contact, tactile stimulation or intricate handwork. Try massage, swimming, rock climbing, planting, sailing, DIY, or contact sports like rugby or judo. Try painting, weaving, printing, model making, working with clay, or ballroom dancing. Walk in the rain or strong wind. If you can afford it, get a sauna, jacuzzi or high-pressure shower.

Start the day with your head in your hands! Sit on the edge of your bed, or the seat of your toilet, and support the weight of your forehead in the palms of your hands, with your fingers in your hair. Allow your chin to fall slowly onto your chest, your hands stretching the skin of your forehead, and your fingers running through your hair.

Sit up again. This time start with your fingertips on either side of your nose. Allow the weight of your head to fall slowly through your hands, which should graze your ears until your fingers touch at the back of your head.

Sit up again and restart with your fingertips under your ears. Again allow your head to fall slowly against the friction of your palms and fingers until your fingertips pass in front of your ears and meet at the top of your scalp.

Repeat with your fingertips passing upwards behind your ears this time, before meeting at the top of your head. This can literally make your hair stand on end.

During the day, brush or comb your hair as often as vanity or local custom will allow.

Sleep, alcohol, caffeine, smoking, drugs, ticks, chocolate and sex

THE EFFECT OF SLEEP ON THINKING

To achieve optimum performance, people need good quality sleep. Horne has found that impaired sleep reduces performance on many mental tasks. Mitler's studies of catastrophes, such as the Three Mile Island nuclear power accident, and the Challenger space shuttle explosion, concluded that poor sleep quality had impaired decision making and contributed to each catastrophe.

The amount of sleep that people need varies greatly from one person to another. It ranges from four to ten hours. For adults, quality of sleep seems to be more important than quantity. Quality of sleep can be impaired by listening for a baby, the return of a missing teenager, or by fear of not hearing the alarm clock. Sleep quality can also be impaired by snoring – yours or someone else's.

Try it now: Sound sleep

Remove televisions and radios from your bedroom. Try going to bed later each night, until you find a time at which you ordinarily drop off to sleep without delay. Talking to a partner prior to sleep can be desirable but such conversations should not involve complicated feats of memory or planning. Use a bedside notepad to park things until the next day. Deep breathing exercises will help you to settle your mind and slow down your brainwaves. If you are physically tense, squeeze and then relax all of your muscles in turn, from your toes through to your ankles, calves, thighs, buttocks, stomach, back, hands, arms, shoulders, chest, neck, face and right up to your scalp. If a massage is on offer, seize the moment! If early sleep is the goal, imagine a line down the centre of the body and another across the body, intersecting at the groin. Taking each quadrant in turn, direct the massage so that the flow of pressure is towards the head or feet, away from the groin. Start by lying face down. You may fall asleep without ever turning over! If you like to make love prior to falling asleep, then ask to be massaged so that the flow of pressure in each quadrant is towards the groin. Avoid any direct contact with the groin.

Many people who work shifts never get the chance for a high quality sleeping pattern to develop. People who work continuous night shifts perform better at mental tasks than people whose shift patterns change. Travel across time zones and the accompanying jet lag impairs performance on mental tasks. Going to bed later than usual has a more deleterious effect than getting up earlier than usual.

Try it now: The dangers of disturbed sleep

Once you have found a convenient time at which you fall asleep easily, without reading, radio or television, try to stick to it. At weekends do not set an alarm. Notice the time when you wake naturally – however early. Record your natural length of sleep time. Notice how short your natural sleep time can be: 4 to 7 hours is often sufficient. Whenever you are forced to sleep less than your natural sleep time, your performance on IQ tests is likely to drop. The consequences can be serious. You may be incapable of learning something you need to learn, or thinking about some emergency that is new or complex or fast-moving. Your reaction to unusual events will be poor. You should minimize your driving after sleep loss or sleep disturbance. Do not negotiate or give presentations at which questions will be asked immediately after travelling across a time zone.

According to Coren, scores on intelligence tests decline cumulatively on each successive day that you sleep less than you normally sleep. The daily decline is approximately one IQ point for the first hour of sleep loss, two for the next, and four for the next. After five successive days of sleeping less than you need, your IQ can be lowered by up to 15 points. This means that a person of normal intelligence could have an effective IQ of only 85, the level at which you would need special education in order to learn. Even a very 'bright' person (IQ of 120 plus) can be reduced to robotic thinking, as though on automatic pilot.

Griffey (2004) claims that, in the UK, in 1910, people averaged nine hours' sleep a night. In 1990, this average was eight hours' sleep a night. By 1995, according to a survey by First Direct, people in the UK were averaging seven hours and 35 minutes' sleep a night. By 2004, the average had fallen to seven hours a night. Are we sleeping less because we are more stressed? Or are we more stressed because we are sleeping less? Certainly, levels of the neurotoxin cortisol are raised, so that the decline in performance is similar to that reported for stress (see Chapter 5).

Remember this: Broken sleep breaks your brain and your bones

A regular pattern of sleep seems more important than how much you sleep – as long as you get enough sleep for you. You can work out how many hours' sleep you need and then try to have a regular pattern for getting them. Five consecutive nights of disturbed sleep can lower your performance on IQ tests by up to 15 points. The deleterious effect of a change in your sleeping pattern can be gauged from its effect on your ability to drive safely. Continuing to drive more than one hour beyond your normal bedtime can lower your judgement, anticipation and reaction times more than if you drive with over the legal limit of alcohol in your blood.

SLEEP-SHORT DRIVERS ARE WORSE THAN DRINK–DRIVE DRIVERS!

Coren tested drivers after they had been awake for one hour beyond their 'normal' bedtime. Their thinking processes and reaction times were worse than a control group who had drunk more than the UK drink–drive limit for alcohol consumption. In countries like the UK, where the clocks are moved forward by one hour in the summer, car insurance accident claims rise by 25 per cent in the first four days following the one-hour sleep loss. Out of all UK motorway accidents, 25 per cent of drivers admit to feeling sleepy prior to their accident. Add to that people not admitting drowsiness for fear of self-incrimination and the drivers who did not live to tell the tale, and the effect of sleep loss may be a more serious contributor to accidents even than alcohol.

EARLY TO BED, EARLY TO RISE

A study at Southampton University in the UK, based on 1,200 men and women, showed no evidence that early to bed, early to rise, made anyone 'healthier, wealthier or wise'! What seemed to be important was to be a regular riser – whether early or late. It is disturbed sleep patterns that disturb health, wealth and wisdom.

POWER NAPS: DO THEY WORK?

New York, the city that never sleeps, has sprouted Metro-Nap salons. Yelo (www.yelonyc.com) offers 20 to 40-minute naps in private cabins, complete with state-of-the-art sound and light systems, with aromatherapy and reclining chairs that give a feeling of weightlessness – and since 2004 more of such things have spread to work places across the Western world as well as more recently in universities such as the University of Perth. Snooze booths are also now appearing either as short sleep stops or overnight stays in airports.

THE EFFECT OF ALCOHOL ON THINKING

Drinking even the occasional glass of wine in pregnancy can damage the brain of an unborn child. Heavy drinkers risk a brain disorder called Wernicke-Korsakoff syndrome, a progressive memory deficit. Sufferers normally recover their ability to speak and walk, but do not recover their ability to think. The condition seems irreversible and untreatable. Alcohol depletes vitamin B1 which is essential for the thinking process. As we have seen already, there are other ways to feel more relaxed and less stressed that do not impair thinking or damage your brain.

Thinking and hitting the bottle?

✻ Minimize your consumption of alcohol, especially during the day. Between one o'clock and four o'clock in the afternoon it can have up to ten times its usual effect.

✻ Do not mix alcohol with analysis. Even small amounts of alcohol lead to a dangerous combination of error proneness, over-confidence and increased risk taking.

✻ Do not drink alcohol on an empty stomach.

✻ Drink plenty of water before and after alcohol.

✻ Drink spirits only with a double mixer plus plenty of ice.

Remember this: Drink talks – and not very well

Apart from the possibility that one unit of alcohol might reduce any inhibitions you may have about starting to tackle your thinking task, there is little evidence that drinking alcohol is good for your brain, or its thinking performance. Not only does alcohol lower your performance, it perversely increases your own estimation of how well you are doing, whether you are writing an essay, driving a car or prospecting at a party.

THE EFFECT OF TEA, COFFEE, COLA AND CAFFEINE

Caffeine is found in tea, coffee and cola drinks and in some food products. Caffeine can quicken your reaction time and prolong your vigilance during demanding tasks. However, there is a need to keep doubling your intake of caffeine to have the same effect and eventually a plateau is reached. The caffeine also acts as a diuretic; you keep urinating, causing dehydration. This produces lethargy and reduces your cognitive performance. Nutritionists recommend that you drink 8 to 15 glasses of water a day, depending on your body size, the weather and your activity level. Water is preferable to tea, coffee, soft drinks or fruit juices. Caffeine stimulates your nervous system and interferes with the quality of your sleep. There is concern about the long-term consequences of caffeine-induced alertness. Work in Israel showed that long-term consumers of caffeine grew spiky protuberances on the cells in their hippocampus. This is an area of the brain that controls memory. David Kerr also found that the caffeine lift, or 'buzz', was an illusion. Within 30 minutes of drinking coffee, he observed that the flow of blood (and hence oxygen) to the brain had reduced by 10–20 per cent.

Watering the brain

* Dehydration has a major adverse effect on mental activity. Coffee, strong tea and cola, like alcohol, make things worse because they are diuretics.

* The adrenal boost from the caffeine in coffee, tea, and cola is short-lived. The first buzz from the first cup is quickly negated by subsequent fatigue.
* Tap water, hot water, fruit tea or herbal tea all produce greater benefits to thinking with less detriment to long-term health than coffee, tea or cola.

Remember this: A cup a day – that's all

One cup of strong coffee, or tea, per day does seem to raise the speed and accuracy of your thinking, but more than that one rapidly produces fatigue and then an addictive tendency to drink more caffeine to try and combat the fatigue. Caffeinated drinks like Coke and Red Bull often exacerbate your thinking problems by producing 'insulin swings' that make it difficult to concentrate. Coffee does contain protective antioxidants but dark chocolate gives more protection and a safer 'buzz'.

THE EFFECT OF SMOKING ON THINKING

Smokers self-report increased mental alertness and improved performance on a host of cognitive tasks after one cigarette. However, this positive effect is soon countered by an adverse effect on the oxygen-carrying capacity of the blood. Smoking ties up the haemoglobin that carries the oxygen in the blood. Damage to lungs limits the body's ability to absorb the oxygen needed to support mental activity. By the year 2000, it had become abundantly clear that pregnant women should never smoke.

THE EFFECT OF DRUGS ON THINKING

▶ Cannabis: the urban myth of harmlessness

Over a three-year period, Mathews studied people who were regularly using cannabis (or marijuana) at least ten times a week. He found that regular users progressively reduced their baseline of brain activity compared to a matched control group. Regular users showed lower proactive energy levels, lower completion rates on personal goals and plans, lower reported pleasure in anything, and reduced interest in using their bodies or their brains.

▶ Ecstasy: no ecstatic legacy in the brain

In *Neurology* in August 2000, Kish reported that users of ecstasy were left with seriously depleted levels of serotonin. This would make it difficult to concentrate, or to complete mental tasks or to sleep. This will, in turn, impair the ability to think.

▶ Cocaine constriction

When an endorphin molecule in your body jumps a synaptic gap and finds a receptor site, you experience pleasure. Normally the endorphin will then detach. A cocaine molecule will lock the endorphin onto the receptor site so that you will continue to experience the pleasure. Once the cocaine has been metabolized, you will be short of endorphins and you will crave a repeat experience. You are hooked. The more cocaine you use the more the blood vessels in your brain will become constricted. This constriction will impair your ability to think and will eventually damage your brain.

'Just a tick': avoiding the brain bug

Lyme's disease was once found only in African countries. It is carried by ticks that bite their prey, suck their blood and sometimes leave a red ring around the bite. Lyme's disease can cause a swelling of the brain (encephalitis), a complication from which about one in 50 victims die. Even if you do not die, you can be left with severe neurological damage and be unable to walk or move your joints. Today there are carrier ticks in 27 countries in mainland Europe, including the UK (in the New Forest, Exmoor, South Downs, Yorkshire Moors, Scottish Highlands and the Lake District). If you are bitten and you get a red ring or flu-like symptoms, you need a large and sustained dose of strong antibiotics immediately. If you wait for a blood test, it can be too late for the antibiotics to be effective.

DESIGNER BRAINS AND COSMETIC NEUROLOGY: THE EFFECT OF SMART DRUGS

In May 2007, Peta Bee, writing in *The Times*, questioned the fairness of students who were buying drugs that enhanced intellectual performance. Taking the case of Modafinil, which was originally developed to treat a sleeping disorder, Bee quoted

Dr Danielle Turner from Cambridge University. Modafinil appeared to improve memory, planning, information processing, emotional and reflective thinking and decision making, and seemed to have only benign side-effects. Bee reviewed a number of other 'smart drugs', including Ritalin, which was originally developed to treat attention deficit disorder in children. It is now claimed to improve alertness, memory and visual and spatial thinking in adults.

However, these drugs cost some $8 (£4) per tablet without prescription on the internet – so will only the rich get smarter? Is it like cheating in athletics, cycling or body building? Mice memorized five times faster when given these smart drugs. Wouldn't that kind of memory acceleration come in handy when you needed to learn a second language, play an instrument, or revise for an exam? But new research into the effects of Modafinil has shown that healthy students could find their performance impaired by the drug.

A recent study, carried out in November 2014, showed the drug had negative effects in healthy people. The researcher Dr Mohamed said: 'We looked at how the drug acted when you are required to respond accurately and in a timely manner. Our findings were completely opposite to the results we expected.'

Yet, be warned, you might also lose your ability to daydream, to muse on what that information might mean. You might remember everything, but understand nothing. What matters is not what you remember, but what you do with what you can remember. What matters most is your ability to think, and your ability to apply your thinking, and 'smart' drugs will negatively affect this ability.

DARK CHOCOLATE BOOSTS THE BRAIN

Dark chocolate boosts your brain while protecting you from heart disease and cancer. Eating approximately 20–150 g a day of dark chocolate can improve your learning and your memory. Improved blood flow carries more oxygen to the brain, enabling you to think quicker for longer. Your blood vessels relax, reducing blood pressure, brain damage and risk of heart disease. In February 2007, the American Academy of Science, from two separate studies, one in the USA and one in the UK, reported that dark chocolate was not an old vice, but a modern-day life saver. Welcoming the news, nutritionists pointed out that the finding applied only to dark chocolate and warned chocoholics to avoid the pale dairy stuff. In a way we have come full circle, because chocolate was originally brought from South America to the court of the Spanish Empire as a medication and brain stimulant. The Spanish court apparently kept this a state secret – on pain of death! High in antioxidants, dark chocolate has more flavonoids even than green tea. Professor Ian MacDonald found the increased blood flows in the cerebral cortex persisted for three hours after eating dark chocolate. Dr Helen Berg of Harvard found that rates of heart disease were lower by 1,280 per cent in parts of the world (for example, Panama) where drinking dark chocolate was part of the everyday diet. Deaths from cancer were 680 per cent lower. Rates for strokes and diabetes were also low. Dark chocolate contains epicatechin – a mineral so vital to health that Professor Hollenberg would like to see it classified as a vitamin. The efficacy of flavonoids like epicatechin are undermined by sugar and dairy products, hence the need to eat your chocolate dark! Although the calorie content of dark chocolate is much lower than milk/white chocolate, it's not calorie-free – this needs to be kept in mind if you are on a calorie-controlled diet.

▶ **Stick to the dark**

Evidence of the deleterious effects of cannabis on the brain is now overwhelming. The adverse effects of heroin, cocaine, and ecstasy are already well documented. The benefits of stimulation obtained from caffeine, or the mood enhancements obtained from other drugs, are more safely obtained by eating a small quantity of dark chocolate.

The brain science of dark chocolate

A heartfelt plea: You need the magnesium in dark chocolate to decrease the coagulation of your blood. This will help your heart to deliver more oxygen to your brain. This will not only raise the thinking speed and thinking power of your brain, it will also protect your brain from the damage caused by high blood pressure. One of the easiest ways to add magnesium to your diet is to eat dark chocolate (Jensen).

Dark chocolate lifts depression: Dark chocolate contains monoamine oxidase inhibitors (MAOIs). These allow the levels of serotonin and dopamine in your brain to remain higher for longer, alleviating depression and producing feelings of well-being.

Dark chocolate: the new vitamin: Free radicals attack and oxidize the DNA in your brain, creating growth points for tumours, as well as the onset of premature ageing. Cheng Lee at Cornell University, USA, showed that dark chocolate is rich in antioxidants, called flavonols. Flavonols mop up the free radicals before they can oxidize your brain. Dark chocolate is twice as rich in antioxidant flavonols as red wine and three times richer than green tea. The flavonols in dark chocolate also make your blood platelets less likely to stick together and thus less likely to cause brain damage through a stroke. Lee found that a normal cup of drinking chocolate, based on dark chocolate, contained about 600 mg of the flavonoid epicatechin.

Dark chocolate is better than broccoli: The US Department of Agriculture compared the ORAC scores of well-known brain foods like spinach, blueberries and broccoli, with dark chocolate (ORAC scores measure the concentration of flavonoid antioxidants in foods):

Broccoli	890
Sprouted alfalfa	930
Plums	949
Sprouts	980
Raspberries	1,220
Spinach	1,260
Strawberries	1,540
Kale/Cabbage	1,770

Blackberries	2,036
Blueberries	2,400
DARK CHOCOLATE	13,120

Dark chocolate: a safer 'buzz' than caffeine: Eating dark chocolate substantially increases your mental speed and energy because it contains the brain stimulant theobromine. (Dark chocolate is virtually free of caffeine, which can also give your brain a temporary boost, but caffeine has fatiguing short-term side-effects and more dangerous long-term side-effects.) Dark chocolate contains about 21 per cent theobromine. Theobromine works as a brain stimulant by relaxing muscles helping to dilate veins and arteries thus allowing blood to flow more easily to the brain. The effect of theobromine is gentler and more sustained than that of caffeine. It lasts four times longer and is kinder to your heart. Theobromine has actually been prescribed for heart patients to help lower blood pressure. Caffeine, on the other hand, is life-threatening to many heart patients, because it raises blood pressure and thus potentially damages the brain.

Get a grip: Dark chocolate contains PEA (phenylethylamine). PEA activates the neurotransmitters in your brain that control mental attention, concentration and alertness. Your levels of PEA go up naturally, without chocolate, when you are gripped by a great movie or are enjoying a good book, or are wholly engrossed in a football match, a work project or a computer game. Elevated levels of PEA can cause you to lose track of time. This is why time seems to fly when you are enjoying yourself. PEA is present in higher levels in 'blissful' people (see Chapter 2). It is also found in dark chocolate. Good quality dark chocolate can contain up to 2.2 per cent PEA.

The brain's BLISS chemical: Dark chocolate contains anandamide – a cannabinoid brain chemical known as a 'BLISS chemical', because it is produced in the brain when you feel good (see Chapter 2). The anandamide released in your brain when you feel good acts on your brain the same way as the THC (tetrahydrocannabinol) in cannabis but because anandamide does not act on the whole of your brain, like cannabis does, then you can feel good without losing your mind. You do not feel 'out of it', like you would on cannabis. Anandamide is a natural brain chemical that is not known to have harmful side-effects, unless you regard BLISS as harmful. In fact BLISS is strongly correlated with good health (see Chapter 2) and the anandamide in dark chocolate is the brain's own BLISS chemical.

The secret of eternal youth? MAOIs (monoamine oxidase inhibitors) in dark chocolate work by allowing increased levels of anandamine and dopamine to circulate in the brain. It is the high level of anandamine and dopamine that distinguishes the brains of children from the brains of most adults because, in general, as you get older the levels of these neurotransmitters decrease. This decrease is associated with a decrease in physical and mental spontaneity and joy. You are as young as you think and feel and the MAOIs in dark chocolate can help to keep your neurotransmitter levels nearer to the levels of your youth (Cousens).

And so to bed Dark chocolate produces endorphins that induce the loving feelings that often lead to sex. The same endorphins also facilitate the euphoria of the 'afterglow'.

THE EFFECT OF SEX ON YOUR BRAIN

The effect of sex on your thinking depends on whether or not your pre-sex stress levels are excessive, whether or not you have an orgasm, and what type of thinking you are concerned about.

▶ The seven steps in the sex life of your chemical brain

1 You and your partner each need to have sufficient testosterone in your brain. Low testosterone is the most common cause of low libido. Stresses, fatigue, disturbed sleep, hormone imbalance due to pregnancy, hysterectomy or menopause, are common causes of inadequate levels of testosterone.

2 Given you have sufficient testosterone, then desire can generate a rising level of oestrogen, triggering the release of pheromones under your armpits. These may create a reciprocal sexual desire in your partner (the jury is still out on this).

3 Sexual desires release dopamine. Dopamine helps you to think visually. Dopamine will help you to visualize, imagine and fantasize about the different possible places and ways in which you might have sex with your partner. This will further raise your level of desire and the level of nitric oxide in your bloodstream.

4 Nitric oxide increases your rate of blood flow. Besides helping you to dilate the labial lips of your vaginal area, or to engorge the tumescence of your penis, the increased rate of supply of oxygen to your brain will enable you to process information faster and to assess problems more quickly. Increased oxidation will leave your head clearer for calculations, decisions and action. Nitric oxide readies you for action!

5 If the action is sexual, your oxytocin levels will rise, causing pelvic contractions and raising the possibility of female orgasm. Oxytocin heightens a sense of being wanted, safe and secure. It is a 'trust hormone'. It increases preparedness to think of novel or riskier solutions. It aids creative thinking.

6 The pleasure of sexual activity, especially following orgasm, raises the levels of serotonin in the brain. Serotonin calms agitation, stress and anxiety. Cortisol levels associated with stress are moderated, making calm, logical decision making and calculation easier. High levels of serotonin favour creative thinking.

7 With stress relieved, head cleared and visual and creative thinking empowered, there is an 'afterglow' of satisfaction associated with a rise in the level of PEA. PEA produces feelings of well-being and a tendency to smile involuntarily! PEA is the brain chemical associated with romance and falling in love. It is also produced by eating dark chocolate. (Sometimes life is less complicated if you just eat the chocolate!)

Remember this: The brain below the belt

The sex cycle – from mutual sexual attraction to the afterglow following orgasm – produces a sequence of seven changes in the chemistry of your brain. Five of these seven stages leave a residue of chemicals that enhance your brain's ability to think well.

Our 'other brains'

THE BRAIN IN YOUR GUT

The gut has a mind of its own, the 'enteric nervous system'. Just like the larger brain in the head, this system sends and receives impulses, records experiences and responds to emotions. Its nerve cells are bathed and influenced by the same neurotransmitters. The gut can upset the brain just as the brain can upset the gut.

The gut's brain is reported to play a major role in human happiness and misery. Many gastrointestinal disorders like colitis and irritable bowel syndrome originate from problems within the gut's brain.

When the central brain encounters a frightening situation, it releases stress hormones that prepare the body to fight or flee. The stomach contains many nerves that are stimulated by this chemical surge – hence the 'butterflies'. On the battlefield, the higher brain tells the gut brain to shut down. A frightened running animal does not stop to defecate!

Fear also causes the vagus nerve to over stimulate the gut, so diarrhoea results. Similarly, people sometimes 'choke' with emotion. When nerves in the oesophagus are highly stimulated, people have trouble swallowing.

THE BRAIN IN YOUR HEART

It is long known that changes in emotions are accompanied by predictable changes in heart rate, blood pressure, breathing and digestion.

The heart communicates with the brain in ways that significantly affect how we perceive and react to the world. Scientists discovered a neural pathway and mechanism whereby input from the heart to the brain could affect the brain's activity.

The heart has a complex intrinsic nervous system that is sufficiently sophisticated to qualify as a 'little brain' in its own right. Information from the heart – including feeling sensations – is sent to the brain where it may influence perception, decision making and other cognitive processes.

The hearts own nervous system that operates and processes information independently of the brain or nervous system is what allows a heart transplant to work.

When the heart has smooth, ordered rhythm patterns, the neural information sent to the brain appears to help brain function. This effect is often experienced as heightened mental clarity, improved decision making and increased creativity. Additionally, this helps support positive feeling. This may explain why most people associate love and other positive feelings with the heart and why many people actually feel or sense these emotions in the area of the heart.

Focus points

* Eat the food your brain needs, when it needs it.
* Minimize damage to your brain from alcohol, tea, coffee, cannabis, cola, ticks and cigarettes.
* The power of your brain is as much a lifestyle choice as a genetic inheritance.
* The brain is adversely affected by mineral and vitamin deficiencies.
* You can improve mental performance by 'grazing'.
* You can improve mental performance by avoiding dehydration.
* Deep nasal breathing enhances imagination and creativity.
* Physical exercise and posture can enhance thinking.
* IQ scores can be improved by changing your sleeping habits.
* Performance on thinking tasks is improved after sex (and by eating dark chocolate).

Dig deeper

Collins, C., 'Behind the label', *The Times* (7 February, 2004), p. 10.

Craven, K., 'We've got the bug', *The Independent* (15 May, 2007), pp. 12–13.

Dharma, D., 'Brain longevity', *The Lancet* (2004).

General Psychology, Fall (1996). 'A contemporary view of selected subjects from the pages of *The New York Times*, January 23, Printed in *Themes of the Times: General Psychology*. Distributed Exclusively by Prentice-Hall Publishing Company.

Griffey, H., 'Ten ways to get a good night's sleep', *The Independent* (22 November, 2004), p. 8.

Guardian, 'Danger to foetus in glass of red wine' (27 January, 2000).

Holford, P., *Optimum Nutrition for the Mind* (London: Piatkus, 2004).

McCraty R (2002), Influence of Cardiac Afferent Input on Heart-Brain Synchronization and Cognitive Performance. International Journal of Psychophysiology; 45(1–2):72–73.

Naam, R., *More than Human: Embracing the Promise of Biological Enhancement* (New York: Broadway Books, 2007).

Piggott, S., 'Seaweed: the tide turns', *The Times* (25 October, 2003).

Next steps

* Keep a food log – are you getting everything you need?
* Check your log for fluid intake – is it enough and of the right kind?
* Keep a sleep log, exercise log and sex log – are you getting enough of all of these?
* If you fancy a bar of chocolate, go for dark chocolate not milk chocolate.

2

Managing your mood

In this chapter you will learn:

▶ *that chemical reactions in your brain determine whether you feel high or low, and this can affect how well you think*

▶ *that you can control these chemical reactions by what you do, what you think, and by what you eat and what you drink*

▶ *that if extremes of mood persist, you should seek medical advice*

▶ *that you can achieve a state of BLISS through Body-based pleasures, Laughter, Involvement, Satisfaction and Sex.*

There is nothing either good or bad but thinking makes it so.

After William Shakespeare

Introduction

In this chapter, you will discover that the chemical conditions in your brain change when you experience emotion, and when you think about the emotions which you and others may be feeling. Thinking thoughts and feeling feelings are both chemical processes. Each affects the other. The need for you to consider what you are feeling, as well as what you are thinking, arises in a number of thinking tasks, for example:

▶ Recalling what was felt, by yourself and others, as well as what was seen and said and done, is important when you need to think reflectively in order to turn your experience into learning (see Chapter 8).

▶ When you need to think creatively, your emotions are an important source of the mental energy you need to generate a long list of novel possibilities. Your emotional response to emerging ideas, yours and other people's, feeds your intuition, and the courage you need to make novel associations and creative connections between emerging ideas and the ideas and images already in your head (see Chapter 9).

▶ An important part of thinking critically and ethically about an idea is the evaluation of its potential consequences for others. How will they feel? (See Final thoughts.)

▶ In general, positive emotions and optimistic expectations correlate with the strength of the immune system, the probability of recovery from serious diseases, like cancer, and the likelihood of successful outcomes on thinking tasks, like problem solving and strategy formulation.

Emotions and thinking

EMOTIONAL INTELLIGENCE

The capacity to link emotions to thinking was described by Goleman as 'emotional intelligence' in 1996, and as 'social intelligence' in 2006. Apparently, emotionally aware children do better in exams and at work, and grow up to have happier marriages and lead healthier lives. Research by both Goleman and Damasio shows that you need to involve your emotions, particularly when thinking about problems and plans (see Chapters 7 and 8).

Emotional information is processed in a part of the brain called the amygdala. The amygdala is constantly sending messages to the prefrontal lobes of the brain. This means that there is a constant flow of emotional information to the parts of the brain involved in calculation and argument. McGaugh points out that the effect is not always beneficial. On the one hand, when fear or anxiety rises beyond a certain level, your ability to think and remember is impaired. On the other hand, when you feel positive or amused, the messages sent by the amygdala appear to improve your ability to think and increase the likelihood that you will come up with original solutions.

To discover for yourself how closely connected your thoughts and feelings are try the following activity.

Try it now: A thinking and feeling experiment

Try the following experiment, either with a partner, or with pen and paper. Look around and write 'I am noticing...'. (write down what you are looking at or listening to) and 'I am thinking...' (write down what you are thinking at that very moment) and 'I am feeling...' (write down a single word describing the emotion). Keep this up for about 15 minutes. Review the results. Notice how many times you can change what you are feeling, even in 15 minutes. Notice what kinds of observations and thoughts are followed by what kinds of feelings. Repeat, trying to increase the number of positive feelings you can experience in 15 minutes. Notice that you can choose what you notice – what you look at or what you listen to. This increases the chance that you can find something positive to think about and this in turn means you feel better. Try to complete the following sentences in succession. When you have completed 3, go back to 1. Keep going around the loop for as much time as you can spare. When you can do it easily, do it as often as you can.

1 Right now I am noticing... (e.g. a person, colour, sound, smell, taste, texture).
2 And right now I am thinking... (e.g. an opinion, judgement, fragment of an internal dialogue).
3 And right now I am feeling... (e.g. an emotion – a single word).

For increased mental suppleness, just keep going around the loop. For increased concentration span, increase the number of repetitions you do at one time. For increased mental agility and thinking speed, try to go around as quickly as you can without hesitation. You may notice that how you feel is changed by what you think and what you think is related to what you notice. Because you can control what you notice by where you choose to focus, you can exert increasing control over your thoughts and your emotions.

Remember this: Heartfelt thoughts

The Chinese script character for thinking combines the separate Chinese characters for 'head' and 'heart'. What the Chinese knew intuitively, thousands of years ago, gained support in 2007 when the human heart was found to contain neurons with axons that reached, via the spinal cord, right into your head. NMR scans of people's brains when they are trying to decide on an action, show that the parts of the brain which process emotion are as active as those which process logic and information.

EMOTIONAL AND VERBAL THINKING

Identifying and labelling the feelings we have is more productive than just expressing the feelings spontaneously or impulsively. This is because when you shout, or otherwise give vent to your anger, for example, you leave a neural pathway between the amygdala and the brain's frontal lobes. This increases the ease with which subsequent stray feelings can disable your ability to think clearly, especially under pressure.

YOUR EMOTIONAL THINKING AS A YOUNG ADULT

In young adults, the hormone-driven dendrite explosion reaches the parts of the brain that deal with stimulation and emotion, well before it reaches the frontal lobes that deal with verbal reasoning. As a young adult this can leave you prey to impulsive and confusing feelings, which you are not yet able to identify, let alone channel.

The amygdala is connected to the prefrontal lobe of the brain, so even when the emotion is expressed, rather than suppressed, it will still disrupt the short-term memory space needed for making judgements, comparisons, calculations, decisions and logical arguments. Emotions need to be acknowledged, recognized, labelled and examined. Gottman realized that the thinking space of many young men is quickly overwhelmed and disabled by emotion. This is especially true following criticism expressed by a female. For a typical male–female relationship to survive, the ratio of her positive remarks to her negative remarks needs to be about 5:1. Even with a 1:1 ratio, the chance of the relationship surviving beyond three years was found to be low.

ARE YOU FEELING ANXIOUS?
Anxiety states can obsess your mind to the point where you are no longer free to lead your life. Specialist therapies are then required. The road to recovery can be tortuous and time-consuming. However, worry in moderation is a sensible preparation and rehearsal for things that may go wrong. It enables you to prepare contingency plans and these are often reassuring and can lower your anxiety. In 126 studies of more than 36,000 students, academic under-performance was often correlated with difficulty in managing emotions, including anxiety.

HIGH HOPES AND HIGHER EXPECTATIONS
We have studied the effect of 'hope' and 'expectation' on the academic grades of our undergraduates. We have found them to be a better indicator of final module grades than A-level entry scores. The handling of feedback on a student's first assignment was found to be a determinant of final performance on the module. It is imperative that tutors seek out positive and encouraging aspects of the student's first attempt.

THE BIOCHEMISTRY OF EMOTION
According to US pharmacologist Dr Candace Pert, your brain signals the release of different chemicals, each of a different

molecular structure, each time your feelings change. These molecules enter your blood and flow around your body until they find a receptor site that exactly fits their shape. These receptor sites will then pick up the messages from your body's hormones, like oestrogen and testosterone, and from your neurotransmitters, like serotonin and dopamine, and from other biochemicals called 'peptides'. Your body's receptor sites also pick up messages from endorphins released by opiates like heroin and morphine and these can enhance your mood. You can release your own supply of endorphins through exercise, thought and sex, with far less damage to your brain than through opiates (see Chapter 1).

Emotional thinking and learning

When students feel over-anxious, resentful, angry or bitter, or when they seem helpless or very sad, this has an adverse effect on their learning. Unmanaged emotion disables learning because it disables some of the thinking skills involved in learning (see Chapter 8). For emotionally distracted students, it is hard to take an interest in new information, or to persist with trying to make sense of information that is confusing or incomplete or to accurately recall material already covered. They find it hard to make decisions. We have been excited to see brain scan evidence of this traffic between the amygdala, processing emotion, and the frontal lobes of the brain that are struggling to think and take decisions. Unmanaged emotions, like fear and anxiety, can lead to a kind of mental paralysis. This happens to some students during examinations or timed tests.

Remember this: Putting theories into practice

The Chinese script character for learning combines the Chinese characters for 'thinking' and 'doing'. Not all thinking involves learning but there is no learning without thinking. For the learning to be 'deep' – i.e. involving future behaviour change – action must be taken. This implies emotional engagement will be important for deep learning and applied thinking.

MENTAL ENERGY AND MOTIVATION

As long ago as the 1980s, Terry Horne found that the development of many mental abilities like mathematics, writing, or playing chess, was a product of the time a person spent on their work. The self-motivation to do homework, to tackle past papers and to practise presentations comes from emotions, such as fear of failure, or the desire to perform well in front of an audience. Emotions provide the mental motivation to deploy your full repertoire of thinking skills. The repetition involved in practice and rehearsal not only contributes to present success, it also thickens the myelin insulation around the neural axons, enabling the brain to think more quickly and more accurately about future thinking tasks. The feeling associated with repetition is often tedium or boredom, and so the motivation to study and practise needs to be based on a strong overriding emotion.

Emotions can sometimes provide a motivation to move too quickly, i.e. to act impulsively or to close down a thinking process prematurely. In order to achieve a more mature, thoughtful responsiveness, emotions like irritation, anger, anxiety and impatience need to be managed. The feelings, as well as the facts, need to be thought about.

In Walter Mischel's famous marshmallow test on Stanford four-year-olds, emotional intelligence (in that case measured by the children's ability to think their way to a double marshmallow reward by delaying the immediate gratification of one marshmallow) has proved a better predictor than IQ alone of their eventual academic success in Maths and English and of subsequent life success. (Children in the top third of Mischel's emotional intelligence test scored 17 per cent higher in their English Scholastic Aptitude Tests (USA) and 25 per cent higher in their Maths Scholastic Aptitude Tests (USA).) These superior results may have been the result of having spent more time on the practice and revision, perhaps because they were able to delay the gratification of their desires for more pleasurable social activities, or perhaps they were able to override one emotion – boredom – with another such as hope or expectation, or even excitement at the thought of doing well. (Or maybe these behavioural traits correlate with having successful, educated, middle-class parents, whose IQs, expectations and networks may have promoted genetically or socially the success of their progeny! Remember, a correlation is not necessarily a cause (see Chapter 7).)

Getting to a 'yes'

If you are trying to get someone to make a decision, act on the assumption that they will need an emotional gain from the decision. Ask them to imagine a good feeling they will feel when they have decided in your favour. Then ask them what convincing reasons they could give to other people for a decision in your favour. People often feel the need to rehearse good reasons to give to others, even when their decisions are intuitive, emotional or irrational. The world often expects people to appear rational, even when they are not.

Try it now: Those old familiar feelings

To understand some habitual but undesirable behaviour on the part of another person, you could test the hypothesis that people will keep repeating behaviours that result in them feeling 'old familiar feelings'. 'Old familiar feelings' are feelings that they have become very used to feeling, possibly since they were children. One person's 'old familiar feelings' will probably differ from another person's 'old familiar feelings'. They may not be feelings that you would consider to be pleasant. This can help you to understand why some undesirable behaviour gets worse when we punish the culprit. Maybe the culprit's 'old familiar feelings' are the ones that result from punishment. Study the pattern of undesirable behaviours. Ask yourself, 'How does this person end up feeling?' Can you organize things so that this person can get these feelings in some other way, preferably in a way that is less disruptive? Can you change how people react to the behaviours, thereby thwarting the suspected emotional pay-off?

FAST SERVE OR FAST TRACK: IS OPTIMISM THAT IMPORTANT?

When the messages we receive via television, radio, the press and the internet are predominantly pessimistic, it is difficult to feel optimistic. Does this really matter? How important is positive thinking?

Yes, the world is full of unhappiness and disease. But there is also love, compassion and joy. Research on selective perception has shown that you observe things with a preconceived notion of how you think they should appear (see Chapter 7). You may find it difficult to change your mind even when you see or hear contradictory evidence (see Chapter 7). Instead of reality, we selectively perceive what we expect and hope to see. This means you will draw false inferences from your mistaken information. You will draw false implications from your false inferences. Garbage in = garbage out. The usefulness of your applied thinking will be seriously compromised.

Milton Ericson and others have shown that thinking is very open to suggestion, including self-suggestion. When researchers told their subjects that everything was bad and that they could not hope to prevail, this increased the chances that they would fail.

Sports psychologists Bull and Rushall were concerned to reverse 'negative' thinking in the players or athletes they coached. They discovered that an optimistic self-confident mood increased their clients' chances of winning. They claimed that optimism improves concentration and speed of thought in sports like tennis and Grand Prix motor racing. In 2012, Wayne Rooney spoke to Gabby Logan about watching from the sidelines during England's 3-2 win over Sweden, and special visualization techniques that helped him prepare for a match. The England striker, said positive thinking the night before a game helps his match performances.

Remember this: You can, if you think you can

For 30 years or more we have known that the intellectual performance of children and students rose or fell when their teachers' expectations rose or fell. More recently we have discovered that your intellectual performance will be low if you expect it to be low. Likewise, optimism, positive mood and high expectations will be important ingredients of high level mental performance.

Memory, too, was found to be very sensitive to suggestion. If you tell yourself 'I'll never remember that', you are more likely to forget it. Feeling anxious or pessimistic about your prospects in a written exam impairs your thinking skills, especially recollective thinking. The main benefits of revision are that you feel more optimistic and the physical condition of your brain will have been enhanced by all the repetition, so long as you don't cancel this out by staying up all night to do it (see Chapter 1). Consequently, you remember and think better even when answering questions on material that you never revised! Formal written examinations best suit people who are optimistic. People who are less confident do better when they are assessed through coursework.

Psych yourself up to learn

Researchers have found that subjects are much more likely to remember test words 50 minutes later, if they are emotionally aroused prior to the task.

Positive thinking: the effect on mind and body

The effect of mood on the chances of recovery from serious traumas to the body, such as major surgery and tumours, has been the object of much study. According to Fosbury, the management of diabetes has been shown to benefit more from mood management by cognitive therapists, than from information from nurse educators. Cohen claims that negative emotions, such as anxiety, increase the frequency with which people suffer from common colds. Colds impair breathing, lower energy, cause headaches and impair clear thinking. Cohen found that swimmers could improve their performance by concentrating on optimistic thoughts. They reported that the optimism affected their cognition and their health as well as their swimming performance. Seven types of thinking increase the pessimistic outlooks that impair health and mental performance. Do you have any negative thinking habits?

Negative thinking

Black and white thinking	Things are good or bad. Pendulous either/or thinking.
Perfectionist thinking	Less than perfect equals failure. Nit-picking. Blemishing.
Comparative thinking	Performance is judged only by comparison with other people.
Generalized thinking	This sees a single event as part of a never ending and inevitable pattern. Characterized by use of 'always' and 'never'.
Telepathic thinking	Believing you can tell when others think negatively about you.
Basket thinking	You give yourself one bad label and then assume any similar or related bad labels also apply to you.
Guilty thinking	Characterized by frequent use of the words 'should' and 'ought'.

Source: Horne and Wootton, 2007

PREOCCUPATIONS

Many people regularly watch popular dramas or 'soaps'. These are frequently tragic. Hyams found that negative preoccupations undermine thinking performance. If you have negative things on your mind, performance will not be as good because your attentional space is limited. The more you preoccupy your limited attentional space with worries or anxieties, the less attention you can give to thinking about the task in hand.

▶ Six steps to overcoming your negative emotions

1 Carry out an audit of your strengths (not your weaknesses). You have skills and resources. You have knowledge. You have learned many things.

2 Forgive someone, if only in your head. Rehearse the imaginary conversation where you forgive them. Let go of the negative memories that steal your head space. You need your head space for more positive thoughts.

3 Visualize how things will look when you have succeeded. Hear the applause success will bring and notice from whom this will be important. Feel now how you will feel when you receive the applause and recognition for the success.

4 Applaud yourself. Discover that you do not need the constant approval of others even though you will enjoy this when you get it.

5 Try things that are difficult and give them your best shot. When you are doing your best at difficult tasks, your best is good enough.

6 Admit that you are not super-powerful. You cannot be the cause of all that is bad, or of all the bad feelings of others.

Try it now: Stop nagging

Stop nagging and nit-picking and complaining. It will lower the mood of people around you. This in turn might lower yours. Moods are contagious. Your good mood will lift the mood of others. Their good mood will then lift yours. When you see something you like, comment on it. Feel good about good things in others. Don't score points at the expense of other people.

Depression

Depression is a black dog that barks in the daytime as well as the night-time, often seven days a week, for months, or even years. In 1999, the World Health Organization reported that neuropsychiatric disorders, like depression and manic depression, had become the world's commonest cause of premature death and disability. Seek professional or medical help if you think you might be suffering from depression. Tell a counsellor or doctor if you have five or more of the following symptoms:

Are you suffering from depression?

You may be, if more than five of the following symptoms persist:

Fatigue	Loss of mental energy
Insomnia	Early waking
Over-eating	No appetite
Loss of sex drive	Increased drinking
Increased smoking	Aches and pains
Piercing own body	Self-harm
Recklessness	Accident prone
Loss of confidence	Loss of enjoyment
Feeling hopeless	Feeling helpless
Feeling guilty	Feeling worthless
Feeling agitated	Unable to work
Unable to concentrate	Thoughts of death

Studies show that the levels of work-related stress are significant (see Chapter 5). Working well with work colleagues and learning to participate in problem solving and decision making can improve mental health.

Remember this: Dealing with depression

Are you depressed? It is important to distinguish between feeling generally fed up, feeling down about something in particular, and clinical depression. The action required is different in each case. Clinical depression is a serious condition for which you should seek professional help. You would not try to mend your own broken leg, would you?

THE BRAIN CHEMISTRY OF DEPRESSION

Adverse social and economic events are associated with biochemical changes in your brain. There is a strong correlation between the amount of serotonin and norepinephrine in your brain and your mood. If your levels of serotonin and norepinephrine get too low, you will experience lowered mental energy, diminished pleasure from normally pleasurable activities and a reduced sex drive. The inclination to be proactive and self-motivated, both of which are essential for applied thinking, are also greatly diminished.

Interview with Robbie Williams – no longer superman

So when I'm lying in my bed .... What's going through my head?

'I used to think my depression was caused by work pressure. It's not. I just get sick. I'm just ill. It's heart breaking. It starts with stopping going out. I come off stage, go home to bed and pull the duvet over my head. In the mornings, I no longer recognise myself in the mirror. Physically it's worse than the worst flu I've ever had, nothing makes it better. That's when I accept I'm not superman and that I need help.'

I'm loving Angels instead...

Robbie Williams was interviewed for *Psychology* in April 2007

The pursuit of happiness

There are many books that offer you happiness in a few steps. Howard asserts that unless you are one of the ten per cent who seem genetically programmed to be happy, no matter what you do or no matter what is done to you, your search for happiness will be fruitless.

A survey of *Time* magazine readers, in December 2004, showed that about half of readers who replied said they were happy 'sometimes'. About a quarter reported themselves as happy 'rarely'.

The difficulties experienced by seekers of happiness are compounded by living in a world that advertises a futile expectation of permanent happiness. In the USA, happiness was included in the Declaration of Independence. Americans have the right to life, liberty and the pursuit of happiness. Such expectations lead to inevitable disappointment for many of us, and this, in turn, lowers our mood.

The pursuit of BLISS (Body-based pleasure, Laughter, Involvement, Satisfaction and Sex) differs because its components are not expected to persist. If they continued for too long, or were repeated too frequently, your chemical receptors would become desensitized; your experience of BLISS would become dulled. In fact, it is necessary, periodically, for you to moderate your state of BLISS so that your receptor sites can clear and you can be aroused again by a new experience.

Try it now: Imagine

✳ A banquet of only meat, or only vegetables – all 20 courses.
✳ Receiving non-stop applause and cheers. A standing ovation for three hours.
✳ Forty-eight hours of non-stop sex with the same partner, in the same position, in the same clothes, in the same bed!

Remember this: A blissful brain

The set of chemical conditions present in your brain at the point you think you are happy is hard to replicate; indeed trying to replicate it seems futile. It is easier, and you are less likely to be disappointed, if instead of pursuing happiness you pursue a state of BLISS: Body-based pleasure, Laughter, Involvement, Satisfaction and Sex.

BODY-BASED PLEASURE

The first component of BLISS is body-based pleasure. This can involve any or all of the five senses: taste, smell, sight, hearing and touch. You will need to become familiar with, and practise using, words that describe the emotions and feelings you experience. Add your own words to this list:

Ecstatic, exquisite, delighted, invigorating, refreshing, uplifting, erotic, arousing, sated, gleeful, joyful ...

Mentally try some of the '30 sensations before you die' below and then try to find a word that describes how the experience would make you feel – what emotion it might engender. Add your new words to your list.

Try it now: 40 or more sensations to try before you die...

Eat: herbs and wild honey, creams and curries ... and dark chocolate.

Taste: lips, skin, liquorice, aniseed ... and dark chocolate.

Smell: cut grass, wood shavings, honeysuckle, pine resin ... and dark chocolate.

Savour: the smell of a barbecue, a baby's neck, seaweed smells ... and dark chocolate.

Gaze: at sunsets, distant hills, the faces of models.

Admire: cathedrals, temples, modern architecture, a well-loved garden.

Hear: babies babbling, Mozart's *Clarinet Concerto in A Major* (2nd movement).

Listen: to running water, wind in trees, a choir and bird song.

Enjoy: Mendelssohn's *Violin Concerto in E minor*, Status Quo, Pavarotti.

Stroke: clean hair, petals, warm sand, smooth skin, soft skin.

Feel: velvet, silk, fine cotton, linen ... and dark chocolate melting in your mouth.

LAUGHTER (AND TEARS)

There is now much neuroimmunological evidence of the benefits of laughter. But the benefits of a 'good cry' have been less well researched. There are many sorts of tears – tears of joy, anger, frustration, relief, hysteria or just of awe at the sight of a DB5 Aston Martin Volante! Witchalls (2007) found that emotional tears contain emotional brain chemicals, like leucine enkephalin, associated with pain, and prolactin, associated with stress. So, crying might be a useful way of cleansing your brain.

So cry me a river

Animal tears do not contain emotional chemicals. Is crying a hallmark of humanity?

People suffering from depression, ulcers and colitis cry less than healthy people.

The ability to cry correlates with prolactin. Women have 60 per cent more prolactin than men.

▶ Is laughter the best medicine?

Laughter may not be the best medicine, but immunology studies confirm that it does augment whatever other medicine you take. The levels of immunoglobin (an antibody found in people's saliva) are predictably:

▶ lower than average in people under stress

▶ higher than average in people who feel loved by others

▶ higher in people whose prevailing mood is optimistic

▶ higher in people who laugh, or who make others laugh.

The effects above are likely to compound each other and be cumulative. Even so, we counsel against abandoning conventional treatments and relying solely on positive emotions to cure disease, even though there are 15 years of studies confirming the beneficial effects of laughter, positive mood and optimism on your immune system.

In research on heart surgery, men basing no optimism on religious beliefs were three times more likely to die, and men basing no optimism on the optimism of others, were four times more likely to die. Clearly the impact of optimism is great. The impact of laughter is even more immediate. Cousins found that the levels of life-threatening sediments in the blood are reduced after only a few moments of laughter. (Laughter also appears to intercept emotional messages from the hypothalamus to the frontal cortex, leaving the frontal cortex free to be logical in its planning and decision making.)

Try it now: Ten things to do to raise your optimism
1 Collect qualifications and certificates.
2 Read any 'suggested further readings' that catch your eye.
3 Commit a random act of gratuitous kindness every day.
4 Reduce the number of stressors in your life (see Chapter 5).
5 Spend time with people who share your sense of humour.
6 Dispose of some assets to release cash for shopping.
7 Contact close family and old friends.

8 Improve appearance, for example through exercise or spray tanning.

9 Collect funny cards to send when people are ill, to say thank you, or for no reason.

10 Keep a file of funny stories or jokes, preferably at your own expense. Share one a day.

INVOLVEMENT

Next you need to get Involved. Involved in what? And exactly what does Involvement entail?

The object of involvement is not sensory pleasure or to get an emotional lift. To get involved is to get totally engrossed and absorbed in an activity, such as a game, a sport, a hobby or a conversation. You need to get so involved that you lose track of time and maybe, even, lose track of where you are, or cease to notice any physical discomfort that you may be suffering. When you really get involved, little else will intrude into your awareness.

The seven elements of Involvement

1 Your goal is clear – you know what you are trying to achieve.

2 You feel up to it – you have sufficient energy and resources.

3 You feel you have a very good chance of achieving your goal.

4 Concentration can push aside conflicting cares.

5 You feel in control of the outcome.

6 Your sense of achievement is immediate.

7 Your sense of time is altered – how time flies when you are enjoying yourself!

Source: Horne and Wootton, 2004

Your chances of getting involved are greatest when the difficulty of the task and the level of skill needed are evenly matched. Too little skill required and you will be bored. Too much skill and you will be frustrated. The beneficial effects of involvement are more enduring than body-based pleasure, or even laughter, because you are active. The activity will help to fix the good feeling in your memory (see Chapter 3). It is you who are playing the game, you are not just a spectator; you are acting on the stage, not just sitting in the audience; you are making the home-made ice cream, not just eating it!

Try it now: Don't just sit there!

Make your own ice cream – don't just eat it!

1 Home made ice cream tastes better than shop-bought ice cream and it does not contain brain-threatening E numbers.

2 Half fill a blender with chilled natural organic yoghurt. Blend with fat-free milk powder (how much depends on how hard you like your ice cream).

3 From the garden, fridge (or freezer), add an equal quantity of your favourite berries, currants, summer fruits, strawberries, raspberries, bananas or coconut cream plus the juice of half a lemon. Keep back a handful of the fruit. Blend until it tastes brilliant.

4 Transfer to a pre-frozen bowl of an ice-cream maker and turn on the machine. When nearly firm, add a handful of the fruit or the juice kept back for the purpose. Stop the machine while the swirl pattern is still clearly visible. Return the bowl to the freezer, or preferably eat as soon as possible!

SATISFACTION

Now you 'just want some satisfaction'. Terry Horne and Tony Doherty found it useful to classify the needs you are seeking to satisfy as:

▶ the need for **Warmth**

▶ the need for **Applause**

▶ the need for **Possession**.

The relative importance to you of each of these areas of need is unique to you, and their relative importance will change as you get older. Your Warmth need is for persistent affection, acceptance, belonging, friendship, support and unconditional positive regard. Many of your needs for warmth are easier to meet outside of work, which is why it is important to strike the right work/life balance.

Your Applause need is for some ephemeral things that require constant reaffirmation, such as approval, admiration, congratulation, gratitude, recognition and success. The scale of your need for applause should determine your choice of partner (see Chapter 10).

Your Possession need is to be able to say 'this is mine' (as in 'this is my space', 'this is my child', 'this is my home, my garden, my hobby, my invention, my poem, my painting, my kind of music, my opinion, my idea').

Clearly you can meet your needs for Warmth, Applause and Possession at home or at work or in the community. It is interesting that you can meet your possession needs just by thinking. For example, 'this is my idea, my poem, my thought...' You need not be dependent on money, or on other people, to meet your need for possession.

SEX

And so to bed. The final S in our state of BLISS is for sex. It is easy to see why sex is such an important source of well-being. Sex combines body-based pleasure (ideally from all five senses), enhanced mood (elevated by endorphin release), very focused involvement (for both the male and the female brain – see Chapter 10), with the satisfaction of all three needs for warmth, applause and possession (lovers literally 'possess' each other).

In Chapter 1, you tracked the chemical changes that take place in the brain during sexual intercourse, and here you have seen how sex can contribute to a state of BLISS. The importance of sex in thoughtful relationships will be explored in Chapter 10.

THE NEUROCHEMISTRY OF BLISS

The neurochemistry of the state of bliss has been studied by Richard Davidson. He wrote about his findings in *Time* magazine in January 2005. When monks self-reported feelings of bliss, Davidson detected a sustained increase in activity in their frontal cortex. The enhanced frontal cortex activity was associated with an increase in the level of dopamine in the brain, combined with a large number of dopamine receptors becoming available in the limbic region. The limbic region is one that records bodily pleasures from, for example, eating food or enjoying sex. Clearly then, bliss is more than just pleasure, because the experience of bliss involves the frontal cortex, which is the seat of logical thinking. Perhaps the frontal cortex is needed to attach meaning to the sensations being reported by the limbic system?

The same pattern of heightened activity in the frontal cortex, plus dopamine flooding in the limbic region, has been observed in students when they come near to solving a difficult, but solvable, problem. This may be why 'involvement' tasks for BLISS need to be demanding but realistic. The 'laughter' is important because it suppresses the stress chemical, cortisol, which can quickly disrupt the conversion of 'body-based pleasure', 'involvement' and 'satisfaction' into good feelings. In Chapter 3, you will find that 'sex' releases many chemical 'memory fixatives'. These help you to remember the 'good times'. You can use 'good time' memories to revive your spirits at some overcast time in the future.

Try it now: Walk tall (well, take three steps at least!)

Step 1. Slump in your chair and hang your head and your chin on your chest.

Step 2. Now try to remember a time when you had a good time and felt good.

Step 3. Now try again, but this time stand with your feet, as wide apart as your shoulders, 'gripping' the ground. Relax your knees. Breathe deeply, suck your belly button back towards your lower spine. Raise your head, pulling your chin back as far as is comfortable. Look straight ahead into the distance and open your arms and chest as though to embrace someone. Notice how much easier it is now to remember some 'good times', and notice how your 'good time' memories can raise your spirits.

OBSTACLES TO FEELING GOOD

While you can't guarantee happiness, you can minimize unhappiness. The five major obstacles to feeling good are: anger, disappointment, fear, sadness and boredom. The table below suggests the things you can do to minimize obstacles to feeling good.

▶ **How to minimize the five major obstacles to feeling good**

The obstacle	What to do
Anger	▶ Have a pillow fight ▶ Run, or walk briskly ▶ Do something physical ▶ Join a martial arts club ▶ Dance, sway or shout to loud music ▶ Talk to yourself, a pet, a tree or a hillside
Disappointment	▶ Watch a heart-warming film, e.g. *Pay it Forward* ▶ Read *Chicken Soup for the Soul* ▶ Perform an act of unsolicited kindness ▶ Write a list of your lifetime achievements
Fear	▶ Keep a diary ▶ Write to someone ▶ Call an old friend, or cousin ▶ Weed someone's garden (it can be yours!) ▶ Rent an action film (not a suspense thriller or a mystery film)
Sadness	▶ Exercise (see Chapter 1) ▶ Watch the film *When Harry Met Sally* ▶ Listen to *La Traviata* or *Madame Butterfly* ▶ Arrange flowers, or photographs ▶ Visit, mourn, discuss or commemorate
Boredom	▶ Join a club ▶ Work with young people ▶ Enrol for a class or a course ▶ Volunteer to visit a hospital, a hospice, a prison, or a school ▶ Become a representative, e.g. councillor, or school governor

So, manage the five obstacles to feeling good and pursue the five elements of BLISS i.e. Body-based pleasure, Laughter, Involvement, Satisfaction and Sex. You may not achieve happiness, but you can reduce unhappiness. And your thinking will benefit.

No longer gazing

As I gaze upon the sky

Vague

Unattributable

Unattached

There descends

A drowsy unimpassioned sadness,

Having no relief in word, or thought, or tear.

In this mood, heartless,

Without thought, thoughtless,

I must gaze no longer on the sky.

For hoping from outward forms to win

The passion and the life whose fountains are within, I might gaze forever.

We win but what we give

And through our lives

Alone

We live

And learn

And might hope to gaze forever.

Terry Horne, 1982

Focus points

* Chemical reactions in your brain determine whether you feel high or low, which in turn can affect how well you think.
* You can control these chemical reactions through what you do, what you think, what you eat and what you drink.
* If extremes of mood persist, you should seek medical advice.
* You should explore what you are feeling before you try to think.
* Emotions can motivate, demotivate, or disable thinking.
* Hope enhances performance. Anxiety and fear diminish it.
* Optimistic self-suggestion increases success in thinking tasks.
* The pursuit of happiness is fruitless.
* Obstacles to feeling good can be minimized.
* The pursuit of **B**ody-based pleasure, **L**aughter, **I**nvolvement, **S**atisfaction, and **S**ex (BLISS), will benefit the speed and accuracy of your thinking.

Dig deeper

Howard, P. J., *The Owner's Manual for the Brain: Everyday Applications from Mind and Brain Research* (3rd edn, Austin, Texas: Bard Press, 2006).

Witchalls, C., 'Join the Blub: The Benefits of Crying', *The Independent* (10 April, 2007, p. 8).

Wootton, S. and Horne, T., *Strategic Thinking* (London: Kogan Page, 2003).

Next steps

We know that our emotions effect our thinking so:

* Make sure you complete the 'thinking and feeling test' at the start of this chapter.
* Ensure you do exercise to help release endorphins as these enhance your mood.
* Keep positive: if you think you can, you can!
* Become emotionally aroused to perform better in a task.
* Stop nagging, it affects the moods of those around you.
* Find time to laugh out loud during each day – laughter is a great reliever of stress.

3

Improving your memory

In this chapter you will learn:

- ▶ *how your memory underpins your thinking*
- ▶ *how to improve your memory, through tips, tricks, tools and training*
- ▶ *how and why memory training expands the cognitive capacity of your brain generally*
- ▶ *how and why expanding the cognitive capacity of your brain helps to protect it against disease and increases its power to support applied thinking and intelligent behaviour.*

> Memory is the warden of the brain.
>
> William Shakespeare

Introduction

In a study of London taxi drivers, researchers from University College London found that the drivers' brains got bigger the more routes they memorized! Your memory is intimately involved in who you are – you are the sum total of what you can remember. However, it is not the role of memory in determining your personality that concerns us. Here, we will deal with recollection as a component of applied thinking.

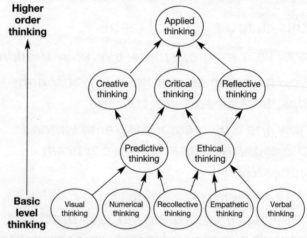

Figure 3.1 The hierarchy of thinking skills.
Source: Horne and Wootton, 2003

First, test what your memory is like now.

TEST YOUR LONG-TERM MEMORY

1 What did you eat at your last meal?

2 Where were you last Saturday?

3 What did you do on the Thursday before that?

4 Where were you at midnight on New Year's Eve?

5 What was the title of the last film you watched?

6 Where were you when you heard about the death of Princess Diana or the 11 September 2001 attack on the World Trade Center?

7 How did you last celebrate something?

8 What was the last book you read?

9 Where were you when you first remember being kissed?

10 Who kissed you?

To score 0–6 is poor; 7–8 is average; 9–10 is good.

TEST YOUR SHORT-TERM MEMORY

Read a row of numbers and look away. How many numbers can you remember?

8						
13						
46	12					
7	10	35				
18	98	84	6			
4	69	25	38	13		
20	22	68	85	16	17	
78	56	88	91	24	46	80

If you can remember three or fewer, then your short-term memory is poor; four to seven, then your short-term memory is average; eight to ten, then your short-term memory is good.

A myth about memory

You are born with all the brain cells you will ever have.

Not true. Memory researchers have discovered that your chemical brain is a complex organ that develops and changes with every thought that you have. This means that old, diseased or deteriorating brains can change and repair themselves with the right diet, exercise and brain training. This explains why it is that the brains of many older people show no deterioration in thinking performance
(*Keep Your Brain Sharp*, Horne and Wootton, 2010).

Remember this: Maximize your memory

You can develop skills in making better use of your brain's capacity to remember. You can also increase your brain's capacity to remember things, e.g. through certain types of physical or mental activities.

Brain training

DOES BRAIN TRAINING IMPROVE YOUR MEMORY?

Carnegie University in the USA reported on male volunteers, of average IQ and memory, who practised brain training for one hour a day, three days a week, for three semesters. A male volunteer who initially could hold no more than seven numbers in his short-term memory could memorize 79 digits by the end of his training. Initially, at the end of a one-hour lecture, like many undergraduates, he could recall nothing within 15 minutes of the end of the lecture! After training, he could recall 80 per cent of the content of a one-hour lecture.

Is it wise to eat sage?

Apparently, if you rip sage leaves into small pieces and add a teaspoon of the ripped leaves to a cup of boiling water and sip your infusion during examinations, tests or presentations, you will feel the benefit. Sage inhibits the breakdown of acetylcholine which the brain uses when it thinks.

DOES SUDOKU BUILD YOUR BRAIN POWER?

Yes. Sudoku requires several different parts of your brain to work simultaneously to support numerical, visual, emotional and critical thinking. As patterns emerge, and fragments are remembered in over 30 different areas of the cerebral cortex, a maze of links to the hippocampus develops. This maze is run over and over again, thickening myelin insulation and improving speed and accuracy of thought. Emotional thinking is also involved in managing impatience, frustration, disappointment and competitive pressure.

THE RULES OF SUDOKU

A Sudoku puzzle is usually a 9 × 9 grid subdivided into 9 squares – like noughts and crosses.

	a	b	c	d	e	f	g	h	i
a						7			
b	8	6			5				
c	4	3	5			8		1	
d				6					3
e		1	4				5	8	
f	3					2			
g		2		9			6	5	8
h					3			2	7
i				5			3	4	1

The puzzle starts with some given numbers called 'clue numbers' already inserted. The object of the game is to fill all the empty boxes so that each row, each column, and each 3 × 3 large square, contains the numbers 1 to 9 – without repeating any number.

See Answers at the end of the book for the solution.

TIPS ON SOLVING SUDOKU PUZZLES

▶ Use a pencil with an eraser at the end, or a ballpoint pen that has more than one colour.

▶ Start by finding the 3 × 3 square that has the most given number clues. Look for the rows and columns going through your most 'clued-up' square that also have several clue numbers already in place. Pick a vacant grid square.

▶ In pencil, or in green ink, enter in small font, in the corner of the square, the 'missing' numbers, i.e. missing from the 3 × 3 square, and the row and the column in which the empty square is sitting. If there is only one such number, you have found your first answer number. Enter the answer number in the middle of the vacant grid square. Write the answer number as big as the clue numbers.

▶ Repeat for all the empty squares in the row, the column and the 3 × 3 square. By elimination, each time you enter a black answer number, you can erase or strike out the small missing numbers that you have entered in other places in the row, column or 3 × 3 squares. As soon as you have only one missing number left in a small square, this is an answer number – overwrite it large and black.

▶ This will get you started and enable you to use basic Sudoku puzzles for brain training. Your brain will get most benefit from doing easier puzzles as quickly as you can. Note your times and note how much quicker you are getting.

The usefulness of Sudoku in training the brain finds support from Susan Greenfield's model of the chemical brain and from David Snowdon's nun study. Oral recitation, repetitive brainwork, and the drafting and redrafting of written work each gives your brain not only a memory upgrade, but also an expansion in general cognitive capacity. The more the capacity of your brain is expanded, the more capacity you have in reserve. This works to protect your memory and your intellect should you become sick with a disease that attacks your brain cells.

Memory

THE MYTH OF DEMENTIA
When the brains of former mentally active people are dissected, pathologists often find that they are riddled with Alzheimer's plaques, and yet those people had shown no signs of impaired memory when they were alive. Michael Valenzuola's analysis (2006), covering 66,000 individuals, showed that people who kept their brains active, for example, through work, leisure activities, or brain training, had half the risk of suffering dementia.

Remember this: The longer the better – it's memory that counts

It is a common misconception that your memory will inevitably deteriorate as you get older. In fact, as you age, your long-term memory will improve and you can boost your speed of memory formation through regular brain training activities, often involving simple numbers.

THE ROLE OF PHYSICAL EXERCISE
Physical training seems to benefit the brain generally and the memory specifically. In 2005, Kramer used an MRI (magnetic

resonance imaging) scanner to show that the normal rate at which the brain loses weight with age can be reduced, or even reversed, as a result of physical exercise. Research has shown that Yoga can also boost your brain activity more than jogging and other conventional exercises.

Try it now: Get physical

If possible, combine physical activity with social and mental activity. Try joining a rambling group, amateur dramatics club, or a ballroom or country dancing club.

MAKING NEW CONNECTIONS

Physical exercise not only results in a stronger flow of blood, glucose and oxygen to the brain, it also stimulates the growth of new neurons, especially in and around your hippocampus, which plays a key role in your memory.

You do have a photographic memory

And it's so good that you can't turn it off – even after two and a half mind-numbing days of looking at over 10,000 boring photographs – many of them similar to each other.

In May 2007, Professor Richard Wiseman took over the ground floor of a branch of Waterstone's in London to expose people to up to 10,000 photographs and slides and then show them that they had remembered them – even though they denied it! Recall rates ranged from 15 out of 16 after flicking through 800 photographs, at about one second each, to recognizing 86 out of 130, after viewing 9,200 images up to three days earlier. The results replicated a study 30 years earlier, in Canada, when subjects scored 98 per cent and 70 per cent in equivalent tests.

All the links between your hippocampus and all the other parts of your brain require the formation of many new neural pathways. If these many new neural pathways are then used repeatedly (as when pupils, for example, chant tables, sing school songs or revise for tests), then the initial connections between the neurons become much stronger.

▶ How to make connections

▶ Create as many links or associations as possible to increase the number of possible starting points for retrieving the memory in future. Since we can only hold up to five (plus or minus two) new items of information in our short-term memory, making notes and associating, linking and mapping are essential (see Chapter 8).

▶ Associations can be simple – the 'g' in stalagmite reminds you that it grows up from the ground, while the 'c' in stalactite reminds you that it comes down from the ceiling.

▶ Sometimes whole sentences (acrostics) can be used to recall the initial letters of a list of words needing to be remembered. The acrostic 'every good boy deserves friends' gives us the musical notes, e, g, b, d, f, while the acronym FACE gives us the musical notes f, a, c, e. The more bizarre the association, the more memorable it will be.

▶ 'I just can't place it' is another way of saying 'I can't remember it'. Over 2,500 years ago, the Greeks propounded the idea of finding a place for things, in order to aid recollection. Here's a way to remember items on a shopping list. You could use a room in your own house where you know from memory the relative positions of all the major items of furniture. You could then imagine a giant hammer on the chest, a teddy bear burning in the fireplace, the steam iron completely filling the sofa, a football bouncing along the piano keys, a hairdryer scattering the chess pieces. As you go around the room in your mind's eye, you can create a shopping list of hammer, teddy bear, steam iron, football and hairdryer.

MEMORIES ARE MADE OF STRAW?

Improving your memory is as simple as stuffing an ass with straw:

> STRAW ASS = Stick To Reading Aloud and Writing
> And Simple Sums

To improve your memory, stick to reading aloud, writing and doing simple sums as quickly as you can. The reading aloud should be about topics that are new and interesting to you, and the writing should preferably involve lots of drafting and redrafting.

After finding that 'bookworms' showless mental decline as they age, scientists believe that reading frequently throughout life may also protect you against dementia.

Remember this: The more languages you speak the better

A study tracking hundreds of Scottish people for decades suggests that speaking an extra language slows the mental decline that can accompany ageing. So how can this be? Possibly by the speaking of more than one language, your brain has to activate your mother tongue words as well as the alternative language word – hence giving your brain a more enhanced workout each time?

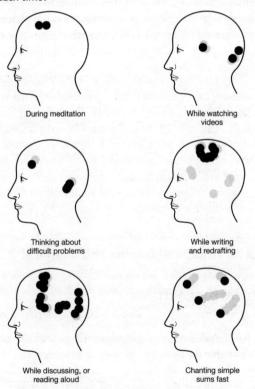

During meditation

While watching videos

Thinking about difficult problems

While writing and redrafting

While discussing, or reading aloud

Chanting simple sums fast

Figure 3.2 Parts of the brain involved during different types of activities.
Source: Based on MRI Scanning Research by Kawashima, 2007. (His electronic exercises are available from Nintendo.)

PASS THE PARCEL: A RELAY RACE DOWN MEMORY LANE

The memory messages from your hippocampus travel through your brain's neural network rather like a baton travels in a relay race. In 2000, Eric Kandel was awarded a Nobel Prize for his work on the Californian sea slug. Kandel's research on the sea slug helped to explain how the baton is passed down your neural memory lane. His work confirmed the central role played by sodium ions, which we first encountered in Susan Greenfield's book, *The Human Brain*. The sodium ions help to transfer the charge along the length of each of your neurons. At the end of the neuron's axon, the baton is picked up by neurotransmitter chemicals which then swim across a synaptic gap to the dendrites on your next neuron. Memory thus corresponds to chemical changes that increase the chances that a given message will be relayed across a given synaptic gap in your brain.

MOLECULES OF EMOTION: THE 'CHEMICAL FIXATIVES' OF MEMORY

Your hippocampus receives messages from all areas of your brain, in particular from your amygdala. Your amygdala controls the production of what Candace Pert described as 'molecules of emotion' (see Chapter 2). These emotional molecules seem to play an important role as 'chemical fixatives' of memory. These chemical fixatives help you to 'burn' your learning into your memory. Hence the importance of emotional engagement in learning activities (see Chapter 8).

Flashbacks, emotional trauma and 'chemical fixatives'

When there is strong emotion like joy, horror or disgust associated with a memory, a release of adrenaline can cause a cocktail of chemicals – norepinephrine, adrenaline, enkephalin and vasopressin – to be released into the brain. Hooper and Teresi have suggested that this cocktail of chemicals has the same effect as spraying varnish onto a chalk pastel painting. It stabilizes the picture or the pattern and reduces the risk of it getting smudged or distorted. The stronger the emotion, the easier the subsequent recall. Thayer and Maguire both separately identified that each emotional state has its own library of memories. When experiencing pride in success, for example, you may well recall a previous success. When expressing anger or resentment, you are more likely to dredge up earlier incidents, or resentments, that had not been expressed at the time. It's a little like collecting similar emotions you have saved up and then cashing them in all at once – thereby intensifying the feelings associated with the memory, either positively or negatively.

DO YOU NEED NEW NEURONS FOR NEW MEMORIES?

Your hippocampus is the only part of your brain known to produce new neurons routinely. This has led to speculation that new neurons might be necessary for new memories. This adds to the importance of physical and mental exercise, because exercise has been shown to accelerate the production of new neurons near to the hippocampus (see Chapter 1).

THE NEUROCHEMISTRY OF MEMORY

In Australia, Clarke Raymond stuck electrodes into both ends of slices of a hippocampus, and recorded the residual voltages in the receiving neurons. When he gave the hippocampus neurons a single charge, the residual voltages in receiving neurons rose slightly. But the effect did not last. The receiving neuron 'forgot' its recent experience. If Raymond repeated the stimulation – another ten times, say – a higher residual voltage was found in the receiving neurons. This time the effect lasted for weeks. In August 2005, the journal *Science* reported that Jonathan Whitlock had replicated Raymond's findings using the hippocampus of a living brain. In the case of the short-term memory effect, molecules of receptor chemicals were modified by the stimulus. The memory faded because modified receptor molecules were slowly replaced with unmodified molecules. In the case of the long-term memory effect, the repeated stimulus not only modified the molecules of the receptor chemicals, it also increased the number of receptor sites, and triggered the formation of new synapses.

The bit that looks like a seahorse

Your hippocampus, the bit that looks like a seahorse, seems to act like a central switchboard. It links fragmentary components of memory that may be stored in many different parts of your brain.

The hippocampus has been the focus of much of the research that has been done on memory and recollective thinking. Why? Is it just because it is so distinctive in its appearance, so easy to see and isolate? In *Stem Cells: Controversy at the Frontiers of Science* (2006) and 'The Labyrinth of Memory' (2007), Elizabeth Finkel jokes about brain researchers' preoccupation with the hippocampus:

'A brain researcher is like a man who has lost his keys in the street. The brain researcher is found crawling about, on his hands and knees, near a street lamp. When asked if he has dropped his keys near to the street lamp, he replies, 'No, but it is too dark to search for them anywhere else.'

Remember this: The Caffeine Buzz

The long-time friend of students cramming for exams, caffeine seems to enhance long-term memory. Studies have shown that caffeine boosts the consolidation aspect of memory function – but it needs to be the right dose of caffeine – two espressos seems to work!

The memory workout

INTRODUCTION

If you find the prospect of a memory workout stressful, you might consider the effects of stress chemicals, like cortisol, on your memory.

▶ The effects of stress chemicals on memory

In 1994, the *Journal of Neuroscience* reported that 19 adult volunteers had been given a stress chemical, glucocorticoid, or a placebo, for four consecutive days. The volunteers listened to a tape and were asked to recollect what they had heard.

The placebo group found this easier and easier on successive days, consistent with the idea of neuromodulation provoked by repetition, whereas the group receiving the stress chemical deteriorated significantly. Worryingly, none of the stressed group noticed any deterioration in their mental performance, even though observers quickly noticed considerable and rapid deterioration, even under low levels of stress!

You might also be tempted by the claims of memory-enhancing chemicals, like Modafinil (Chapter 1).

Cosmetic neurosurgery and brain enhancement

Is this a lifestyle choice, or just cheating? Research into drugs to treat Alzheimer's, narcolepsy and attention deficit disorder has shown that these drugs improve the memory and mental performance of healthy, able people. If you took some of these so-called 'smart drugs', you could speed up the rate at which you learn a new language or a musical instrument or revise for an exam by up to five times. Among our students, claims to double speeds of learning or to quadruple periods of night-time revision are commonplace. Other drugs have been found to have side benefits for risk taking and creativity. Should you take drugs that may shape your personality, your relationships and your mental ability? Is it ethical or is it cheating? If 'smart drugs' were banned, banning research into performance-enhancing drugs would interfere with research into drugs which are desperately awaited by millions of people.

So, we have evidence from Snowdon's nun study; from human brain dissection; from studies of occupation and mental activity; and from the neurochemistry of the brain, that brain training not only improves your memory, it also improves your brain's capacity to resist and reverse the effects of disease, and increases the power of your brain to support more effective applied thinking and more intelligent behaviour. Time to train your brain.

Try it now: pre-test your memory for words

Take exactly two minutes to memorize as many as possible of the 30 words in the table. Then cover the words and write as many of them as you can remember in two minutes on a sheet of paper labelled 'before visualization'. Note your score.

story	midday	slice	tube	corner	fruit
tiger	folder	ceramic	extract	thought	music
dew	office	point	shop	watch	life
sister	cardboard	relax	honey	colour	braces
brain	rain	hole	puzzle	magic	secure

Re-read the original list and create an image in your head associated with each word – an image as large, colourful and weird as possible. Connect that image with an equally colourful image of another word, until all the words are interlinked into a story, or a grand collage or picture. Imagine it hanging on a wall near where you are. Again cover the words and, this time, write as many of them as you can remember in two minutes on a sheet of paper labelled 'after visualization'. Note how much better your score is.

You can count on your memory

Remember to repeat to remember.

* Count aloud to 99 in threes as fast as you can. Note the time you take. Note how you get faster every successive day you do it.
* Count in fives as quickly as you can while cleaning your teeth with your wrong hand. Notice how much further you can get in successive days.
* Repeat 'Remember to repeat to remember' as quickly as you can for one minute.
* Once a week, count aloud from 1 to 130 as fast as you can. Notice how much faster you get each week. This uses both sides of your prefrontal cortex.

Try it now: quick, do some simple sums!

Take exactly two minutes. Total your correct answers and multiply by two. That is your percentage score.

18 – 10 =	8 + 7 =	2 × 5 =
6 + 6 =	13 – 8 =	4 + 2 =
2 × 10 =	0 × 8 =	12 – 5 =
14 – 9 =	8 – 3 =	7 + 10 =
3 × 7 =	3 × 10 =	5 × 2 =
9 – 6 =	6 + 7 =	5 × 4 =
1 + 7 =	10 – 3 =	3 + 6 =
15 – 8 =	1 + 10 =	10 – 9 =
2 + 8 =	9 × 9 =	9 + 5 =
10 – 4 =	7 – 3 =	6 × 8 =
9 + 9 =	6 × 7 =	6 × 9 =
9 – 4 =	6 – 1 =	12 – 4 =
6 × 6 =	4 + 8 =	1 + 8 =
7 + 9 =	7 × 6 =	9 × 10 =
8 × 6 =	4 × 5 =	11 – 8 =
5 – 5 =	5 + 4 =	8 + 9 =
3 + 8 =	10 – 8 =	
	Total score =	× 2 score =

See Answers at the back of the book. You will be able to repeat an equivalent test at the end of Chapter 6 on numerical thinking. By then your score will have improved.

I CAN REMEMBER YOUR FACE, BUT I JUST CAN'T PLACE YOUR NAME

People are irrationally offended, or delighted, by whether or not you forget or remember their names. The names – the words – especially if foreign, are hard to remember because they are only letters devoid of meaning or of any associations that could be placed in your brain to be picked up later as cues. You must repeat the name out loud. Check the spelling. If it is a foreign name, ask what it means and, if appropriate, ask why their parents chose it, etc. The more you talk about it and repeat it the more likely you are to find a way to associate it with a feature in their face.

JUST ADMIT IT

If you have forgotten a name, you've forgotten a name. It's not surprising and you just need to admit it. You will probably find the person has also forgotten yours and will be grateful for a second chance to swap names. Also you will then be able to associate their name with the embarrassment of forgetting it and having to ask a second time. You are far less likely to forget it again.

PINS AND PHONE NUMBERS

Numbers are hard to remember because they are even more devoid of meaning than letters and words. You have to create a meaning, a strong visual meaning. Try going on a 'memory walk'. For example, one (1) might be a mast or a tower near your home or work, two (2) a pair of white swans on black still water, three (3) moist pink lips, four (4) a white sailing yacht on blue water against the green edge of a seaweed-smelling coastline, and so on. You can then connect these images in a silly story to make a sequence, or place them with the objects on your memory walk.

If numbers have more than three digits, they may exceed your cognitive limits, that is, 5 ± 2. The first task is to 'chunk' them, i.e. break them up into groups. Get into the habit of reading numbers like 8922196833369 as, say, 89, 22, 1968, 333, and 69. Read them aloud to add sound and rhythm to what you are trying to remember. The next task is to make each chunk personally meaningful. For example, 89 might be a parent's age – picture the parent as you say 89 aloud; 22 might be the number of a house – visualize the door number as you say 22. Now imagine your 89-year-old parent going into the doorway of the house numbered 22. Perhaps 1968 was the year of a famous sporting event – picture it taking place on the television inside the house numbered 22, and already you can remember 89221968. Continue the process, by associating 333 and then 69 with people, addresses, historic dates, birthdays, etc., and then connect all these images in a story or sequence, adding movement, colour, sound, smells and tastes wherever possible.

LEARN THE LINGO

Joining a conversational language class ticks many brain training boxes. Learning a second language involves social and emotional intelligence (see Chapter 10), as well as recollective thinking, speaking aloud and much useful repetition. It also involves a different part of your brain from the part that you use to speak your first language, and develops some of the parts you need for mathematics and for music. This is very good for synaptic growth generally and for myelination. By making the learning of a second language in school an option rather than mandatory, schools make an important route to brain development optional. If many such 'options' are created, it becomes possible for young people to opt out of brain development altogether! You can make up for this deficit through brain training.

SPELL IT OUT

Obtain a list of the 100 most common misspellings, or generate your own. Stick it up in the bathroom and learn one a day. Recite the ones you have already learned. After 100 days, find a new list, e.g. 100 words that describe emotions. Important as it is to spell accurately, the practice of memorizing – even a word a day – is as important as what you memorize.

Your verbal thinking (see Chapter 10) is limited by your vocabulary, so it is a good idea to expand it. A word a day = 1,000 new words after three years. To put the value of a 1,000 words into perspective, some daily newspapers can be read with a vocabulary of 100 words!

REMEMBER WHAT YOU READ – IT'S OKAY TO SNIFF

In a book, find a paragraph you would like to remember. Then:

1 Inhale a favourite scent (e.g. sage, lavender, basil).

2 Underline the key words.

3 Give the paragraph a newspaper headline.

4 Read the paragraph aloud, as if you were a newsreader – stand up and give it the same drama and emphasis.

5 You might be able to sing the entire paragraph as though it were an emotional ballad.

6 Close the book and write out all you can remember.

7 The next day, inhale the same smell and write out the paragraph again.

GROUP THINGS TOGETHER

Group all like things on your shopping list together, for example, fresh, tinned, chilled, dairy, sweet, frozen, hardware, magazines, etc. Use a mental map of a familiar store to help you. Later, as you walk from section to section in the store, each section will prompt you to recall the items that you grouped together. If there are more than three items in each category, cluster them together in groups of three connected items.

REMEMBERING NOT TO FORGET

Remember that to forget is normal and healthy. It is your healthy default to forget, unless you deliberately decide to remember. Remembering not to forget involves conscious exaggerated concentration on what is to be remembered.

Give yourself a fighting chance to not forget. Put your car keys or door keys on top of what you must remember to take with you. Put your watch on the other hand or a rubber band on your wrist to remind you that there is something to remember.

Remember this: Remember to remember

Your brain has evolved to routinely forget things so as to keep its working space clear to deal with the next threat, or to take the next direction you need to take to get on with your life. Forgetting is your brain's natural default behaviour. Forgetting things does not mean that you are losing your marbles. You will only remember if you remember to override your brain's natural tendency to forget.

BE AFRAID, BE VERY AFRAID

Emotional molecules are the chemical brain's best fixatives. And fear is the best fixer. To remember a route, imagine yourself following the route in fear that a mugger is following you and might attack you at any of the key landmarks. Visualize yourself turning (and cowering) as you pass each of the landmarks.

MAKE A NOTE OF IT

> 'The horror of the moment', the King went on, 'I shall never, never forget.'
> 'You will though,' the Queen said, 'if you don't make a memorandum of it.'
>> *Through the Looking-Glass and What Alice Found There*,
>> 1872, after Lewis Carroll

Always make notes. Take a pad, or ask for a page from someone else when you need one. Map what is being said, or read. Use three chunks of three. Most people can remember three new things $(5 - 2)$, but rarely seven new things $(5 + 2)$. Add matchstick people or colours to your notes, if you want to be able to recall them without reading them.

SLEEP ON IT

If you have forgotten something, remind yourself of the context (subject, person, place, time, occasion, key letter, sound, emotion) and then sleep on it. Put a pen and pad by your bed. If you wake up and remember what you had forgotten, jot it down immediately.

A WALK DOWN MEMORY LANE

Go for a walk that you can reliably reproduce in your head. As you go around your walk, identify, say, 27 distinctive objects on your way from A to B. Be sure that you can see, or imagine, each object clearly, as you go for your mental walk. Then associate each object with a point you want to remember, for example, a point in a presentation, speech, exam question, sales pitch or job application. The crazier, more bizarre or more emotional the association, the better. You will be able to recall your points in any order or even amaze your audience by telling them what points you are skipping over, so as to finish on time. You can, of course, remind them in reverse order of the 27 points (three groups of three groups of three points = 27 points) you have just covered. What a speaker, and without notes!

THE FUTURE OF MEMORY

It has previously been thought that Alzheimer's is principally caused by the build-up of plaques in the brain. Drugs aimed at dispersing these have failed to bring about any improvement in memory and cognitive abilities. Research now suggests that high levels of an inhibitory neurotransmitter that dampens the firing of neurons in people with Alzheimer's is considerably decreased in an area of the brain that is the gateway to the region responsible for learning and memory.

The next ten years is likely to see memory implant chips being inserted into human brains. The Restoring Active Memory project run by the US Defence Advanced Research Project Agency (DARPA) is currently recruiting!

Try it now: Post-test your memory for words

1 Re-do the mental arithmetic exercises as a warm-up.
2 Study the words below for two minutes. Use image associations to connect the words into a picture or a story.
3 Cover the words and write as many of them down as you can in two minutes.
4 After exactly two minutes, check your score.

fruit	bowl	coin	elastic	diamond	eye
list	crowd	field	stamp	taste	wind
frame	poem	ink	garden	water	correct
price	swim	pole	mouth	dress	litre
sweat	finger	wake up	inside	dance	Boat\

▶ How did you get on?

The post-test has been designed to be equivalent in difficulty to the pre-test memorization exercise you did at the start of the workout (see above).

Our students typically remember around five words without visualization and do very much better after visualization. Their scores usually improve by at least 30 per cent; their scores average eight words, thereby exceeding their theoretical cognitive limit of 5 ± 2. Often they can remember many more words than that.

Focus points

* Your memory underpins your thinking.
* You can improve your memory, through tricks, tools and training.
* Memory training expands the cognitive capacity of your brain.
* Expanding the cognitive capacity of your brain helps to protect it against disease and increases its power to support applied thinking and intelligent behaviour.
* Your memory can limit your thinking power.
* Forgetting is normal and necessary. When you need to remember, you must take deliberate steps to counter your natural tendency to forget.
* Effective strategies for countering forgetfulness exist and can be learned.
* Forgetfulness is not an inevitable consequence of getting older.
* Memorizing new things stimulates new neuron growth and forges new synaptic connections.
* Memorizing involves repetition, which strengthens myelination. Memorizing thereby develops intelligence and spare cognitive capacity. This helps to protect your ability to think, as well as to remember, should you develop a disease like Alzheimer's.

Dig deeper

Finkel, E., *Stem Cells: Controversy at the Frontiers of Science* (Sydney: ABC Books, 2006).

Finkel, E., 'The Labyrinth of Memory' (*Cosmos*, 13, 2007).

Kawashima, Dr, *Train Your Brain* (London: Penguin, 2007).

McKay, R., and Cameron, H. A., 'Restoring the production of hippocampal neurons in old age', *Nature Neuroscience*, 2 (1999), pp. 894–7.

Otten, L., *Journal of Neuroscience* (February, 2006).

Rupp, R., *Committed to Memory* (London: Aurum Press Limited, 1998).

Wiseman, J., *Quirkology* (London: Macmillan, 2007).

Next steps

* Make sure you do brain training exercises: number activities such as electronic games and sudoku are good.
* Combine physical activity with social and mental activities, for example amateur dramatics, dancing clubs.
* Learn a new language.

4

Developing intelligence

In this chapter you will learn:

▶ *how to exploit multiple intelligences to make your behaviour more intelligent*

▶ *how to improve your scores in IQ tests*

▶ *how to exploit aspects of your intelligence that improve with age*

▶ *that you can preserve your ability to think by creating spare cognitive capacity as a buffer against disease*

▶ *that you can use puzzles and games to develop spare cognitive capacity.*

Intelligence is what you use when you don't know what to do.

Jean Piaget

Introduction

WHAT IS IQ AND HOW IS IT MEASURED?

Early ideas about intelligence were discredited when they were used to justify slavery, discrimination and sterilization of the 'feeble minded'. We now know that there are multiple types of intelligence, many of which continue to develop during your lifetime. Unfortunately, IQ continues to be measured by traditional tests which are based only on verbal, numerical and spatial reasoning. While these are very important contributors to your overall intelligence, they ignore other important contributors to intelligent behaviour, such as creativity, ability to predict, and skills in reflecting on general knowledge and experience. All of these improve as you get older.

Remember this: Feeling right

Success at work and satisfaction in life have been found to be more closely related to emotional intelligence than high scores on mental, numerical and verbal tests of IQ.

THE USE OF IQ TESTS FOR JOB SELECTION

Traditional tests are still being used to assess people for jobs, despite having been shown to be poor predictors of success. If you go for a job with an employer who uses selection tests, you are likely to be given a battery of tests – often called psychometric tests. The tests will almost certainly include some traditional IQ tests. These may be pen and paper tests or, more likely, they will be screen-based. You must attempt as many questions as you can within a limited time, which will be strictly enforced. There are always more questions than you can complete within the time and the questions will usually become harder as you work through the test. Since incorrect guesses do not count against you, you should try to attempt all the questions. Your scores for numerical, verbal and visual thinking will then be combined into an overall IQ score and added to a profile of your aptitudes and abilities.

IQ PRE-TEST

Try to answer the following ten questions in ten minutes:

Q1   Fill in the blank space.

17	35	3	21
26		19	

Q2   2.5 is to quintuple as 2 is to…

Q3   Which is next in the series?

▶ 5 minutes before 3 o'clock

▶ 15 minutes after 5 o'clock

▶ 25 minutes before 7 o'clock

Q4   Infant is to infancy as adult is to…

Q5   Which is the odd one out? 684.5, $\sqrt{100}$, 13.4, –1, $\sqrt{49}$, 72

Q6   Which is the odd word? Through, thought, thorough, trough, tough, brought

Q7   Add a word made up of four letters so that it completes a word beginning forth_ _ _ _ and starts another word ending _ _ _ _out.

Q8   Who is the odd one out in the following list of artists? Dali, Da Vinci, Van Gogh, Verdi, Picasso

Q9   What is the next number in the series? 1, 2, 3, 5, 9, 12, 21, 22… (Hint: Write out the numbers as words.)

Q10   Complete the series Bach 4/17, Brahms 6/19, Britten 7/20, Beethoven _/_

See Answers at the back of the book.

▶ How did you do?

If you were able to answer these questions in ten minutes, then you are likely to perform well on the sorts of IQ exercises that are typically used in job selection tests.

Modern tests of multiple intelligences

To try to overcome the limitations of traditional IQ tests, there has been a move, especially in US organizations, towards tests that provide a better assessment of multiple intelligences.

Older people generally perform better than younger people on these tests. This is because the tests involve using lifetime-acquired general knowledge and information to infer the most likely answers. Older people generally have more lifetime-acquired information than younger people. These tests involve verbal, visual and creative thinking.

However, even these tests are still an imperfect measure of intelligence, because they do not measure numerical, predictive or reflective thinking, which are important contributors to intelligent behaviour. Older people tend to score higher than younger people on numerical, predictive and reflective thinking. Predictive and reflective thinking are key components of 'streetwise' intelligence.

A MORE MODERN IQ TEST

Answer as many questions as you can in five minutes.

Q1   Woman is to X as criterion is to criteria. Is X: child, father, gender or women?

Q2   Past is to X as spun is to spinning. Is X: present, participle, predictive or rotation?

Q3   Planes is to X as lines is to cross. Is X: arc, eclipse, intersect or chord?

Q4   Breakfast is to X as meal is to hearty. Is X: continental, full English, light or eat?

Q5   Plane is to X as polish is to stone. Is X: flight, hydrofoil, timber or wheat?

Q6 Buddhism is to X as median is to average. Is X: séance, monk, meditation or religion?

Q7 Submarine is to X as helicopter is to air. Is X: yacht, fish, lake or water?

Q8 Meaning is to X as category is to homogenous. Is X: acronym, anonymous, synchronous or synonymous?

See Answers at the back of the book.

THE DISADVANTAGES OF YOUTH

Young people who have high verbal IQ scores can sometimes think and talk so quickly that they can defend the intellectually indefensible. They can argue for an unreasonable inference or gloss over an impractical implication, especially when they get a quicker reward for doing a clever demolition job on your ideas than they would if they took time to examine their own.

Intelligent people are used to getting things right, from school onwards. Getting something wrong is unfamiliar, and intelligent people generally do not like the unfamiliar feeling of getting things wrong. Delusions of infallibility are often intact in younger people and the preservation of these delusions is sometimes more important to them than entertaining the possibility that they may be wrong.

▶ 'Streetwise'

Awareness of other possibilities and other possible consequences increases as you get older. According to Sternberg (1997), this leads to 'streetwise' intelligence, which shows its wisdom through having 'good' or 'bad' feelings about people and situations. 'Streetwise' intelligence depends on broad general knowledge linked to experience. Both of these increase as you get older.

Remember this: Streetwise

Your 'streetwise' intelligence – your practical ability to solve problems, or to learn things quickly – has at least eight components, only three of which are routinely measured in IQ tests.

▶ Eminence

To be eminent, you need only exhibit one type of intelligence. Eight possible types of intelligence have been identified:

Intelligence	The capacity... type
Environmental	to observe and see patterns
Interpersonal	to compartmentalize and respond
Intrapersonal	to know your motives, goals, feelings
Kinaesthetic	to manipulate concepts or to use your body
Linguistic	to use language, oral or written
Musical	to use tone, accent, rhythm, pitch
Logical	to think logically, calculate scientifically
Visual	to use graphics, to think spatially

Source: after Gardner, 2004

William Wordsworth, Ludwig van Beethoven, Albert Einstein, J. M. W. Turner, Pablo Picasso, Sigmund Freud, Winston Churchill, Mahatma Gandhi and Charles Darwin displayed intelligences that lay dormant until specifically exercised later in life.

Try it now: Which intelligence could be pre-eminent for you in later life?

Study the table below and then check out 'Steps to eminence'.

Types of genius in later life

Masters	Know all there is to know in a particular field. Masters are people with whom others feel privileged to work, or to whom others seek to be apprenticed, or under whom others seek to serve. One thinks of master painters, like J. M. W. Turner.
Makers	Know enough about the rules of a particular discipline to be able to break them. Like writing sentences without verbs! Makers bring new ways of thinking. People like Charles Darwin and Sigmund Freud.
Influencers	Work through others, often behind the scenes. Influencers are the power behind thrones, like the 'Silent Accountant' behind Richard Branson. Philosophers like

John Locke influenced Thomas Jefferson, who wrote the American Constitution. Karl Marx, Martin Luther King and Mahatma Gandhi illustrate how powerful an idea can be – sometimes quietly spoken in small circles (witness the influence of the Quakers).

Introspectors Keep detailed diaries, write long letters or make extensive notes and leave them for posterity. Novelists, poets and politicians sometimes do this. People like Virginia Woolf, William Wordsworth and Tony Benn.

Source: after Gardner, 2004

▶ Steps to eminence

Step 1 First decide which of the following would interest you most. Ring the letter below your choice.

If...	Groups Management	Individuals Psychology	Nature Biology	Engineering Maths
Ring	A	B	C	D

If...	Bodies Sport	Words Teaching	Sounds Music	Appearance Art
Ring	E	F	G	H

Step 2 Next decide which of the following you think describes you best. Put a ring around the number below it.

Planning Organizing Controlling	Articulate Numerate Logical	Good at learning Reflective	Curious Experimental Risk taking	Adaptable Easygoing Streetwise
1	2	3	4	5

Step 3 You now have a number/letter combination, e.g. A2. If you find the position of your number/letter combination on the matrix below, it will be at the epicentre of career words that enable you to explore the opportunities open to your particular intelligence.

	1	2	3	4	5
A	Production control	Manufacturing management	Quality control	Research development	Sales services
B	Planning administrator	Counselling Therapy	Academic research	Writing Editing	Social work Youth work
C	Middle management	Editor Publisher	Academic research	Inventor Designer	Environment Ecology
D	Project management	Systems analysis	Purchasing Logistics	Design engineer	Team leader
E	Own business	Commentator Sports writer	Dance Performance	Outdoor Active	Trainer Journalist
F	Literary PR agent	Actor/Editor Teacher	Critic Professor	Poet Writer	Journalist PR/ media
G	Agent, arts management	Lyrics Advertising	Music critic	Composer Musician	Teacher Accompanist
H	Arts admin. Museum	Designer Trainer	Exhibitor Development	Artist Creative	Director Innovation

Increase your intelligence and IQ score

Reviews of more than 200 studies, including studies of adopted siblings and twins, have shown that less than 50 per cent of your IQ is limited by your genes – although good genes clearly get you off to a good start! In the longer term, you can improve your IQ score by 4 points just by what you choose to eat and drink (see Chapter 1). You can add another 6–7 points by regular thoughtful conversations (see Chapter 10). You can avoid short-term deficits of up to 15 points, by following regular patterns of sleep (see Chapter 1). According to Ostranger, you can add up to 14 points to your test score by preparation and stress reduction (see Chapter 5). An increase of 14–15 points is significant when related to a 'normal' IQ score of 100. A reduction of 15 points, to an IQ of 85, would be to a level where special educational provision is needed. An increase of 15 points, to an IQ of 115, would normally allow access to 'white collar' jobs.

Remember this: It's not just genes

IQ does not appear to be determined solely by your genes – though it does no harm to have high-IQ parents and grandparents. The extent to which you develop high IQ seems to be a lifestyle choice, rather than a genetic determinant. What you eat, what you do and how you predominantly feel, are lifestyle factors over which you can exercise control.

▶ Preparing for IQ tests: a seven-point plan

1 If your diet has been haywire recently, then take the stipulated daily doses of vitamins B1, B5 and C, plus mineral supplements boron, zinc and selenium. Take with plenty of water (see Chapter 1).

2 Practise mixing yourself booster drinks to find the mix and concentration that suits you. You may need a boost on the day, especially if the tests are held in the afternoon. Booster drinks can be made from hot water and a spoon of honey mixed together in a mug. Add the juice of a lemon. Drink it with a capsule of vitamin E. Experiment the week before, with one to four capsules but do not exceed the daily dose. Take the drink and the vitamin E capsules about one hour before the test. Sip sage tea during the test (see Chapter 1).

3 Make sure your prior sleep pattern is stable and sufficient (see Chapter 1).

4 Raise or reduce your stress level so that you enjoy a sense of well-being. Use lavender oil if you need to calm yourself. On the day, put peppermint, basil, sage or rosemary oil on a tissue so that you can control your level of mental alertness (see Chapter 5).

5 If you think you may be over-tired and low in energy on the day, practise making 3G cocktails. A 3G cocktail comprises the herbs ginger, ginkgo and ginseng. It is important not to exceed the stated dose.

6 Use visual thinking and emotional thinking to experience, in advance, a good feeling in the test room (see Chapters 2 and 8).

7 Careers advice services, or job centres, will often let you practise taking tests under 'test' conditions. This is a good way to desensitize yourself to test trauma. Learn a breathing exercise to control your stress (see Chapter 1).

This seven-point plan will also help you with the job selection tests in Chapters 6, 7, 8, 9 and 10.

DOES LIFELONG LEARNING HELP?

In 2001, in a basement in Scotland, Professor Ian Bard discovered 70,000 test papers that were taken when the candidates were 11 years old. The university tracked down 1,500 of the original candidates (who at that time were then over 70 years of age) and invited them to resit their 11+ examination. The candidates agreed to the use of MRI (magnetic resonance imaging) brain scans and to provide a life history. The results did not surprise those of us with extensive experience of working with mature students. The mature students scored on average about 10 per cent higher than when they had first taken their IQ tests at the age of 11! As we saw earlier, a 10 per cent shift, e.g. from 100 to 110, or 110 to 121, or 120 to 132, is a very significant gain. Other gains, especially among the physically fit candidates who had remained mentally active, were very high indeed. This 'elite' group is still being studied. It is already clear that ongoing learning and ongoing mental activity correlate strongly with these larger gains in IQ. The only vitamin/mineral supplements that appeared to have any long-term correlation were B12 and folic acid. The implication for those who wish to improve their IQ as they get older is to carry on learning formally, or informally, no matter at what age, and, of course, to train the brain as much as the body.

First, what you learn will likely add to the breadth of your general knowledge and this will support many of the thinking skills that contribute to your intelligent behaviour – like your capacity for critical, creative and reflective thinking. Second, how you learn can promote the formation of new neural pathways, newly connecting different parts of your brain.

Remember this: New tricks

Learning new things is a good way to put new neuron connections in place, as well as thickening up the insulation on existing neural pathways. The more often a neural pathway is run, the thicker the myelin insulation becomes on the axons of the neurons on that particular pathway. The thicker the insulation, the lower the risk of corruption or interference.

▶ **Choosing courses**

▶ Check *how* you will learn, as well as *what* you will learn.

▶ Avoid programmes that rely heavily on a traditional lecture/ seminar format, especially if seminar numbers are too high to support the kind of one-to-one conversations that foster cognitive development (see Chapters 8 and 10).

▶ Be wary of academic courses that rely heavily on information transfer via information technology (IT), distance learning packs or handouts.

▶ Ask how much one-to-one, face-to-face contact you will have.

▶ Ask if paired learning will be used (see Chapters 8 and 10).

The neuromodulated neural pathways created by your learning will enhance and extend the neural networks that support your growing intelligence.

Neurochemistry of intelligence

So far we have only considered ways to improve traditional IQ scores, but a multi-faceted model of intelligence leaves open the possibility of activities that can further enhance intelligent behaviour. The work of Haier (1995) and Miller (1994) suggests that the better connected the different areas of your brain, the more intelligent you will be.

Exercises like the ones in this book may work in part by stimulating the growth, thickening and replacement rate of the myelin, the insulation that surrounds the nerves in the brain. This is like replacing the poor quality leads that come with a boxed set stereo, or home cinema system, with a more expensive set of leads. The more expensive leads enhance the quality of the sound from your speakers and the definition of your TV picture.

The density of the neuron connections in your brain can be increased not only by learning new things (see Chapter 8), but also by tackling tasks and exercises that require you to use different parts of your brain in combination. As you saw in

Chapter 3, activities that involve remembering and repeated recall involve an extensive network that radiates out from the hippocampus, rather as if it is a central switchboard. The brain training exercises in this book are purposely designed so that you can exercise different thinking muscles, separately, and then in different combinations.

COMBINATION THINKING TASKS

Here are three sample combination thinking tasks for you to try.

Q1   Combining visual and numerical thinking

What's the missing number?

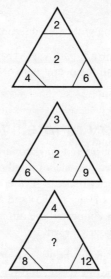

Q2   Combining visual and emotional thinking

A young child has returned home from school to find seven pebbles, a carrot, and a wet scarf on the grass outside the house. Why is the child crying?

Q3 Combining visual, numerical and creative thinking

Because it is a chocolate cake, all eight people at the party want an equal slice of the cake. You are allowed three cuts.

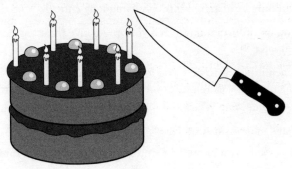

▶ **How did you get on?**

Students doing these kinds of thinking combination exercises as part of their brain training workouts have often complained to us that such exercises make their 'heads hurt', a little like muscle fatigue after working out in a gym. This book helps you to create your own mental gymnasium. (Answers at the back of the book.)

Remember this: Get connected

The physical basis of your intelligence or cognitive capacity seems to be the extent to which there are residual connections in place between different areas of your brain. You put these connections in place by thinking about problems that require you to use more than one area of your brain simultaneously.

AFTER THE INITIAL BURN...

Haier's (1995) work, using brain scanners, has shown that when more intelligent people start thinking about a problem, many different areas of their brains light up and link up simultaneously. During this initial stage the brain burns lots of energy while feeling its way around the problem, but it quickly delegates its work to those areas of the brain that support the kinds of thinking needed to address the problem. This local area network then takes over, allowing the rest of the brain to relax.

GROWING OLD GRACEFULLY AND INTELLIGENTLY

As you get older:

▶ you have the advantage of information and experience that can only be acquired through living long enough

▶ you use information to feed your predictive thinking (see Chapter 8)

▶ when it begins to take you longer to do certain things – like calculate, for example, or memorize new material – start sooner

▶ keep learning and trying new things (see Chapter 8)

▶ make sure you know a lot and about many different things

▶ use the full 'hierarchy of thinking skills'

▶ each time you do exercises in this book, you will open new neural pathways and this will add to the processing power of your brain. As you complete more chapters, you will combine the processing power of different parts of your brain. You will become more intelligent.

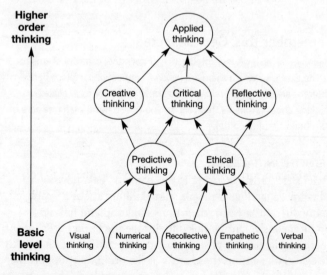

Figure 4.1 The hierarchy of thinking skills.
Source: Horne and Wootton, 2003

The IQ workout

INTRODUCTION

The following sets of activities will stretch and work different combinations of your mental 'muscles'. Each activity can leave a different neural pathway in place. The more neural pathways through the neural maze of your mind, the greater your intelligence. Activities like the ones below force your brain to think about the problems they pose. This is called 'metacognition'. Metacognitive activity thickens the front of your cerebral cortex. This is the thinking cap – the top layer of your brain, sometimes called the 'learning brain'. The two layers below are often called the 'reptilian' or 'mammalian' brains. Your cerebral cortex is the part of your brain that works out the best way to think about a problem.

▶ **Puzzles**

A good 'puzzle' or 'problem' requires virtually all of the ten component thinking skills (see Figure 4.1). If you find some of these puzzles hard, so you should. They were contributed by many of James Fixx's friends from MENSA in the USA (see Taking it further). Fixx is keen to point out that one of the key components of intellectual power is the power to work and keep going. Intelligent work is often 90 per cent perspiration and 10 per cent inspiration.

Q1   Boxes and coins

| All copper coins | Copper and silver coins | All silver coins |

Each label is incorrect. You are required to re-label each box correctly after removing one coin only without looking into the box.

Q2 The spider and the fly

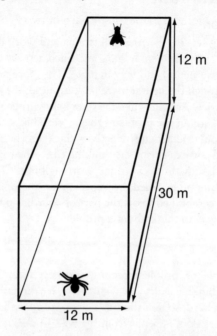

What is the shortest distance from the spider to the fly (the room is 30 m × 12 m × 12 m)? The spider is 1 m from the floor. The fly is 1 m from the ceiling.

Q3 Getting to the root of the problem

A garden has 12 trees in a row.

How could they be uprooted and replanted to make six rows with four trees in each row?

Q4 Swinging between beach showers

A 12 m rope is secured to the tops of each of two 8 m tall beach showers and the rope hangs down between them so that, at its lowest point, the rope is 2 m from the ground. What is the separation between the two posts?

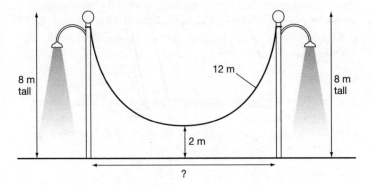

Q5 Give me one honest man

The man in the road needs to find one honest man. He knows that one side of the road is Truth Land, where everyone always tells the truth and the other side is False Land where everyone always lies. He asks Mr A to ask Mrs B which side of the road she lives on. Mr A returns saying that Mrs B says she is from Truth Land. Is Mr A an honest man?

Q6   Job selection: does colour matter?

Three candidates for a high-IQ job are asked to close their eyes while a mark, either black or white, is placed on their forehead. They are asked to open their eyes and raise a hand if they can see a black mark on the forehead of another candidate. All three raise a hand. The first candidate to identify the colour on his own forehead will get the job. After a while, one of the candidates does this and is given the job. How did he work out what his colour was?

Q7   Cash

You are a cashier and one customer has shaved 1 g of gold off each of the gold coins in one of their ten bags. All the bags contain the same number of coins. How can you find the bag with the shaved coins in one weighing?

Q8   Seven-year itch?

Not very long after it was bought second-hand, a sports car was fitted with a new, more powerful engine. Now the car is twice as old as its engine had been when the car was as old as the engine is now. How old was the car when the more powerful engine was fitted? The combined age of the engine and the car is 49 years.

Q9   Eight small squares

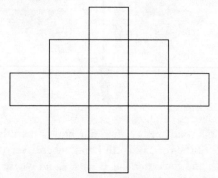

Remove four lines to leave eight small squares.

Q10   What time is it Mr Wolf?

Which clock, A, B, C, or D, completes the series?

Series

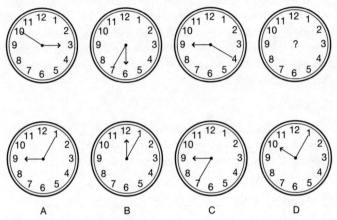

A   B   C   D

Q11   Stacking pyramids

Move three lines only to make five triangles.

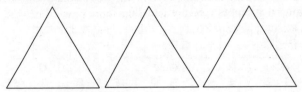

Q12   Eternal triangles

Add three lines to make eight triangles.

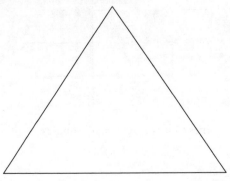

Q13 Where next?

Where should the next • go (given that the first • was placed in the top triangle)?

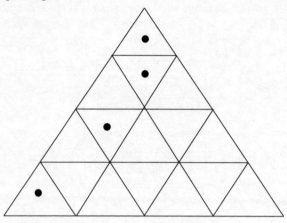

Q14 Topsy-turvy words

When you insert the missing letters you will discover a way of thinking that makes you more intelligent.

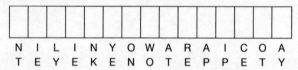

N	I	L	I	N	Y	O	W	A	R	A	I	C	O	A
T	E	Y	E	K	E	N	O	T	E	P	P	P	E	T	Y

Q15 The one-match trick

Move one match to balance the equation.

Q16 Saving trees

The swimming pool is square (area 900sq metres). How can
you keep the pool square but increase its area to approximately
3,600 sq metres, without felling the trees (or surrounding them
with water)?

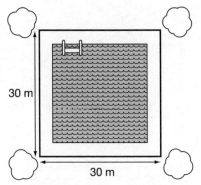

30 m

30 m

Q17 Half full and half empty

How can you change this line of seven glasses so that they
alternate full and empty? You may only touch one glass of the
seven.

Q18 Water bottles

Three Bedouins travelling together in the desert decided to go
their separate ways. Between them they had seven full, seven
half full and seven empty water bottles. The bottles each held
5 litres. They decided to divide their water and the 21 bottles
equally between them. How did they do that?

Q19 What day is it?

In summer, water lilies double their area every 24 hours, so
that on day 30 the pond is covered. The first lily appeared on
the first day of the month and the pond is already half covered.
What day of the month is it?

Q20 Moat width

At its narrowest point, the castle moat is 10 m wide and you have only two planks 1 m × 9 m and no means to join them. How can you use the 2 planks to cross the moat? (The planks must not touch the water.)

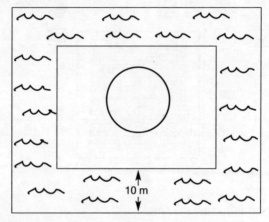

Q21 Segments and life support

What life support could be chemically represented by the following segment of the alphabet?

HIJKLMNO

Q22 Refusing to pay for bad service

A restaurant's royal customer waited 43 minutes for the waiter to take her order. Finally she got up and left. The doorkeeper asked her if she had paid her bill. She said no and offered to write the manager an explanation. She wrote:

10004180204

What did she mean?

Q23   A load of balls

A blindfolded man takes a ball out of Box A and then a ball out of Box B. What are his chances of picking at least one black ball?

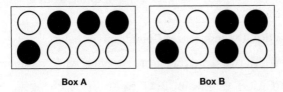

Box A   **Box B**

Q24   A big chest

A big chest holds two chests, that each hold three chests, that each hold 4 chests. Only one chest contains gold. How many chests must be opened to be sure which one has the gold?

Q25   Bottles and tops

A bottle top costs one-tenth the cost of a bottle. Together they cost £2.20. What does the bottle cost?

Q26   The knights of the round table

In how many different ways can eight knights be arranged around a round table?

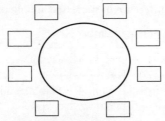

Answers are at the back of the book.

IQ POST-TEST

After completing the IQ workout, allow a day's rest before this post-test. Follow the advice on taking IQ tests from earlier in the chapter.

You are allowed strictly ten minutes for ten questions.

Q1 Fill in the same five letters, in the same order, to complete the words:

_ _ _ _ _ weight and news _ _ _ _ _

Q2 Which word in brackets is closest to the word in upper case?

ORIGIN (unique, zero, point, species, source)

Q3 Which two word fragments are edible when combined?

(GAR; SAL; LIK; BUR; GER; AME)

Q4 Which word in brackets has a meaning most opposed to the meaning of the word in capitals?

INTRICATE (involved, circuitous, straight, direct, simple)

Q5 B, F, J, P, V – which letter is immediately to the right of the letter which is three to the left of the letter P?

Q6 Pond is to field as island is to (waves, current, rocks, reefs, water)?

Q7 What tidy piece of civil engineering would be an anagram of MANDATE?

Q8 What is the next number in the series 1, 3, 7, 15, 31, 63 …? (Hint: difference in successive numbers)

Q9 What is the missing number X?

5	9	14
7	3	10
12	12	X

Q10 Which word in the brackets could replace any of the following?

faultless, rectify, discipline (accurate, correct, admonish)

Answers are at the end of the book. Compare your score with the pre-test. If it has improved, that bodes well.

Focus points

❋ You can exploit multiple intelligences to become more intelligent.

❋ You can exploit aspects of your intelligence that improve with age.

❋ You can preserve your ability to think by creating spare cognitive capacity, as a buffer against disease.

❋ You can use puzzles and games to develop spare cognitive capacity.

❋ IQ tests measure some important thinking skills that contribute to your intelligent behaviour.

❋ In addition to the critical thinking skills measured in IQ tests, creative thinking, reflective thinking and predictive thinking are major contributors to your intelligent behaviour and these will improve as you get older.

❋ Your scores on IQ tests can be easily improved by up to 14 points – a very significant improvement.

❋ A high IQ score is no guarantee of intelligent behaviour. For example, some fast-thinking people are more adept at defending poor thinking than they are at thinking well.

❋ Speed and accuracy of thinking are correlated with the quality of the myelin insulation surrounding the axons of the neurons in your brain, and this can be improved through diet and brain training exercises.

❋ Intelligence is linked to the number of neural pathways in your brain and these can be increased by working through this book.

Dig deeper

Fixx, J., *Games for the Super Intelligent* (New York: Doubleday, 1972).

Gardner, H., *Changing Minds* (Boston: Harvard Business School Press, 2004).

Haier, R., *Newsweek*, Associated Press (27 March, 1995).

Howard, P. J., *The Owner's Manual for the Brain: Everyday Applications from Mind and Brain Research* (3rd edn, Austin, Texas: Bard Press, 2006).

Miller, E. M., 'Intelligence and brain myelination', *Personality and Individual Differences*, vol. 17 (1994), pp. 227–55.

O'Keefe, J., *Mind Openers for Managers* (San Francisco: Thorsons, 1994).

Sternberg, R. J., *Successful Intelligence* (New York: Plume, 1997).

Next steps

* Check your diet – are you getting the stipulated doses of vitamin B1, B5 and C, plus minerals Boron, Zinc and Selenium?
* Drink plenty of water – at least two litres a day.
* Ensure you get plenty of sleep and follow your natural sleeping and waking times seven days a week – the lie in at the weekend doesn't help your IQ!

PART TWO
AT WORK

The brain at work

In this chapter you will learn:

▶ *how to use music, temperature, lighting, colour, smell, touch and fresh air when creating a space to think*

▶ *how to protect your brain from computers, photocopiers, fax machines and air conditioning*

▶ *how to limit the brain damage caused by stress*

▶ *how to use mindfulness to help your brain*

▶ *how to concentrate and control interruption – the myth of multitasking*

▶ *how to not disturb the brain at work.*

There tends to be a terrible cleavage between thinking and doing.

Laurens van der Post

Introduction

THE RISE AND DEMISE OF THE KNOWLEDGE WORKER

In the remainder of the book, we look at how to train your brain to think well at work and in relationships. To work successfully and to form close relationships, are two of the primary challenges of adult life. During the last century in the Western world, the nature of work – whether as a paid employee or an unpaid parent – has changed dramatically and is now changing rapidly for millions of people in Asia. Muscle is needed less and less as machines take over labour. Machine minding is done by microchips. As databases expand, 'knowledge' workers are paid less for what they know, and more for how well they think about what they know. In this chapter we discuss the conditions that favour economical, efficient and effective thinking.

Environmental factors

NOISE AND MUSIC WHILE YOU WORK

In 2007, Professor Deepak Prasher found that noises exceeding 75 decibels raise your blood pressure, which damages your brain. In 2006, loud noises caused 3 per cent of fatal heart attacks. Sudden intermittent noises are more distracting to your brain than consistent high background noise. It is the level of intermittent noise relative to the background noise level that seems to be important. So, sometimes, one way to reduce distraction is to raise the level of background noise. Music while you work has been used to do this, but not all music has the same beneficial effect for all people. Ideally, music while you work should be through individual headsets. Background music has been found to reduce mental fatigue and improve concentration only if it is well matched to the thinking task in hand, and to your preference as an individual. Communal background music actually impairs the thinking ability of 20 per cent of people, because 20 per cent of people can only think if it is absolutely quiet.

> **Remember this:** Thinking skills
>
> Thinking involves chemical reactions in your brain. How well these reactions take place depends on other chemicals present in your brain. The chemical balance within your brain responds to what is going on around you. You can learn to control what is going on around you in order to create a good space in which to think.

▶ **Music for the mind**

▶ **Buy, borrow or record the following music:** Mozart (e.g. *The Marriage of Figaro*, *The Magic Flute* or a piano concerto), Beethoven (e.g. any of the nine symphonies or the five piano concertos), Wagner (e.g. the *Ring Cycle*), Mendelssohn (e.g. Violin Concerto in E minor), Liszt, Chopin or Grieg (e.g. their piano music), Vivaldi (e.g. harpsichord music), ballet (e.g. *Swan Lake*, *Coppélia*, *The Rite of Spring*), Verdi (e.g. 'Chorus of the Hebrew Slaves' (from *Nabucco*) or *La Traviata*), Ravel (e.g. *Boléro*), Rolling Stones, Status Quo, Tina Turner, Eagles, Queen or Meat Loaf, King's College Choir (e.g. early plainsong), 1920s jazz (e.g. King Oliver).

▶ **If you need to raise your mental energy** try King Oliver, Rolling Stones, Status Quo, Motown, disco, Meat Loaf or Tina Turner. If you don't like rock, try Ravel or Vivaldi.

▶ **If you need to process new information,** and you like orchestral music, try Beethoven. If you prefer piano music, try Liszt. If you like the sound of the violin, try Mendelssohn. Try Wagner if you like big choral sounds. In order to maintain your energy levels, choose music that is suited to the type of thinking you need to do and that you find most rhythmic.

▶ **If you need to calculate,** or to draw networks, or flow charts, choose Mozart, Vivaldi or the King's College Choir.

▶ **If you need to analyse accounts,** try listening to baroque or King's College Choir plainsong.

- **If your work requires creative thinking,** do not use music that you have found to be energizing. Choose music that you find calming, or use a relaxation tape. Try *Jonathan Livingston Seagull* (Neil Diamond), *Tubular Bells* or Jean-Michel Jarre.

- **If you need to think creatively about new information,** try the second movement of Bruch's First Violin Concerto or Mendelssohn's *Violin Concerto in E minor*. If there is some element of calculation involved, listen to Mozart's *Clarinet Concerto in A major*.

- If you have been asked to take a test, listen to Mozart beforehand.

- Radio channels or compilations of 'hits' are too varied in mood and rhythm to support a particular kind of thinking. (Teenagers who play general popular music while doing homework learn 50 per cent less.) Classical music usually comes in longer movements which can sustain the same useful mood for longer periods.

ARE YOU UNDER THE WEATHER?

Changes in air pressure can alter your behaviour and trigger poor performance. In southern Europe, public examinations are postponed if the wind direction changes so that it blows from the Sahara desert. This particular wind makes it impossible for some students to think.

Sunlight can also affect performance. The length and brightness of daylight affect your body's melatonin and hormone levels and this influences the release of neurotransmitters in your brain. This affects your alertness, responsiveness and mood. Each, in turn, can affect your ability to think.

Lack of exposure to sunlight can create a specific condition called Seasonal Affective Disorder (SAD). Artificial light therapy can alleviate SAD if the dosage of light is strong enough. SAD triggers carbohydrate cravings and eating the carbohydrate creates excessive levels of serotonin in the brain, and this reduces speed and performance in thinking tasks that involve complex analysis, calculation and decision making.

US defence studies report that heat stress (a combination of high temperatures and humidity) dramatically lowers scores in intellectual and physical tasks. High temperatures reduce performance in tasks that require accuracy and speed. A rise of only 1° in brain temperature is enough to disturb cognitive functioning. At work, you should push for comfortable, breathable clothing for the back office; and whatever the dress code needs to be for the front of house. Evaluations of non-uniform days have found a marked improvement in creative thinking.

LET THERE BE LIGHT

Light affects your mood and hence your mental energy. Light also affects your mental alertness and speed of thinking. Light tells your pineal gland to stop producing melatonin. This is a good thing because melatonin literally sends your brain to sleep.

Do not dim the lights to make your computer screen easier to read. If you need to think about what you are doing, brighten your screen instead (or, better still, do your thinking away from your computer). For brainwork you need bright light, preferably natural light. If this needs to be supplemented by artificial light, use full spectrum 'blue' tubes. Many lightbulbs emit too much red and violet light. Absence of the blue end of the spectrum causes measurable fatigue and eye strain.

If you fly to work across a time zone, try taking a 'light shower' to help reset your body clock, otherwise your brain may still be half asleep as you struggle to think on your feet. Pierce Howard reports that three schools in North Carolina improved their average test scores by up to 14 per cent, by increasing their use of natural lighting. If you need to buy your own full spectrum light for brain work, check out www.sltbr.org or www. naturallighting.com.

DO YOU SEE RED AT WORK?

Howard finds little evidence to support a general view that pale green, pale blue, pale pink or pale yellow are more conducive to brain work than pure white, or than dark colours like brown, grey or purple. Some findings are contradictory, but most agree that primary colours are energizing. Given the range of individual responses, pale green and pale blue seem safest.

Howard recommends adding touches of red, but in March 2007 the *Journal of Experimental Psychology* reported that scores dropped for students who were given a red motif to attach to their test papers (control groups were given green or grey motifs). Japanese researchers reported similar effects when they fitted red surrounds to computer screens. (Contrary to urban myth, researchers found that drivers of red cars were less likely than others to break speed limits or jump traffic signals.)

DO YOU SMELL OF SEX, STRESS OR SUCCESS?

Howard has identified two scent-detecting systems in the brain, one for sexual scents and another for non-sexual scents. The detection of non-sexual scents is routed via the cerebral cortex, enabling some rational evaluation of their significance. Sexual scents on the other hand, are routed directly to the limbic system and so have no rational mediation.

In animals, the sexual scent system detects pheromones, but the jury is out on whether this happens in humans. Men and women wearing 'guaranteed to pull' pheromone perfumes report success. However, the placebo effect may be strong, because increased confidence is itself sexually attractive.

Your smell system is sensitive to more than 10,000 odours. Compare this with your retina, which can distinguish only a few hundred different colours.

Be wary of thundery weather which causes you to sweat because this kind of weather also heightens everybody's sense of smell. 'Bad' smells cause distraction and lower concentration.

Certain 'good' smells, on the other hand, produce a well-researched improvement in thinking speed and accuracy. Lavender, for example, may work because it lowers stress-induced cortisol levels. Lavender enhanced concentration levels by around 20 per cent. Jasmine saw a 33 per cent improvement in the same trial, and lemon smells – like melissa and citronella – produced an uplift of 55 per cent.

Baron reports that home baking smells, and fresh coffee smells reduce unhelpful feelings of competitiveness. Perhaps this is why estate agents suggest brewing coffee and spraying vanilla before showing people around your house?

Other mood-enhancing smells that raise mental energy include mint and cypress. Mint can be found in toothpaste (clean your teeth at lunchtime), or it can be grown in a pot on your desk. (Just squash a leaf between your fingers.) Cypress smells can be found by sniffing a decongestant, or from an indoor plant like rosemary. Swartz reports that the smell of spiced apple lengthens the alpha brainwaves that aid creative thinking (see Chapter 9). So take spiced apple, camomile, lemon, jasmine and peppermint teabags to work. Pick the smell and flavour you need for the task in hand.

Try it now: creating space to think

The spaces in which people think best are very personal to them. For this reason, if you are to get and give good value for your thinking time, you must insist as far as possible on the kind of thinking space that suits your personality. In the chart below, score the word cluster that suits you best. The kind of space in which you might think best will be found next to your highest scores.

Create your personal space to think		
Which word cluster describes you best?	Score (1–9, where 9 = Best)	Your space to think might include...
Content, secure, cool, chilled		You won't mind – whatever
Sociable, chatty, happy, in control		Window view, open plan, low partitions
Curious, liberal, imaginative, likes stimulus		Lots of books, resources, pictures and posters
Accepting, nurturing, helpful, agreeable, sympathetic		Separate seating, low table, sofa, comfortable armchairs
Decisive, productive, organized, reliable		Lots of files, memory sticks and storage compartments
Alert, edgy, quick, jumpy, eager		Will keep changing suddenly
Reserved, private, planner, inhibited, writer		Closed office, quiet room or library with writing desk
Assertive, loud, proud, competitive, big ego		Access to latest databases, computer equipment, systems
Spontaneous, flexible, multitasker		Lots of horizontal surfaces and large shelves to house piles

EVERY BREATH YOU TAKE

Computers, mobiles, Wi-Fi, photocopiers, fax machines and air conditioning can have damaging effects. Electrically-charged particles called 'ions' are present in the air all the time and they can carry either a positive or a negative charge. The concentration of negative ions in the air – the number in each cubic centimetre – affects the level of serotonin in your blood, and, according to Harper, this affects your ability to do thinking tasks that require quick thinking and calculation.

The concentration of negative ions in mountainous areas is, on average, 35 per cent higher than in lower lying areas. This might explain why some people 'take to the hills' when they want to think about a problem that is worrying them. (There are other benefits that come from the exertion of climbing up and from the relaxation that follows coming down again, so it would be unfair to attribute all the improvement in thinking to an increase in negative ions.) Air conditioners and the ventilation systems in cars remove negative ions from the air. The average concentration of negative ions inside air-conditioned offices is commonly around 150 per cubic centimetre. This should be compared to an average of around 4,000 ions per cubic centimetre in the mountains, and 3,000 ions per cubic centimetre in unpolluted air at ground level. Soyka investigated the effect on mental performance of adding back the missing negative ions. The percentage of people whose performance showed a marked improvement varied between 57 per cent and 85 per cent.

Try it now: Keep an eye on your body

Each hour try to squeeze all the breath out of your body, especially your lower body, and tense every muscle you can, as tightly as you can, for as long as you can. When you relax, you will automatically breathe very deeply. Repeat this three times.

* Having relaxed your body, you can relax your head by alternating your eye focus between, say, the texture of a surface a long way away and the texture of your own fingertips. This will not only relieve eye strain, it will be mentally refreshing.

* Keep your chin back and your head still, and then move your eyes to look as far to the left as you can and then as far to the right as you can. Repeat this alternation, counting one, and two, and three etc., as you do it. Count until you reach 60. This is a one-minute neurobic exercise.
* Still keeping your head still, and this time your eyes still as well, see how far to the left, and to your right, you can see, using your peripheral vision to the left side and right side simultaneously. Use your imagination to complete the 360° view to your rear. Notice how amazing new space appears in your head.

PASSIVE SMOKING, VENTILATION AND POLLUTION

Neurons depend on oxygen for the production of adenosine tri-phosphate (ATP), the fuel that energizes the cell. Without an adequate supply of oxygen and ATP, your neurons quickly begin to malfunction. In some cases they die. Normally you can get enough oxygen from air, but ventilation, traffic pollution and people smoking can reduce the proportion of oxygen in the air.

Oxygen is carried in your body by the haemoglobin in your blood. When the air contains carbon monoxide (for example, from traffic pollution or people smoking), the carbon monoxide combines irreversibly with the haemoglobin in your blood to form carboxyhaemoglobin. This permanently reduces the capacity of your blood to carry oxygen to your brain.

Inspire to be inspired

Creative thinking is directed towards the chance that you will be 'inspired'. The word 'inspire' literally means 'in breath'. To breathe in is to be inspired! Breathing very deeply washes the brain with the negative ions that are attached to the oxygen. Fresh air is best, having 3,000–4,000 negative ions per cubic centimetre. The air in cars or in some air-conditioned buildings, especially near fax machines or photocopiers, can be as low as 50 negative ions per cubic centimetre. Negative ions promote alpha waves of longer amplitude in your brain. These are associated with creative thinking. The Japanese inventor Nakamats breathed very deeply, then held his breath and worked under water with a metal pad and underwater pen. He is credited with more inventions than Thomas Edison.

COMPUTERS, PRINTERS, FAX MACHINES AND PHOTOCOPIERS

Cardinali has investigated mental fatigue and apathy in people who spend long periods working close to computer screens. He suggested that one of the adverse effects might be due to the removal of negative ions by visual display units (VDUs), because VDUs become positively charged. Many photocopiers, printers and fax machines work by carrying powder on electrostatically charged drums, and these also may disturb the ionic balance in the air.

Many computers emit a debilitating humming noise. Do your thinking away from your computer. Remove copiers, printers and fax machines from your thinking space.

Your bottleneck brain: the myth of multitasking

DON'T TALK AND DRIVE

The discovery in 2007 of a 'bottleneck in the brain' finally confirmed what many men had suspected for a long time, namely that no one – not even a woman – can do two things at once! The myth of multitasking was laid to rest. Writing in the *New Scientist*, in April 2007, Alison Metlock reported David Strayer's finding that talk-drive should become the new drink-drive, for all drivers, male or female. The problems caused by talking and driving include an impaired reaction time, and hands-free sets for phones do not improve this. In 2005, in the UK, 13 people were killed and 400 seriously injured by drivers who thought that they could talk and drive. The equivalent figures for the USA were 2,600 dead and 330,000 injured. Rene Marois thinks that self-styled multitaskers are simply underperformers of parallel tasks. You can get better at parallel processing, which in reality involves rapid alternation between parallel tasks, but the evidence says 'one thing at a time' is best for optimum performance. The problem, even for those who practised (twice a minute for an hour a day for 14 days) was that doing even just two tasks, both very simple, involves negotiating three bottlenecks in your brain:

1 Deciding to what to give your attention. This is called the 'Attention Blink'.

2 Holding two sets of information in a short-term memory that is already limited (see Chapter 3). This is called the 'Cognitive Limit'.

3 Selecting a response to each situation and then deciding which selection to implement first causes a further delay. This is called the 'Selection Blink'.

Do you brake because of that child in the road, or do you tell your sister on your mobile not to leave her husband?

None of the researchers found any significant difference between men and women, but it did turn out to be one of the few thinking tasks where younger people fared better than older people, whose cognitive performance in most other areas improves with age (see *Keep Your Brain Sharp*, Horne and Wootton, 2010).

Remember this: One thing at a time

Multitasking – in practice, rapid switching between parallel tasks – raises cortisol levels. When the task involves thinking quickly or clearly, it is better for your brain if you can do one thing at a time. This has implications for conversations in cars whether hands-free or not. Concentrate on one thinking task at a time. Get it finished. The resulting satisfaction will produce chemicals in your brain that aid further thinking, especially creative thinking.

Cortisol kills: the chemistry of stress

Excessive stress increases the levels of cortisol in your body, which can cause you to feel confused and can reduce your ability to distinguish between what is important and what is not. You can appear to revert to familiar 'tried and tested' ways of thinking. Your brain can lose some of its ability to sort out new information, to retrieve old information, and to perform certain kinds of numerical thinking tasks. Your thinking becomes more automatic, your brain struggles to perceive patterns and relationships and it is hard to learn anything new. The cortisol is impeding the deployment of your thinking skills.

Yet some people lead busy, tightly scheduled lives without building up cortisol. They appear not to suffer from excessive stress. Others have routine predictable lives and yet they feel very stressed.

Try it now: Boats, boots and trains

Reorganize your holidays so that you can take one long weekend break every month. Use public holidays to create evenly spaced one-week holidays. These will be less stressful than one long break in the summer. (Preparing for a long holiday is stressful. The long holiday itself can be stressful. Trying to catch up after a long holiday can be the final straw.) Favour breaks based on non-competitive physical activities like walking, riding, climbing, dry-stone walling, path building, canoeing, rock climbing or dancing (see Chapter 1). Try to minimize driving or travelling great distances. Favour boats, boots and trains over cars and planes.

Research by Ostrander on over 4,000 students demonstrated that excessive stress impairs learning, thinking, memory and problem solving and reduces IQ scores by up to 14 points (this is a very significant reduction – see Chapter 4). This effect was illustrated by Benson (see Figure 5.1).

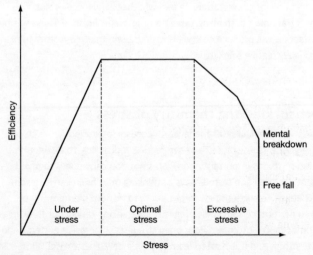

Figure 5.1 Stress and efficiency.
Source: Horne and Wootton, 2003, after Benson

Beware of falling in love: good news is stressful

Watch for precipitating events – unexpected things and good things can add to stress. Because stress in others can raise stress levels in you, you should be aware of stressful events for other people as well as for yourself. Since it is the total strain that determines the level of stress experienced, you should be alert to the possibility of excessive stress caused by deaths, illness, accidents, a missing child, neighbour disputes, separations, legal actions, a new partner, new children, a new address, outstanding achievements, wonderful holidays, religious celebrations, major family gatherings of any sort... and falling in love!

Remember this: Win some, lose some – it's all stress

If you find you are suffering excessive stress, you should check out what is going on in your life. Whether stressful events take place in or out of work, the build-up of cortisol in your brain will be cumulative. Both positive events, e.g. falling in love, and negative events, e.g. losing something, or someone, important to you, can raise your stress levels.

ARE YOU STRESSED?

The symptoms of stress are many. The physical symptoms include:

▶ general aches and pains, including backache

▶ excessive sweating, constipation, diarrhoea

▶ frequent indigestion or heartburn

▶ insomnia and constant tiredness

▶ lack of appetite or overeating

▶ sexual impotence

▶ migraine attacks

▶ asthma attacks.

Try it now: Hit the bottle and take a walk

Fill a bottle with water in the morning. Keep it with you. Drink it before evening. Reduce tea, coffee or cola intake; caffeine causes the body to lose water. Dehydration makes stress worse. Drink *before* you are thirsty. Go for a 15-minute walk, morning, afternoon and evening, whatever the weather.

The psychological symptoms of stress include:

▶ feeling inadequate

▶ difficulty in concentrating

▶ feeling anxious, apprehensive or irritable

▶ increasing difficulty in making important decisions.

Many of these symptoms are similar to symptoms of depression (see Chapter 2), which is why it is important to seek help with diagnosis. Excessive stress can be prevented, or at least managed. If it is not, it may lead to depression, which is then much more difficult to manage.

Remember this: Cortisol kills creative thought

High levels of cortisol in your brain can make it very difficult for you to think at all, let alone think clearly, quickly and well. Cortisol is produced in your brain when the environment in which you are trying to think is excessively stressful. You can learn to detect when excessive stress is producing too much cortisol in your brain; stress produces a range of physical and psychological symptoms which you can check.

Try it now: How stressed are you?

Complete the questionnaire below to see how stressed you are. Tick the boxes that apply to you.

Do you ever suffer from ...?

	Rarely (score 1)	Sometimes (score 2)	Often (score 3)
Irritability			
Restlessness			
Tension			
Anxiety			
Lack of concentration			
Panic			
Frequent crying			
Finger or foot tapping			
Scratching			
Lethargy/fatigue			
Accident proneness			
Insomnia			
Headaches			
Nausea			
Constipation/ diarrhoea			
Skin problems			
Sweating			
Rapid breathing			
Allergies			
Frequent colds			
Working long hours			
Dreading things			
Boredom			
Lack of communication			
Unfinished work			
Concern with trivia			
Nail biting			
Not having free time			

If you scored 25–35: You seem to have things under control.

If you scored 36–60: You are affected by stress – see the next section.

If you scored 61–100: You should take professional advice.

MANAGING STRESS

Before acting precipitately to reduce stress, you need to distinguish between helpful levels of stress and excessive levels of stress. A violin string is useless unless it is tense, but it will break if it is over-stretched. Stress levels must be tuned not eliminated. Stress is helpful in releasing some adrenaline and noradrenaline. Both these hormones have been shown to improve perception, motivation and performance on certain thinking tasks.

Things that can push stress beyond helpful levels include embarrassment, perceived loss of status or a belief that a task is impossible. Unhelpful levels of stress are more likely when you think there is not enough time to complete a task to the standard required. Where a task involves decision making, the extra time needed to do the work could be gained by taking the decisions more quickly but, because thinking becomes slower under excessive levels of stress, it takes longer to make the decisions! This creates a vicious circle. If you try to make up for the shortage of time and the slower thinking speed by giving less thought to the decision, you increase the number of thoughtless decisions. This raises anxiety about the risk of mistakes and raises further the level of stress experienced.

Exacerbating factors include thinking about problems you do not wish to think about; thinking about the consequences of not taking decisions on time or of making a mistaken decision; and having little control over the way decision making takes place.

Try it now: Getting to 'No'!

You may need to say 'no' to those who want to load up your thinking space. Often you can say 'yes' to achieving a particular outcome, but say 'no' to a proposed time scale. 'How' and 'when' might be negotiable, even when 'what' is not. Try not to give more than one reason for saying 'no'. Multiple reasons invite stressful questions. The questions can be more stressful to answer than doing the work! Just say, 'Right now, I do not have the head space to work out how to include something else on my list' or 'here is my list of top priority items, which would you have me drop to make room for your request?'

Sixty per cent of your 'no' message does not come from *what* you say, but from *what you look like* when you say it. Plant both your feet firmly on the floor, about the same distance apart as your shoulders. Relax your knees and imagine that you can squeeze the carpet between your feet. This will solidify your position and make it difficult for you to shuffle from one foot to another. Look the other person fully in the face and say 'Sorry, but no.'

MINDFULNESS

At the core of each person is a space that knows pure peace. But as we grow, we start to be drawn away from this deep sense of self as a result of social conditioning, trauma, time, and a host of other personal factors. It becomes easy for us to feel detached and to start making choices based on external factors as opposed to being true to ourselves.

Mindfulness means maintaining a moment-by-moment awareness of our thoughts, feelings, bodily sensations, and surrounding environment.

Studies have shown that practising mindfulness, even for just a few weeks, can bring a variety of physical, psychological, and social benefits. Some of the benefits reported, include:

▶ After just eight weeks of training, practising mindfulness meditation boosted people's immune systems' ability to fight off illness.

▶ It increases positive emotions while reducing negative emotions and stress and may be as good as antidepressants in fighting depression and preventing relapse.

▶ Mindfulness appears to changes our brains as it has been found that it increases density of grey matter in brain regions linked to learning, memory, emotion regulation, and empathy.

▶ Mindfulness helps us to focus: mindfulness helps us tune out distractions and improves our memory and attention skills.

▶ Self-defeating negative thoughts

One of the easiest ways to be disconnected from our core selves is through habitual negative thinking. It can be easy to feel like negative or worrisome thoughts are capable of 'kidnapping' our minds and taking us out of the present moment, especially when we're stressed or anxious.

Try it now: Challenging negative thought patterns

Mindfulness, according to Jon Kabat Zin allows us to become more aware of our thoughts without labelling or judging them. When we are able to be still, and be anchored in the now, we notice our thoughts more clearly. And when we become *aware* of our thoughts, we're able to begin challenging them.

It's easier to challenge negative thoughts when the process is broken down into steps. The next time you observe yourself stuck in a negative thought pattern, try practising these four steps.

1 Recognize that you are having a negative thought or pattern of negative thoughts. Say 'Stop!' in your head (or out loud if it feels socially appropriate).

2 Challenge the thought by probing it with questions. Ask yourself, 'What evidence do I have to support this thought?' Odds are, you'll notice that the evidence isn't strong.

3 Replace the thought with something more rational or positive. For example, if you're thinking, 'I am ugly', try thinking instead about the individuals in your life who would disagree, or browse through flattering photos on Facebook™, Snapchat™ or Instagram™.

When we release negative thought patterns and become mindful of the present, we allow ourselves to fully experience all the joy that is available to us in a given moment.

BECOMING MINDFUL – AN ACTION PLAN

Mindfulness may *feel* great, but that doesn't mean it feels easy to achieve. To help you start on the path to mindfulness, try the following actions.

▶ Action 1: Imagine how young children and animals act in the world

They're so connected to whatever's going on in the present. Set an intention to bring a gentle curiosity to life, as animals and children do. When you approach your thoughts in this way, you don't feel a need to attach to them or push them away. Instead, you can explore them, with childlike wonder, and let them be nothing more than what they are – thoughts.

▶ Action 2: Practise yoga – especially the hard poses

Yoga is a meditation of the body. In yoga, our bodies help to 'anchor' us in the present, as our awareness is focused on the changes happening within our bodies. A particularly useful paradigm for those struggling with anxiety or depression is to hold a challenging pose, and to bring attention to the discomfort, embrace it, and breathe through it. When we experience a depressive or anxious state, we feel that it will never end, that the pain will not lift. Challenging poses teach us to accept the challenge and to trust that, just like anything else, it will pass, and the pain will subside.

▶ Action 3: Eat mindfully

When was the last time you sat down for a meal and really enjoyed the flavour, texture, smell, and presentation of your food? So often, we eat on the run or in front of a screen. In contrast, eating mindfully means paying attention to our five senses in conjunction with *slowing down*. Think about where your food came from – who made it? What processes occurred to bring the food to the plate in front of you? Look, smell, explore, feel, smell again, take a small bite, chew, taste, savour, and swallow. Challenge yourself to eat a meal mindfully (and maybe in silence) at least a few times a week.

▶ Action 4: Take a mindful shower

The activities that we perform on a daily basis, such as showering, often become the most mindless, because we learn to cruise through them on automatic pilot. The next time you're in the shower, focus on the water on your skin. What is the temperature? How is the pressure? Use your sense of smell to enjoy the scent of your shampoo or body wash. Really bring yourself into the moment and actually think about what you are doing. Notice how this experience differs from your usual routine.

▶ Action 5: Practise mindful listening

What does it mean to listen mindfully? It means to listen, *just* listen, without judgement and without preparing or thinking about your response or opinion. Instead, just listen and allow the person space to express their ideas and feelings. Don't interrupt, add your opinion, or agree or disagree. Decide to neither attach to nor reject whatever the other person is expressing. Simply let the expression be what it is. The simple practice of mindful listening can enhance relationships by promoting mutual respect and creating a deeper understanding of the messages being communicated.

MENTAL CONCENTRATION AND THE CONTROL OF INTERRUPTIONS

Try it now: you need time to think

Even once you have lowered your anxiety, raised your expectations and maybe removed some of the sources of excessive stress, it still requires a deliberate effort on your part to improve your ability to concentrate. Take a few moments to study Figure 5.2 and to plot the natural rhythm of your concentration levels through a typical working day.

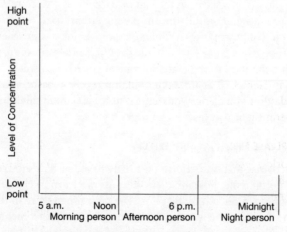

Figure 5.2 Concentration levels in a typical working day.

▶ How did you get on?

Is your best time to think in the morning? The afternoon? Or at midday? Whenever it is, according to researchers at Surrey University, UK, there is a gene for it, and so you cannot easily change your daily pattern of concentration; you have to work around it. That means, if you can, scheduling long tasks that require sustained individual thought for your peak times, and allocating activities where you can react to the stimulus of others, such as meetings, phone calls and interviews, to your off-peak times.

GOOD DAYS AND BAD DAYS

A self-reported survey of US professionals revealed that Tuesday was their most productive day, followed jointly by Monday and Wednesday, with Thursdays and Fridays being doldrums days. Does this pattern fit you? What are your good, bad, and best days to think?

'I just can't think!'

If your concentration curve is pretty low most of the day on most of the days of the week, then check your eating pattern (see Chapter 1), check your prevailing mood (see Chapter 2) and check your level of stress (see earlier in this chapter). Then check your sleep pattern. Insufficient or disturbed sleep plays havoc with concentration. Buysse found that it took at least four days of sleeping in late for people to recover from even one night on the tiles. Re-read Chapter 1.

So, having matched your key thinking tasks to the best times of the day for you to think, you need to protect your thinking spaces from interruption.

'CAN I PLEASE FINISH MY SENTENCE?'

In a world of diminishing courtesy, you may have to say 'I need to finish what I'm saying/doing/writing/thinking' more often, and remind yourself constantly to extend the same courtesy to others. People often think aloud to clarify their thoughts. When you interrupt their sentences, you break their train of thought. It can take them a long time to recover that train of thought and some fleeting creative ideas may never be recovered. That's how most of Samuel Coleridge's poem 'Kubla Khan' got lost. He was interrupted when writing it. He was never able to remember it again. So, the 'Kubla Khan' we have is only a tantalizing fragment of what it might have been.

You might also want to think about whether you interrupt yourself.

Remember this: Back to the beginning

If you are interrupted in a thinking task, like solving a problem, deciding what to do, or making a plan, you will generally have to start again. This produces frustration, more cortisol, and lack of satisfaction. Repeated interruptions will lower your mental energy and your mood. Both will impair your ability to think well. Your thinking can be interrupted by others or even by yourself: in either case these interruptions can cause stress and should be avoided.

Try it now: Do you interrupt yourself?

On a scale of 1–6 (1 = rarely; 6 = often), do interruptions cause you to do the following:

	A		B
Stop everything you are doing?		Ask why it needs to be now?	
Do what you can to answer questions?		Help them to answer their own questions?	
Enjoy feeling needed and wanted?		Feel annoyed that you hadn't anticipated these questions?	
Empathize with their situation?		Explain their impact on you?	
Carry on discussing other aspects related to the question?		Fix another time to review the wider situation?	
Total A		**Total B**	
		Overall score B – A = _____	

A negative score suggests that you are not minimizing the frequency with which you are interrupted. Look at your high-scoring As and work out how to convert them to Bs. The higher you score, the less likely you are to interrupt yourself. If you still get interruptions, you need to pause for thought.

The practice of management

A THOUGHTFUL APPROACH

In a knowledge economy, enabling workers to think well is a priority for all managers. Thinking at work poses specific difficulties:

▶ Working in groups or teams raises anxiety. Anxiety works against clarity and creativity when you try to think.

▶ Many models of work-based learning are deeply flawed unless you pay attention to the thinking skills required.

▶ Thinking thrives best in open, exploratory, non-competitive cultures, but these must be deliberately engineered.

Remember this: Confused thinking costs lives

How well you can think at work is strongly affected by the way your managers behave. Certain styles of management are more conducive to thoughtful work than others. Thoughtful work by employees creates competitive advantage in commerce. Thoughtless work cost lives in hospitals, transport and child protection.

YOU CAN WORK IT OUT

One of the ways to relieve stress is through exercise. Exercise has other benefits too. It helps thinking; it develops the brain (see Chapter 1); it lifts mood (see Chapter 2) and it improves memory (see Chapter 3). Try walking, running, cycling – maybe to and from work – or a park and ride. Many employers provide showers and lock-ups for bikes. A workout or a swim at lunchtime will clear your head for the afternoon. Eat a working lunch that has predominantly raw ingredients and is low in salt, chemical additives and refined flour. Hot water, weak tea or herbal teas are the best drinks (see Chapter 1).

Bad relationships at home and at work

Get out of excessively stressful relationships. They are not good for you. If you feel that now is not the right time to end a stressful relationship, then use a 'bell jar' to limit the drain on your energy.

Try it now: The bell jar technique

When that stress-generating person approaches, imagine that a large glass bell jar is slowly descending over you. From inside your imaginary bell jar, you can now watch that person's energy-draining behaviours and rituals. You can hear the same old statements being made, often thinly disguised as questions. When you watch from inside your bell jar, you are impervious to the energy-draining stress. Observe the scene intently. Later you will be able to recall it, in detail, on your history screen. Then you will be able to turn down the brightness and the contrast. You will be able to turn off the screen and watch the scene reduce itself to a dot. Let it fade away.

Source: Horne and Doherty, 2003

SEX AT THE OFFICE

If the stressful relationship is at home, it can be tempting to seek solace at work (see Chapter 10). This can lead to sex at the office. Sex at the office can be of three kinds:

1 Acquaintanceship sex.

2 Companionship sex.

3 Admiration sex.

Research has found that the average length of a work-based affair is six months. When it ends, you will almost certainly lose a close working relationship and you may have to move jobs. At the very least, it will be a major mental preoccupation and certainly a distraction from being able to think clearly at work. Sexual partners are easier to find than good friends and good working mates. Think before you bypass your cerebral cortex and go with your amygdala!

Remember this: Sex on the brain

Better, closer, more intimate relationships can be cultivated by having thoughtful conversations. Close intimate relationships, especially sexual relationships, produce a cocktail of chemicals in the brain, most of which greatly aid your ability to think. However, it is better to develop sexual relationships outside of work: research into workplace affairs points to a six-month cycle of events that frequently results in a diminished capacity to think straight.

Focus points

* You can use music, temperature, lighting, colour, smell, touch and fresh air to create a good place to think.
* You should protect your brain from computers and air conditioning.
* You can limit the damage to your brain caused by stress.
* You can learn to concentrate.
* You should avoid disturbing your brain at work.
* You cannot multitask but you can control interruptions – your own and those of others.
* You cannot think well if you suffer excessive stress.
* You can recognize the signs of excessive stress.
* You can do many practical things to reduce excessive stress.
* You should avoid heavy lunches and bad relationships at the office.

Dig deeper

Horne, T. and Doherty, A., *Managing Public Services – Implementing Changes: A Thoughtful Approach to the Practice of Management* (London: Routledge, 2003).

Howard, P. J., *The Owner's Manual for the Brain: Everyday Applications from Mind and Brain Research* (3rd edn, Austin, Texas: Bard Press, 2006).

Janda, L., *The Psychologist's Book of Self-tests* (New York: Perigee, 1996).

The Mind Gym, *Give Me Time* (London: Time Warner Books, 2006).

Davidson, R. J., et al. (2003). Alterations in brain and immune function produced by mindfulness meditation. Psychosomatic Medicine, 65(4), 564–570

Weinstein N et al. (2009) A multi-method examination of the effects of mindfulness on stress attribution, coping, and emotional well-being. Journal of Research in Personality 43, pp374–385

Hölzel, B.K et al. (2011). Mindfulness practice leads to increases in regional brain grey matter density. *Psychiatry Research: Neuroimaging*, 191(1), 36–43.

Next steps

* When working and when you need to keep focused, try putting on music – not too loud – as this may help blank out surrounding distractions.
* Different music seems to encourage different thinking needs – look at the section on environmental factors in this chapter and experiment with what you are doing.
* Light affects your mood and hence your mental energy – so try getting sunlight if you need to be alert – you can brighten your computer screen (but better get away from this if you need to think!)
* Try the 'creating space to think' section in this chapter as you may benefit from changing your desk layout and location.
* To be inspired, deep breathe in fresh air as it washes in lots of oxygen.
* Focus on one thing at a time rather than multi-tasking.
* Become mindful (look at the action plan in this chapter) – become more aware of of your thoughts, feelings, sensations and environment.

6

Numbers at work

In this chapter you will learn:

▶ *about the workings of your numerical brain*

▶ *how to speed up your mental arithmetic*

▶ *how to pass tests of numeracy and numerical thinking*

▶ *how to make and take chances at work (and at play)*

▶ *how to use number puzzles to build intelligence and spare cognitive capacity.*

The prosperity of our state is ultimately connected to advancement of mathematics.

Napoleon Bonaparte, 1792

Few subjects are as important to the future of the nation as mathematics.

Keith Joseph, 1982

Introduction

In a commercial business, the need for numbers seems self-evident. After all, profits, returns and cash at the bank are all numbers. The relevance of numeracy to workers in charitable organizations and public services may be less obvious. Yet the need to 'crunch the numbers' turns up quickly in service planning, quality control and project management, as well as the more obvious areas of grant applications, fundraising and budgeting. Despite this, when many workers in charities and public-service organizations are confronted with the need to estimate, forecast and quantify, they disempower themselves by deferring to accountants, engineers and 'technical' people, and by asking others to 'do the numbers'.

Remember this: You need to know the score

All organizations – even charities, public services and care providers – have to be able to quantify their activities. It is not just commercial businesses that need to know the score. Charities compose bids. Public services need a business case. They all need to balance their books.

CAN YOU DO THE NUMBERS?

While the ability to make reasonable estimates and give good enough guesses lies at the heart of numerical thinking, actually doing the sums – the mental arithmetic – is also important.

Mental arithmetic is a quick and easy way to do your daily dozen 'neural reps'. Quick repetition of simple sums thickens the myelin insulation around the axons in your brain. This is necessary for fast, accurate thinking. 'Neural reps' also refresh the connections between your neurons. This increases your intelligence and your cognitive capacity to learn and to solve problems, thereby protecting your brain from the mental debility that might otherwise occur if you contracted a disease which attacked some of your brain cells. It is helpful to have spare cells that are already connected to your neural network, just in case.

Try to do the following sums in two minutes. Recite your sums aloud as you write in your answers.

18 – 8 =	8 + 7 =	2 × 3 =
6 + 6 =	13 – 3 =	4 + 0 =
2 × 10 =	0 × 6 =	12 – 3 =
14 – 7 =	8 – 1 =	7 + 8 =
3 × 5 =	3 × 8 =	5 × 0 =
3 + 6 =	6 + 5 =	5 × 2 =
9 – 4 =	10 – 1 =	3 + 4 =
1 + 5 =	1 + 8 =	10 – 7 =
15 – 5 =	9 × 7 =	9 + 3 =
2 + 6 =	7 – 1 =	6 × 6 =
10 – 2 =	6 × 5 =	6 × 7 =
9 + 7 =	6 – 0 =	12 – 2 =
9 – 2 =	4 + 7 =	1 + 6 =
6 × 4 =	7 × 4 =	9 × 8 =
7 + 7 =	5 + 2 =	11 – 6 =
8 × 4 =	10 – 7 =	8 + 7 =
5 – 3 =	4 × 3 =	

Total score =

×2 score =

Answers at the back of the book.

▶ **How many did you get right?**

Note your score. Compare it with your earlier score in Chapter 3.

Numerical thinking

ARE YOU NUMBER-PHOBIC?

Consider in how many areas of your life numbers are already at work. In the last year, for example, have you done the following? Tick the boxes that apply to you.

Tick

1 Placed a bet
2 Planned a hill walk
3 Bought shares
4 Refused a flu jab
5 Compared insurance quotes
6 Decided to go out without a coat
7 Worked out the best holiday deal
8 Worked out how long until pay day
9 Followed a cricket or baseball match
10 Told someone what time to expect you
11 Compared sales prices with normal prices
12 Worked out when you need to refill something
13 Compared price per 100 g with store's own brands
14 Played darts, dominoes, bridge or backgammon
15 Refused product or breakdown cover because it's not worth it

▶ Scores

0   = You are a number-phobic!
5+ = A closet numerate?
10+ = You probably enjoy numbers
15 = You are numerate

Remember this: Can't count – won't count

If you have a below-average capacity to think numerically, you will be dependent on professional number crunchers and prey to persuasion, manipulation or bullying, by your more numerate colleagues.

YOUR NUMERICAL BRAIN

Butterworth reports on studies of four-week-old babies that suggest that numbers – at least up to five – come much earlier than was previously thought. In which part of your brain is this numerical ability located? Studies of stroke victims sometimes report an inability to calculate in patients whose general intelligence and memory remains high. Inability to calculate is associated with damage to the left parietal lobe of the brain, which also controls the fingers on which you first learn to count. By the year 2000, brain scans of people doing calculations had detected activity not only in the left parietal lobe, but also in the visual, auditory and motor areas of the brain. The scan data helped us to understand why brain training exercises which involve only the recitation of simple sums are so effective in developing the cognitive capacity of your brain. The recitation of simple sums first establishes, and then strengthens, neural connections between four major areas of your brain. There are clear implications for the use of recitation and 'times tables' with young children, at home and in schools.

Tests on numerical thinking

INTRODUCTION

Re-read the general advice given in Chapter 4 on preparing for a brain-based test. If you haven't done any numeracy work since you left school, or are otherwise number-phobic, allow four to six weeks' preparation time. Even if you are reasonably confident numerically, you can still improve your test score with about 12 hours of practice, up to and including the day before the test. Try to avoid using a calculator. It is important to practise on questions similar to the tester's questions. (Testers normally provide sample questions, often on a website. Publishers often sell 'mock' tests.) Split your practice time so that one-third is time constrained and two-thirds is open ended, allowing time to read up and/or ask about the types of questions you find difficult. See the end of the chapter for test practice books.

Remember this: Maths matter

Numerical thinking not only confers the ability to compute, estimate and quantify, it also develops parts of the brain that are involved in memory and logic. It is no accident that tests of numeracy, or numerical IQ, are routinely included in the battery of psychometric tests given to job applicants.

Attempt every question. Guesses should be 'educated', that is, only made after eliminating obviously incorrect responses.

These questions are diagnostic. Try the questions and then check the Answers at the back of the book. If you get a question wrong, study the topic indicated in the answer.

Q1   Complete the table.

½		
	0.75	
		60%
		33%
	0.25	

Q2   A median is...

Q3   What is the mean of 3, 7, 10, 13, 14, 19?

Q4   For $21 \leq T < 70$, is T = 18, 36 or 73?

Q5   If you tossed a fair coin and rolled a fair dice, what is the probability of getting heads and a six?

Check it for sense

✻ Make estimates prior to electronic calculations. Ask people whether they expect something to be much bigger or much smaller? Ten times as much? More than a 50/50 chance?

✻ Check answers for sense. 'So, for every person who did X last year, we can expect Y, can we?'

✻ Work through the practical implications of figures. 'So how much space would that take up?'

Q6   What is 3 to the power 5?

Q7   The area of a square is 36 square metres. What is its length?

Q8   What is 3.142 as a fraction?

Q9   How many factors (including 1 + 32) does 32 have?

Q10 A prime number is...

Q11 What is the distance around the equator? Radius of the earth = 6,377 km.

Q12 Uplift 85 by 15 per cent.

Q13 A reduction of 75 per cent in the selling price of £20 gives a sale price of?

Q14 If £300 = cost price plus 20 per cent, what was the cost price?

Q15 Divide 63 in the ratio 3:6.

Q16 If 5 (X + 6) = 75, what is X?

Q17 What is the equation for the line?

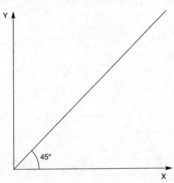

Develop your capacity to calculate

To expand your capacity to calculate on the move, volunteer to cook at a barbecue, run a charity auction or to organize games at a party. These activities develop mental agility, mental arithmetic and your ability to think on your feet.

Q18 Your sales this month were £2,000 increasing at 10 per cent per month. What will your total sales be at the end of another two months?

Q19 What is the surface area of the cube?

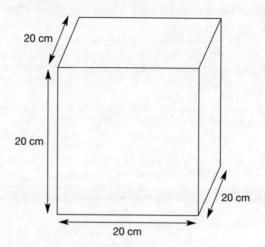

20 cm

20 cm

20 cm

20 cm

Q20 What is the volume of this house?

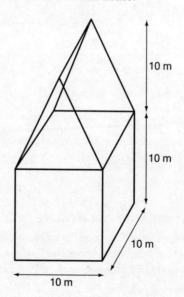

10 m

10 m

10 m

10 m

Making your number skills count

Numerical thinking can be developed by playing games like backgammon or the African game Umweso, which involves counting seeds into small holes scooped in the ground or carved into a piece of wood. The counting skills involved in backgammon or Umweso develop your ability to recognize numerical patterns.

Q21   If you toss two fair coins, what is the probability that one will land heads?

Q22   If you toss three fair coins, what are the chances of three heads?

Q23   Teams A, B, C, D, E, F play in a local football league. Study the results table so far.

Team	Played	Lost	Drawn	Won	Points
A	3	0	0	0
B	2	1	0	1
C	2	0	2	6
D	2	0	2	6
E	1	0	3	9
F	0	1	3	10

a   *How many points are given for a win?*

b   *How many games have been played?*

c   *How many games remain to be played?*

d   *How many teams could win the league?*

e   *What is the maximum possible total points (across all the teams) that could be scored now?*

Q24

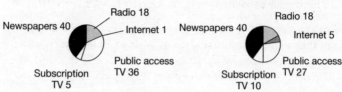

1995

Newspapers 40

Radio 18

Internet 1

Public access
TV 36

Subscription
TV 5

2005

Newspapers 40

Radio 18

Internet 5

Public access
TV 27

Subscription
TV 10

a *Which source has gained the most share between 1995 and 2005?*

b *Which source has lost the most share?*

c *Which has shown the greatest percentage gain?*

d *What would you forecast for the internet share in 2015?*

▶ **How did you get on?**

The questions were representative of those you will find on employers' recruitment tests on numeracy, numerical thinking and numerical reasoning. Revision notes for mathematics examinations are often helpful. See also 'Taking it further' at the end of this book. For managerial posts, the numerical reasoning tests will include questions on forecasting, planning, budget control and business judgement.

Remember this: Tips on testing

When you apply for a job, expect to be given a test on your numerical aptitude. You can improve your performance by practising all the common questions used in numerical tests.

GIVE YOURSELF A CHANCE AT WORK AND AT PLAY

As a member of a criminal jury, you will be asked to convict someone if you believe their guilt has been established 'beyond all reasonable doubt' and, in a civil case, 'on the balance of probabilities'. These are examples of numerical thinking. You are estimating – attempting to quantify and compare – the likelihood of one outcome compared with another.

One way to assess your capacity for probabilistic thinking is to consider how extensive your relevant vocabulary is, since this can limit your capacity to talk to yourself (see Chapter 10).

You can also talk about past events: 'The chances are 20 per cent that a given play attributed to William Shakespeare was not, in fact, written by Shakespeare at all.' This is the kind of judgement that might be made by a literary scholar.

The probability that you ascribe to the likelihood that a particular statement is true is, in a sense, a measure of the strength, extent, depth and degree of certainty of your belief in that statement – and that measure involves you thinking numerically. The stronger your belief, the higher the number you may be prepared to ascribe to it.

IN THE LONG RUN
Just because, in the long run, if you toss a coin enough times the proportion of heads will tend to be towards 50 per cent, it does not mean that you can expect the same 50 per cent behaviour in the short run. Do not make predictions or estimates of probability in the short term that would only come to pass in the long term. The 'law of averages' only applies in the very long run. It does not help you to decide what is likely to happen next.

WEATHER OR NOT...
With the weather, you can only stand and stare out of the window at the rain! You cannot do 'weather or not' experiments! What you can do is to keep making guesses like, 'the chance of rain tomorrow is 60 per cent', and then keep records of the actual rainfall plus satellite maps, historical patterns, wind pressures, etc. and then maybe use a computer to model the interactions and correlations. In the long run, you can improve your success at guessing that 'the chance of rain tomorrow is 60 per cent'.

ON AVERAGE
When trying to think numerically about decisions, John Haigh (1999) has some good illustrations of the use of averages to simplify numerical thinking. For example:

A prize of £1.50 is offered for each correct guess of who will be drawn to play whom in the second round (last 16) of the World Cup. What would you pay for a card on which you can enter a predicted draw?

▶ **How did you get on?**

What did you decide?

Discussion

For 16 teams you will predict 8 pairs, so the most you can win is 8 × £1.50 = £12.00. You could write out all the possible combinations to find out the chances of one winning pair, two winning pairs, etc. multiplied by the winnings for each, but that would be tedious and time-consuming. This is where your good friend 'average' is very helpful. If you select your first team, there are 15 choices for the pair, so, on average, you have a 1 in 15 chance of winning £1.50 – an average win of 10p (× 8 = 80p). So if you paid 80p for an entry card, on average, you'd get your money back, so that seems fair. Of course you could get nothing, or up to £12.00 (in steps of £1.50). If a well known charity was selling the entry tickets for £2 a go, you might still be happy knowing that, on average, more than half of your ticket money was going to the charity. You might not be so happy if you later found that the person selling the tickets was taking £1 for each ticket sold!

SUGGESTED ACTIVITIES

▶ **1 Watch a film**

Watch the film *The Sting* (1973) and work out how you could always win against Doyle and why Doyle is always bound to lose.

▶ **2 Coin it for charity**

Ask a group for the most likely result of tossing a coin, say, 50 times. They will likely say 'equal heads and tails'. Raise money for charity by offering to double the money of each member of the group if an even number of them simultaneously toss a coin and if, between them, they get an equal number of heads and tails. If they don't, you collect all the coins for your charity. Why will you coin lots of money for your charity?

▶ 3 Play last days in Marienbad

The following game, played with any 16 objects, is an excellent way to diagnose how you, or others, think. Arrange the objects in rows of 7, 5, 3 and 1, as follows:

$$I\ I\ I\ I\ I\ I\ I$$

$$I\ I\ I\ I\ I$$

$$I\ I\ I$$

$$I$$

Alternate who starts. Players take turns to remove as many of the objects as they like from any one horizontal row. The player who is left with the last object loses. By playing often, you will develop your ability to recognize numerical patterns.

▶ 4 Do tricks

Get a book of magic tricks. Practise the ones that involve numbers.

▶ 5 You can be serious!

Get books on algebra and geometry and work your way through them.

HOW TO SCORE ON A BLIND DATE

You have arranged to meet a blind date at around 9 p.m. tonight. Naturally the rendezvous is a public place and you have told someone your plan and the latest time to expect you back.

If you are both early, or both late, neither of you will be offended and it increases the chances you will be compatible, for example, like-minded in relation to the importance of punctuality. You could assign both these cases an outcome value of plus 2.

If you are early and he or she is late, you are likely to be seen by someone else, who will get into conversation with you and confuse your pitch when your date arrives. You could tell people that you are waiting for a date, but then, if he or she doesn't turn up, you will lose face. Either way, you could assign this case an outcome value of minus 2.

Finally, if you arrive late and your date is kept waiting, or worse, is already in conversation with someone else, this outcome is not good. Assign an outcome value of, say, minus 1.

You can use a pay-off table to try to work out your best chances of scoring with your new date.

The pay-offs for blind dates

Possible strategies	Historical success	If date late	If date early	If date on time
You go early	1 in 10 times	−2	+2	+1
You go late	7 in 10 times	+2	−2	−1
You go on time	2 in 10 times	−1	+1	+3

Q1 Ignoring your history, which strategy gives you the least chance of a good outcome?

Q2 Ignoring your history, which strategy would give you the best chance of a good outcome?

Q3 Taking your history into account, which strategy gives you your least chance of a good outcome? (Whatever that might be!)

Q4 Taking your history into account, which strategy would give you your best chance of a good outcome?

Answers are at the back of the book.

The numerical thinking workout

Numerical thinking – the source of all the rest

René Descartes claimed that mathematics was far more than a particular numerical science. For Descartes, mathematics was more than arithmetic and geometry. He saw astronomy, music, optics and mechanics, for example, as branches of mathematics. These subjects are all numerical. They all involve the principles of sequence and measurement. For

Descartes, numerical thinking contained the rudiments of reasoning and reasoning is necessary, but not sufficient for the discovery of truth in every field.

Numerical thinking helps to develop the basic tools of the applied thinker's trade – the tools of logic, sequence, reasoning and proof. The history of twentieth-century science is replete with examples of 'discoveries' in astronomy, physics, chemistry, biology and geology that had been predicted years earlier by mathematicians.

INTRODUCTION

This numerical thinking workout goes beyond the development of your numeracy skills, important though these are for everyday living. The workout also aims to go beyond numerical reasoning, important though this is for getting a job. This numerical thinking workout will develop your general intelligence and cognitive capacity by encouraging you to link at least four different parts of your brain as you struggle to find solutions to the numerical puzzles. If you can talk to yourself about the puzzles, preferably aloud, so much the better. If you can discuss them with someone else, even better still (see Chapter 10).

Remember this: Connections you can count on

Mental arithmetic, especially when you give a verbal commentary out loud on how you are doing the calculation, is a great way to develop your brain. Mental arithmetic establishes neural pathways between important areas of the brain involved in memory and logic. Because arithmetic can involve a lot of rapid repetition, the axons of the neurons, along these neural pathways, develop thicker myelin insulation. These well-established, well insulated, neural connections then enable you to think quickly and accurately about other things that do not involve numbers.

Q1 The Tutonton pyramid

This is a sketch of the profile through the centre of the pyramid.

How tall is the pyramid? How broad is the pyramid? How many metre cube blocks were needed to build the Tutonton pyramid? It had a square base of area 81 square metres. Each block weighed approximately 1212 kg.

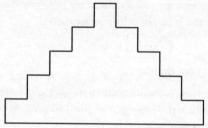

Q2 Balancing act

How many triangles to balance scale C (distance from fulcrum is not a factor)?

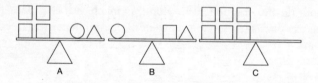

Q3 Fill the squares

You have 36 squares to fill with numbers 1–9. You may use each four times, but the same numbers may not be adjacent horizontally or vertically.

		8				8, 8 not 3.
		7				4, 4, 7, 7.
		6				6, 6, not 1.
		5				8, 8, not 1, 1.
6	5	4	3	2	1	
4						

| 39 | 21 | 33 | | 33 | | |

Q4 A distance too far

How far away is London?

York 50 km

Oslo 60 km

Paris 70 km

Madrid 80 km

Q5 Balancing the numbers

Using the numbers 1–9 only once, balance the 6 equations.
Calculate from left to right and then top to bottom.

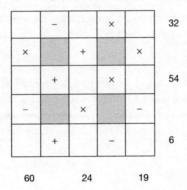

Q6 Cracking the code

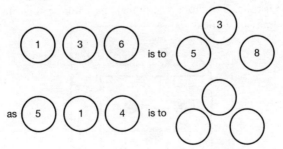

Q7 Clocking on

If A = 3 o'clock, what time will Clock F show?

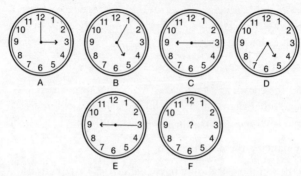

Q8 Roll out the barrel

You have only a torch to determine whether a wooden barrel is more than, or less than, half full. How will you do it?

Q9 Sands of time

You need to measure a quarter of an hour and you have two sand glasses. One takes 11 minutes the other 7 minutes to empty. How can you use them to measure your quarter hours? (Hint: At what point in the sand glass is 4 minutes left in the other glass?)

Q10 Seeing spots

This is the top dice of a single stack of ten. How many dots are visible on the stack?

Q11 The magic shrinking flute

A musician doesn't want to check in his precious 48 cm flute, but an officious security officer is limiting the length of hand luggage to 40 cm. How can the musician legally carry his flute on board as hand luggage?

Q12 All the threes

Put 2 in the centre and then select from only three other numbers, other than 2 and 3, to make each row, column and diagonal total ten. What three numbers will work?

3		3		3
	3	3	3	
3	3			
3				
	3			

Q13 Tripletons

How many routes through the maze score more than 300? At each number you must go North or East. You must enter the maze at IN and exit at OUT. You can add together any of the numbers on your route, except 27 which you must subtract.

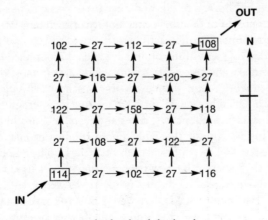

Check your answers at the back of the book.

Where have all the bright ones gone?

In 2008 in the *Journal of Educational Psychology*, Professor Michael Shayer announced what he considered to be a 'staggering result'. He reported that certain cognitive abilities of 11- and 12-year-old children had deteriorated by, on average, two to three years compared with 15 years ago. Yet they had been expected to rise! The fall was so drastic and so unexpected that the results of the 10,000 children in the study had to be checked and rechecked. A fall of this magnitude is expected to impact on general IQ, as well as numerical IQ.

The difference between boys and girls recorded over 15 years ago has now nearly disappeared. Both boys and girls have deteriorated so sharply that the difference between them is not as concerning as the overall deterioration of both groups.

Professor Black of University College London thinks that Shayer's results are a wake-up call. Shayer's results challenge UK government claims that standards in, for example, SATs (standard assessment tasks) and GCSE and A-Level examinations have been rising. Professor Black thinks that school test results and exam results reflect performance incentives, 'teaching to test' and syllabus options that make it possible to avoid topics that are experienced by pupils as 'hard'.

Many lecturers in further and higher education were not surprised by Shayer's results and have been forced to question assumptions about the intellectual ability of even our better-graded students. Learning activities that used to be important for the development of the brain have been discontinued in many primary and secondary schools. However in most of the developed world, more people are now in school for longer, and teaching methods have evolved, moving away from the simple memorizing of names, dates and facts. It seems like a reasonable assumption that education is training people to think better. And recent research at the Kings College London in 2015 suggests that IQ may be increasing now. This may also be down to profound shifts in society as well as education over the last century, which have led people to think in a more abstract, scientific way – the kind of intelligence measured by

IQ tests. However, there is no need to despair. Brain training can develop missing thinking skills and expand cognitive capacity. Throughout this book we have noted the damaging effects of TV, computer games, calculators and mobile phones on the development of the brain. Yet we also consider how enhanced information search and visual and spatial thinking among young people can be used to develop creative thinking and help them to recover from the deficits revealed in the Shayer Report. It is possible to develop the new and burgeoning talents of children.

Remember this: Children's mental development may suffer

Because mental arithmetic done out loud makes such an important contribution to developing the cognitive capacity of the brain, we are concerned that children will suffer unless the reduction in mental arithmetic at school, and in counting games (cards, dominoes, backgammon, Mr Wolf), is compensated for with other activities.

Focus points

* You can understand the workings of your numerical brain.
* You can speed up your mental arithmetic.
* You can make and take chances at work (and at play).
* Number puzzles build intelligence and spare cognitive capacity.
* Recruitment selection tests usually include tests of numeracy.
* Scores on numeracy tests can be improved.
* You can build mental arithmetic into shopping, travelling and planning.
* You can improve your chances of taking the right decisions at work, and in life.
* Numerical thinking is the root of logic, reasoning, argument and proof.
* Numerical brain training improves intelligence and creates spare cognitive capacity as insurance against disease.

Dig deeper

Al-Jajjoka, S., *How to Pass Professional Level Psychometric Tests* (London: Kogan Page, 2004).

Barrett, J., *Test Yourself* (London: Kogan Page, 2000).

Bryon, M., *How to Pass Graduate Psychometric Tests* (London: Kogan Page, 2001).

Bryon, M., *How to Pass Advanced Numeracy Tests* (London: Kogan Page, 2004).

Butterworth, B., *The Mathematical Brain* (London: Macmillan, 1999).

Haigh, J., *Taking Chances: Winning with Probability* (Oxford: Oxford University Press, 1999).

Parkinson, M., *How to Master Psychometric Tests* (London: Kogan Page, 2000).

Tolley, H., *How to Pass Numeracy Tests* (London: Kogan Page, 2000).

Tolley, H., *How to Succeed at an Assessment Centre* (London: Kogan Page, 2001).

Next steps

❋ Practise mental arithmetic – relearn your times tables but go beyond 12 × 12 and go up to 20 × 20!
❋ Practise selection tests if you are having job interviews.
❋ Whilst shopping, compare prices per 100g with the store's own brands.
❋ When travelling, build in mental arithmetic challenges by doing algebra, newspaper sudokus and numerical ladders.

Applied thinking at work

In this chapter you will learn:

- ▶ *how to become an applied thinker*
- ▶ *about the role of critical, creative and reflective thinking in applied thinking*
- ▶ *how to use logic to assess the truth of information and the reasonableness of inferences*
- ▶ *how to train the frontal lobes of your brain to think logically, solve problems and make decisions.*

We know the science. We have predicted the threat. It's time for action.

Governor Arnold Schwarzenegger, January 2007

Introduction

Applied thinking involves the use of critical, creative and reflective thinking to assess the truth of information, and the reasonableness of inferences on which implications for action can be based. The 3 'I's (the way you move from Information, via Inferences, to Implied action), and the roles played by your critical, creative and reflective thinking are shown in Figure 7.1.

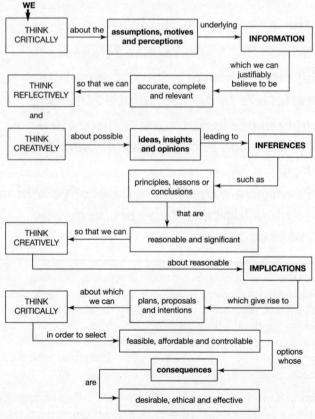

Figure 7.1 Information, inferences and implications (the 3 'I'S).

The brain training you need to improve reflective thinking will be considered in Chapter 8, and the brain training you need to improve creative thinking will be provided in Chapter 9. In this chapter, we look at the way critical thinking can support your applied thinking as you solve problems, take decisions and make plans at work.

Remember this: Past, present, future

Applied thinking is the kind of thinking you need to turn information into knowledge on which you can take action. Applied thinking enables you to take the kinds of actions that other people see as intelligent, such as learning things, solving problems, making decisions, and making practical plans. Applied thinking helps you to avoid getting stuck in the past. It helps you to form a present-day opinion and plan a future action.

Applied thinking – the 3 'I's

The quote at the beginning of the chapter is what Arnold Schwarzenegger said about climate change. In it you can see applied thinking at work. Schwarzenegger's 1-2-3 pattern of thinking is the thinking pattern of all applied professions, from medicine to management. Arnie's thinking pattern (science, prediction and action) mirrors the medic's (symptoms, diagnosis, treatment) and the manager's (data, decision and plan). Schwarzenegger, the medic and the manager are all following the 3 'I's of applied thinking: Information, Inference and Implication.

Information: You need to use critical thinking to assess the extent to which you justifiably believe in the accuracy, completeness and relevance of the information you have about the problem, decision or proposal. (Is it 'the truth, the whole truth and nothing but the truth'?) This will involve uncovering implicit assumptions, being sceptical about the motives of sources, and finally cross-checking your perceptions with those of other people.

Inferences: You will need to use creative and reflective thinking to generate a long list of the possible insights, interpretations, principles, opinions, lessons, ideas and even conclusions that you might reasonably infer from information that you justifiably believe to be true. To test the reasonableness of your inferences, you may rely on deductive, or inductive, logic.

In Deductive Logic:

> Reasonableness = A justified belief + A valid conclusion

In Inductive Logic:

> Reasonableness = A justified belief + A probable conclusion

Implications: You will again need to think creatively and reflectively in order to formulate feasible and practical plans of action soundly based on reasonable inferences you have drawn and soundly based on justifiably believable information you have assessed. You will need critical thinking again before you move to implement your plans or proposals – are these plans affordable, ethical and likely to be effective, and will you be able to control their implementation?

Remember this: Is it the truth, the whole truth ...?

Applied thinking enables you to assess whether you believe information and whether you could justify your belief. It develops a repertoire of challenging questions you can ask.

▶ **Applied thinking: ten questions to ask**

Concerning the believability of **information:**

1 Which word or phrases are ambiguous or imprecise?

2 What assumptions are not admitted?

3 What assumptions are admitted?

4 Why is this being said or written?

5 What statistics are offered?

6 Are the statistics skewed?

7 What is omitted?

8 Who might construe this information differently?

9 What concepts underpin the collection, or analysis, of this information?

10 Is the use of these concepts valid?

Concerning the reasonableness of **inferences**:

1 What internal contradictions can we see?

2 What counter examples can we think of?

3 What opinions are being offered as facts?

4 What evidence is offered?

5 How authoritative, or biased, are the sources of evidence?

6 What conflicting evidence is offered?

7 What flaws are there in the reasoning?

8 Have counter-arguments been considered?

9 Is the evaluation fair and their rebuttal convincing?

10 Does the conclusion over-stretch the evidence available?

Concerning the practicality of **implications**:

1 If the implied action were taken, would it so change the situation that it would invalidate the assumptions on which the argument for action is based?

2 How controllable is the behaviour of the key actors?

3 Do we have the skills needed to take the implied action?

4 Are all the consequences beneficial? Judged by what criteria?

5 Are there unwanted side-effects?

6 Does the implied action confer the greatest benefit to the greatest number of people?

7 Does the implied action waste the least resources?

8 Does the implied action do least harm?

9 Thinking about resources, how feasible is the implied action?

10 What risks are associated with the implied action? What is the probability of the risk and the extent of the consequence? Is the worst case acceptable, and by what criteria is acceptability judged?

Assessing the believability of information

▶ **On being a Critical Friend: ten questions to ask**

1 Can you distinguish what you know from what you believe?

2 Are you open to the possibility that you may be wrong?

3 Who might disagree with you and what would they say?

4 Can you understand why they might think this way?

5 Can you see any connection between these things?

6 What do you personally have to gain if people agree with you?

7 Are you offering me opinions or facts?

8 Have you considered this counter example?

9 How will you stand up to the ridicule of others?

10 Are you settling because it seems hard work to question it?

ON BECOMING A GREAT THINKER

Aristotle said, 'You are what you habitually do.' When you change what you habitually do, you change! When you habitually ask questions like the ones above and below, you will become a great thinker.

▶ **Ten questions great thinkers often ask**

1 Could you elaborate a little?

2 Can you give me an example?

3 How could we check that out?

4 How are those two things connected?

5 How does that follow from what you said earlier?

6 Why do you think that is important or significant?

7 How does that information help us to make progress?

8 Can you think of a different way to explain that to me?

9 Can you be more precise? How much, how many, how often?

10 What do you think X would say in reply to that? (Where X can, for example, belong to another race, culture, gender or socio-economic group.)

INTELLECTUAL VIRTUES

When people hear you habitually asking the questions above, they are more likely to say that you have persistence, integrity, empathy, courage, humility and the confidence to think for yourself. These are intellectual virtues. These intellectual virtues will help you to reduce hypocrisy, indifference, cowardice, arrogance, injustice and conformity. Your developed virtues and habits of mind will show themselves in the way you question what other people have written, or in the way you question what you have written yourself.

▶ **Ten ways to question what you have read or written**

1 Why do I think the author wrote this?

2 What question is the author trying to answer?

3 Are there any clues to the author's intentions?

4 What kind of information is being brought forward here?

5 Why am I expected to believe that this information is true?

6 What assumptions are being made explicitly, and also implicitly?

7 What principle, general truth, or conclusion does the author want me to accept?

8 Are all the inferences reasonable and supported by valid reasons or examples?

9 If I accept these conclusions, what actions are implied that I, or others, should take?

10 What would be the consequences for others, if these actions were taken?

BEWARE BIAS IN THE MEDIA

Commercial news is produced to make money for its producers. The owners of the media generally receive money from advertisers and so they seek as large an audience or readership as possible. Usually, viewers, listeners or readers will not listen to or read things that make them feel bad. For this reason, the presentation of information in the media is usually biased towards making their audience feel good about themselves. Even the language used can reflect bias.

Try it now: are you biased?

In the following word pairs, underline the words that you think would bias you against the people about whom the words were said, or written.

intervene; invade   walk tall; brag

proud; arrogant   plan; plot

Questioning the media

❋ Which stories have been 'buried'?

❋ Which stories have been promoted to the front page and why?

❋ Who stands to gain from this promotion or from this demotion?

❋ Whose interests are being served or whose agenda is being furthered?

❋ Whose opinions or political beliefs are being given priority over others?

❋ Whose points of view are belittled or go unreported? Why might this be so?

❋ What counter-arguments, or counter examples, can be found elsewhere in the media?

BECOME A CRITICAL WRITER

Plan before you write. Put yourself in the shoes of a critical thinker reading what you plan to write.

Questions for critical writers

✳ What question can I use as my working title?

✳ Why do I want to write this and who do I hope will read it?

✳ What assumptions underlie my position and should I make them explicit?

✳ When my reader has read my writing what do I hope they will be convinced of?

✳ From what role, position or vested interest am I arguing? How can I own this?

✳ What information can I give readers to increase the likelihood that they will be convinced?

✳ Can I back this up with figures, examples, experiences or endorsement by sources that my reader is likely to view as credible?

✳ What do I hope readers will do differently if I can get them to accept my conclusions?

▶ **Ten rules for everyday critical thinking**

1 **Ask** yourself what assumptions you are making.

2 **Articulate** as clearly as possible criteria you use to make judgements.

3 **Remember** to own what you feel, as well as what you think.

4 **Treat** initial reactions, your own and other people's, only as tentative positions.

5 **Enquire** whether other people share your perceptions.

6 **Empathize** with the feelings and thoughts of other people.

7 **Decide** whether you have enough justifiably believable information to support a tentative conclusion. Could more information be gathered easily? What kind of information is needed? Is there a reliable source that is readily available? What credibility would the source have and why?

8 **Recognize** that all interpretations, including your own, are subjective.

9 **Admit** the limitations of your information, or of time spent gathering or checking it.

10 **Contextualize** your conclusions. Don't over-claim universal truths or principles.

Here are four problems for you to consider. When you have considered them, turn to the discussion of the problems below.

▶ **Problem 1: Is seeing believing?**

Do you see the hexagon and the cube?

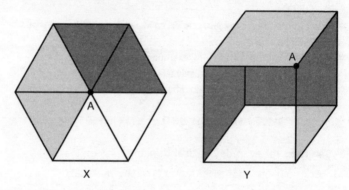

▶ **Problem 2: Are you seeing things?**

Roughly what is the size of the side of the white triangle? 3 cm, 5 cm or 7 cm?

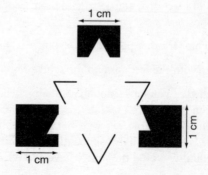

▶ Problem 3: But I saw them with my own eyes!

Can you spot the faint grey circular blobs at the corners of these black squares?

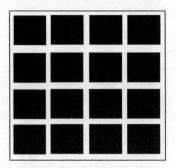

▶ Problem 4: It's down in black and white

Copy the disc. Push a pencil through the centre and spin the disc. What colours can you see? If the disc were stationary (and black and white again) and you moved around it fast enough, would it still be black and white?

▶ Discussion of the four problems

Sometimes you do not see or recognize things that really are there, like the cube (in diagram X) in Problem 1, because the way they are presented to you is unfamiliar. Sometimes, we see things that are not there because we are predisposed by other clues or experiences to see them, like the large white triangle in Problem 2. Sometimes, we are just mistaken, as in the circular blobs between the squares in Problem 3, which are not there, or the colours on the disc in Problem 4, which you would only see if you, or it, were in a great hurry!

A SCEPTICAL DISPOSITION

▶ **Are people incompetent, mistaken, lying or confused?**

You have seen how easily you can make genuine mistakes in what you think you have observed, for example, triangles, dots and colours that were not there. You have seen how easily you can mistakenly identify things, like a cube as a hexagon, because you are not used to looking at things the way other people do.

That said, according to a survey in *Time* magazine, the average American lies 200 times a day! So yes, people do lie, sometimes to protect others, sometimes to protect themselves. 'If there's no real harm done', they argue, 'what's the harm in it? After all, little white lies are better than hurting people.'

Yet there are others who would have no compunction in lying for personal gain, and who would have no regrets unless found out (and perhaps not even then). Clearly the scepticism of the applied thinker is justified.

Don't take lying, lying down

According to a *Time* magazine survey:

✳ The average woman lies about 180 times a day

✳ The average man lies about 220 times a day

✳ Apparently, 40 per cent of lies are to conceal things that would reflect badly on you

✳ Apparently, 20 per cent of lies are seen as social lubrication

✳ One in five job applicants withdraw their applications when told that their CVs are going to be authenticated

✳ Body language – for example, unnatural eye contact (evasive or fixed), blushing, a hand touching the face, throat or mouth – might indicate lying

✳ A euphemism is a lie. A child, killed by a soldier trained, and often paid, to kill, is not 'collateral damage'.

✳ They say, 'We made significant savings.' Applied thinkers say, 'Give me the numbers.'

Source: John Middleton (2006)

Assessing the reasonableness of inferences

You can use critical thinking to assess whether inferences are reasonable. Having borne in mind the need for caution and scepticism and having diligently verified the accuracy, completeness and relevance of information, you now need to infer your own opinion, and to do so reasonably. These tests of reasonableness involve logic – deductive and inductive logic.

Remember this: Using logic

Applied thinking enables you to question whether the steps that lead from believable information, or assumptions, to inferred opinions, conclusions, ideas or lessons are reasonable. Both deductive and inductive logic can be used to test the reasonableness of these inferences.

DEDUCTIVE LOGIC: TEST OF REASONABLENESS

In the case of deductive logic, the inference (for example, a conclusion) is reasonable *if* you can justifiably believe that the information in the premise is true *and* there exists no case where, the premise being true, the conclusion is not.

i.e. *Deductive reasonableness = A justified belief + A valid conclusion*

INDUCTIVE LOGIC: TEST OF REASONABLENESS

In applied thinking, we rarely enjoy the luxury of a deductively reasonable inference. In the real world, because our samples are too small or our experience is too short, we often have to settle for the probability that the information on which our premise is based is true, plus a greater likelihood than not that, if our premise is true, the conclusion will be also. Although we would prefer deductive reasonableness, inductive reasonableness may be sufficient for us to risk some action that may help us to solve a problem, make a decision or make a plan. Often it is sufficient just to be less 'imperfect' than one's competitors.

To be inductively reasonable, your inference must have a justifiably believable premise combined with a conclusion that has a greater than 50:50 chance of being right.

i.e. *Inductive reasonableness = A justified belief + A probable conclusion*

Common difficulties with accepting inductive reasonableness arise where a premise is based on a sample that may not be representative of the population to which it refers, or where conclusions have been drawn about an individual who may not belong to the population sampled.

So, while in the case of deductive reasonableness the conclusion must be inescapable to be valid, in the case of inductive reasonableness, the test is less severe because the conclusion must simply be more probable than not.

HOW LOGICAL ARE YOU?

Q1 Hello, hello, hello!

In a clampdown on drinking alcohol under the age of 18, you are to ask for proof of age ID from persons consuming alcoholic drinks. A's ID shows that she is 17. B's ID shows that he is 22. C is drinking water. D is drinking alcopops. From whom do you require further information?

Q2 All red square?

Four cards, A, B, C and D, are either red or blue on one side, and have either triangles or squares on the other side.

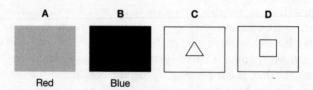

Which card(s) need you turn over to be sure that the red cards each have a square on the other side? (Answers at the back of the book.)

Many students continue to assert that their intuitive wrong answers to the questions are right, even after they have had the correct solution explained to them. This is a warning to you about accepting other people's knowledge 'in good faith' based on their 'justified belief'. Our experience with students shows that even highly intelligent people can persist in beliefs that are not justified.

> To verify is diligence, not to question is negligence.
>
> Horne, 2003

Even if logic does not seem natural to you, it is essential to train your brain to think logically when the need arises, for example, if you work in a nuclear power plant, a food factory, or a hospital or a public service.

Try the following exercises. They will strengthen the frontal lobe of your cerebral cortex – the part that deals with logic and rational analysis.

EXERCISES TO DEVELOP DEDUCTIVE LOGIC

Decide if the following arguments are deductively reasonable. The arguments are deductively reasonable if the inferred conclusions inescapably follow from the information in the premise (irrespective of whether or not you believe the premise to be true).

▶ Lies, damn lies and statistics

All spin doctors need to lie. No honest person becomes a spin doctor. Therefore no honest person lies.

▶ Are you crazy?

If bungee jumping is dangerous, then it is silly to try it. Bungee jumping is not dangerous. Therefore it is not foolish to try it.

▶ The bear facts

If you were causing climate change, the ice caps would be melting. The ice caps are melting, therefore you are causing climate change.

▶ How did you get on?

To save you looking at the back of the book for answers, none of the arguments were deductively reasonable. They were all invalid. Go back to any you thought were deductively reasonable and think again.

INDUCTIVE LOGIC

Pedantry in everyday speech can be irksome and inappropriate. But pedantry in deductive logic, used by a critical thinker at work, is very useful. Sometimes pedantry can help you to infer a definite conclusion, implying a clear plan of action to make things better. Failing that, you may have to settle for the use of inductive reasonableness.

Are any of the following arguments inductively reasonable? (i.e. could belief in the truth of the premise be justified and is there a likelihood that more people than not would accept the conclusion if they believed the premise to be true?) If necessary, add qualifying words to the premise that would make it more believable and change 'therefore' to 'probably' (but only if you think the probability of the conclusion is greater than 50:50).

Q1   Child abuse

Child abuse is committed by people who have themselves been victims of child abuse. Mr X has been found guilty of the crime of child abuse. Therefore Mr X has been himself a victim of child abuse.

a   *Is this deductively valid?*

b   *What qualifiers might be helpful?*

c   *Is the argument now inductively reasonable?*

Q2   Brazil for the cup?

Consider the following, overheard on the street. 'Brazil have a better chance of winning than Germany, or France, or even Argentina, therefore they will probably win the World Cup.'

a   Is this statement deductively valid?

b   Is this statement inductively reasonable?

c   What change could you usefully make?

Q3   English football fans abroad

English fans will probably cause trouble at the World Cup and then England could be expelled from the competition. Maybe not from the World Cup itself, but certainly from the next European Cup. Therefore, it is unlikely that England will be playing in the next European Cup.

a Is this deductively valid?

b Is this inductively reasonable?

c How could you write it as an inductively reasonable argument?

d How would you need to write it as a deductively reasonable argument?

Remember this: More likely than not

In the practical world of applied thinking, inductive logic is more useful than deductive logic. This test is not so severe; it is sufficient that, the premise being true, there is a greater likelihood than not (i.e. greater than 50:50) that the conclusion is true.

How to spot flaws in arguments

✻ Check whether the arguments offered contradict what has been said elsewhere.

✻ Examine evidence offered in support of each step in the reasoning. Is the evidence current, from a reliable source, and authenticated?

✻ Check whether correlations are being offered as though they were causes. Are assertions being offered as facts? Are they non-sequiturs?

✻ Ask whether there are possibilities that are not being considered. For example, there are usually more than two possibilities.

✻ Ask: 'On what does this all hinge?' 'What is the crucial point of the argument?' 'On what does it turn?' 'What is the *sine qua non*?' 'What is it that would invalidate a key conclusion if it were shown to be untrue?' Discard all that may be irrelevant, or unimportant – a sop or a smokescreen – of what remains, judge the parts of the argument you regard as pivotal to the soundness of the assumptions on which it rests. How strong is the reasoning that leads from these assumptions to the conclusions you are being invited to accept? Is it flawed, rocky, telling or compelling?

TRAINING YOUR BRAIN TO BE CRITICAL AND LOGICAL

There is more to critical thinking than its role in assessing whether information is justifiably believable, and in assessing whether inferences are deductively or inductively reasonable. It also has a practical role in evaluating proposals for action. But critical thinking is not in itself sufficient. You will also need to deploy creative and reflective thinking (see Chapters 8 and 9) to look at the Implications of your proposed action.

Remember this: Becoming a critical friend

To help you move from the past, via the present, to the future, applied thinking relies heavily on three high-order thinking skills: creative thinking, reflective thinking and critical thinking. It is very important that all three are developed. Critical thinking is not destructive; its aim, and the aim of becoming a critical friend, is to support and help the person whose work is being subjected to your critical thought.

A logical workout

INTRODUCTION

Your brain will certainly benefit from this cerebral workout. Many parts of your brain will be exercised, including the frontal lobes of your cerebral cortex, which is needed when logic and rationality are required. The logic puzzles are similar to puzzles that appear every week in the broadsheet newspapers. The answers are at the back of the book.

Warm up with one of these Sudoku puzzles and then tackle the logic puzzles.

A

		3		8	7	6	4	
	1	6				9		
9			6	2	1			8
3		2			5			
6		5	4		9	3		7
			2			8		4
7			1	4	6			5
		1					8	3
	2	9	7	3		4		

B

	3	9		2	1		8	
8			7					2
		2			4	5		7
5		7	2		6		4	
9				5			6	1
	1	3	9		7	2		8
4		6	1			8		
3				9	8			5
	9			6	7		1	3

Q1 Monthly ménage

Tri is to sex as quad is to what?

Q2 Who went into the UK Labour Party before and next?

… James Tony …

Q3 Theatrical confusion

When you say 'Go Nurse', which medic stirs?

Q4 Moon starer

At certain times of the month he (or she) may be a moon starer.

Q5 Hearing

Can you hear four vowels and a D, if not 'goodbye'?

Q6 Letter puzzle

These letters ZAYXWBCDEFGVUTSRQHIPJONMK scream Christmas.

Q7 Can you throw any light on this?

Which of the three switches control which lights? The switches are outside the room and you can only enter the room once. How will you find out?

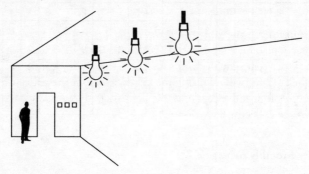

Q8 Is this fair?

If he were to give her £300 of what he earns per month, they would earn the same, but if she were to give him £300 of what she earns, he would earn five times what she earns? What do they each earn?

Q9 Will you blow it?

The bridge will be blown up at midnight. It is now 22:50. You can only cross with a torch. There is only one torch. You are fit and it only takes you four minutes to cross the bridge. Your colleagues are slow, B takes 8, C 30 and D 40 minutes. Can you get everyone safely across the bridge before midnight? (Only two people can share the torch at one time.) How?

Q10 This is a drag board meeting

How many queens could you put on a chess board without one threatening another?

Q11 And the last shall be... Last

Runner 4 is faster than 1. Runner 2 is faster than 3. Runner 3 is slower than 1. Who will be last?

Q12　Who's Lying?

Larry always lies. Tommy always tells the truth. Which one of them said of the other: 'He claims he's Larry'?

Q13　Have room for a DB5 Volante

A collector of fine vintage fast cars wants to expand his collection so he increases the size of his air-conditioned garage by 50 per cent. Each car on average is 15 ft (4.5 m) long and 6 ft (2 m) wide. During the auction season, the collector acquires four more cars and fills the garage. How many cars does the collector have now?

Q14　Lord of the ring cycle

Richard Wagner is said to have enrolled for a course and was asked a question to which he replied '9-W'. What was the question?

Q15　The brain train

The brain trains run from A to B, one a minute, 24 hours a day. The return journey, at the same speed, takes one hour. How many trains do you pass on the journey from A to B?

Q16　This really could be the final one – it could blow your brains out

You are to be shot but your inquisitor offers you a way out. You can blow your own brains out! You are to be offered the choice of three pistols to put against your temple and fire. Your inquisitor demonstrates that each of the single shot pistols is empty by firing each one into your head! He then loads just one bullet into one pistol. You know he only loads one pistol, but you do not know which one. You indicate your choice of pistol 1. Surprisingly 'to show good faith', your inquisitor places pistol 2 against his own temple and pulls the trigger. Surprise, surprise it does not fire. Even more surprising, he now offers you the chance to change your mind about your choice of pistol 1. Should you?

Thinking critically about education

William Sumner suggested that education was 'good' only in so far as it developed the ability to think critically because 'it is a way of taking up the problems of life'. We do not entirely agree. Critical thinking is a necessary, but not sufficient, condition. In order to 'take up' the problems of life, you need applied thinking, and this requires that you combine critical thinking with reflective thinking and creative thinking. We do not underestimate, however, the benefits to society of a population educated in critical thinking alone. As a critical thinker you could not readily be mobilized by propaganda to serve undesirable ends or unjust wars. You would be sceptical and slow to believe what others say or write. An education that prioritizes the development of critical thinking may not be a sufficient preparation for active citizenship, but it is a great start!

Focus points

✻ You can become an applied thinker.

✻ Applied thinking is the kind of thinking you need to turn information into knowledge, on which you can take action.

✻ You can train the frontal lobes of your brain to think logically, solve problems, take decisions and make plans.

✻ Applied thinking helps you make changes to make the world a better place.

✻ Applied thinking is supported by critical, creative and reflective thinking.

✻ Critical thinking can empower people who would otherwise be easily impressed, or oppressed, by people in positions of power.

✻ Critical thinking is not negative. Its intention is to support the person whose ideas are the subject of the critical thinking.

✻ Critical thinking develops personal characteristics, like courage, intellectual independence and social self-reliance.

✻ Critical thinking uses deductive and inductive logic to assess the believability of information, the reasonableness of inferences and the practicality of implied actions.

✻ Logic involves the use of the frontal lobes of the cerebral cortex, which can be developed by solving brain training problems.

Dig deeper

Baggini, J. and Stangroom, J., *Do You Think What You Think You Think?* (London: Granta Books, 2006).

Cohen, M., *Philosophy Problems* (London: Routledge, 1999).

Horne, T. and Doherty, A., *Managing Public Services – Implementing Changes: A Thoughtful Approach to the Practice of Management* (London: Routledge, 2003).

Middleton, J., *Upgrade Your Brain* (Oxford: Infinite Ideas, 2006).

Middleton, J., 'Ground rules for telling lies', *Time* (3 April, 2006).

Thompson, A., *Critical Reasoning* (New York: Routledge, 1999).

Wootton, S. and Horne, T., *Strategic Thinking* (London: Kogan Page, 2003).

Next steps

Applied thinking is the kind of thinking that you need in order to turn Information into Knowledge on which you can take Action. So:

✳ Look at the 'ten questions to ask' at the start of the chapter and apply them to situations.
✳ When assessing the believability of information, use the 'ten questions great thinkers often ask' in this chapter.
✳ Critical thinking supports applied thinking so consider the 'ten rules for everyday critical thinking' in this chapter.

PART THREE

AT PLAY

8

Looking and learning

In this chapter you will learn:

▶ *how to use visual thinking to help you predict and learn*

▶ *how to use reflective thinking to help you learn from your experiences*

▶ *how to improve your performance on tests of visual and spatial reasoning*

▶ *how to use visual thinking puzzles to develop your visual intelligence and cognitive capacity.*

Thinking visually is more important than knowledge.

Albert Einstein

Introduction

Patients who undergo surgery in both eyes, and have both eyes bandaged, can suffer dangerous delusions. They tear at their bandages and sometimes attempt suicide. Such is the importance to your brain of visual processing and visual thinking that visual deprivation can be used as a punishment or torture. Prisoners in prolonged solitary confinement often resort to imagination in an effort to stay sane. The routine processing of visual images, real or imagined, seems to be important for the health of your brain.

Visual images are also important in memory (see Chapter 3), creative thinking (see Chapter 9) and in ethical thinking and empathy (see Chapter 2 and Final thoughts). In this chapter, we will look at the role of visual thinking in prediction and reflection.

Remember this: The basis of belief

Reflective thinking helps you to turn experiences and past events into lessons or ideas that you believe to be true today, and which can indicate how you should behave tomorrow.

Try it now: Reflective thinking

Notice how you think visually as you answer the following two questions:

1 How many windows are there in your house or flat?

2 What shape are a horse's ears?

Now think about packing a car. You can create images of what you need to take and you can manipulate them in your mind to test out which arrangements will fit, and which won't.

A room of your own: creative visualization

When you laugh, scream or cry when watching a film, the images are not real but your emotions are. You can use visual thinking to create or recall images in order to feel the way you want to feel. You can visualize images that will make you feel excited and creative or calm and reassured, or that can lift vague unattached despondency that settles on you out of nowhere. Virginia Woolf's plea was that a woman might have £60 a year and a room of her own, in fact a choice of rooms whenever you want.

Try it now: Relax and breathe very deeply

Close your eyes and imagine a large white house near a lake. See the light on the water and smell the garden plants as you approach the door. Notice what large windows the house has. You have a key; hear yourself turning it in the lock. As you walk through the rooms, notice how they are decorated and the changing views from the large windows. They are all wonderful. Breathe in and sit down at a desk by the window when you are in a room that will have the answers to your questions. When you have what you want and when you are ready, come back to your own real desk in your own good time.

Visual thinking: foretelling the future

Visual thinking can be foresight sensing what something should look like in the future. Many historical leaders appeared to have had a vision of the future that they followed. In the Bible's Old Testament, Moses had a vision that he would lead his people out of bondage. Alexander the Great foretold the expansion of his Macedonian Empire. Mahatma Gandhi foresaw that India would be independent. Martin Luther King had 'a dream'.

Remember this: Envisaging the future

Reflective thinking relies heavily on visual thinking. When recalling the experiences on which you need to reflect, it is important to recall what you saw, heard and felt as real. Non-verbal clues can help you to interpret what was meant, as well as what was said. Visual thinking will help you to envisage a spectrum of possible actions, or to develop a 'vision' of the future.

VISUAL THINKING AND SCIENCE

The history of science contains innumerable reports of scientists having an image in their mind immediately prior to a major discovery. Faraday and Maxwell visualized electromagnetic fields as tiny tubes filled with fluid. Kekulé saw the benzene ring in a reverie of snakes biting their tails. Watson and Crick mentally rotated models of what was to become the double helix. Einstein imagined what it would be like to ride on a beam of light. He once wrote, 'My particular ability does not lie in mathematical calculation, but rather in visualizing effects.'

VISUAL THINKING AND SUCCESS

Since the mid-1990s, visualization has been used in sex therapy, weight loss, sports enhancement, memory improvement, life planning and complex problem solving.

Lazarus has reported on the connection between being able to think visually and success in day-to-day living. Many of the top 150 UK business leaders were reported by Alder to be good visualizers. Ernest Hemingway thought that, 'Cowardice, as distinct from panic, is the inability to suspend imagination.' Ambition, sexual arousal and jealous rage can all be triggered by images.

VISUAL THINKING AND IMAGINATION

Kosslyn used positron emission tomography (PET) scanners to see which parts of the brain were most active when people had mental images. He found that the area of the brain that handled vision was the same as was active when patients were asked to imagine things.

Try it now: Visual thinking

* Close your eyes when trying to bring information together.
* Sketch out the information people give you as they talk. If it is a one-to-one conversation, or a small group, make sure that your sketching is visible to whoever is speaking. Encourage them to add to the emerging picture.
* Play solitaire or, better still, chess. Maybe join a chess club. If you don't like chess, try the game Go. Games involving other people are better because conversation encourages you to think aloud, which is much more developmental for your brain (see Chapters 6 and 10).

▶ Psychometric tests for job selection

Tests for employment almost always include tests of visual thinking. Figure 7.1 and Appendices A, B and C show that visual thinking is an important component of each of the three pillars of applied thinking (Critical, Creative and Reflective Thinking).

Remember this: Visual and spatial IQ

Applications for employment routinely involve psychometric tests that assess visual and spatial aptitude. Visual IQ is seen as a component of overall IQ. Your performance on visual aptitude tests can be improved by practising typical questions.

Visual thinking tests

PATTERNS, ANALOGIES, SEQUENCES, CLASSIFICATIONS, REASONING AND DIAGRAMS

Try the following six sets of questions. These are examples of each type of question that you will find in a typical job selection test. Check your answers at the back of the book.

▶ Type 1: pattern recognition

Q1   The hole in the boat

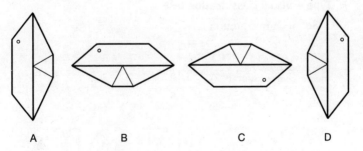

| A | B | C | D |

Which is the odd one out?

▶ **Type 2: visual analogy**

Q1   Some breed, some die

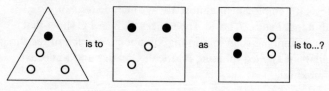

Q2   The great survivors

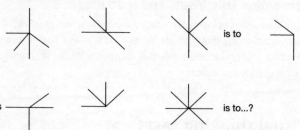

▶ **Type 3: visual sequence**

Q1   Which comes next?

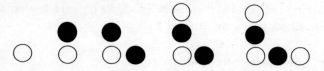

▶ **Type 4: visual classification test**

Q1   So much in common

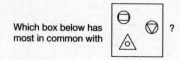

Which box below has most in common with [ ] ?

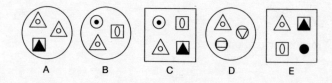

A   B   C   D   E

Q1   No pack

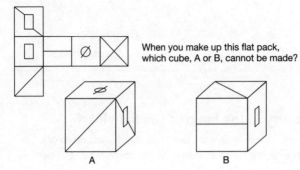

When you make up this flat pack, which cube, A or B, cannot be made?

A   B

Q2   Like this or like that?

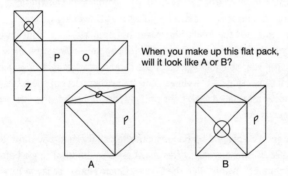

When you make up this flat pack, will it look like A or B?

A   B

▶ **Type 6: numeric diagram**

Q1

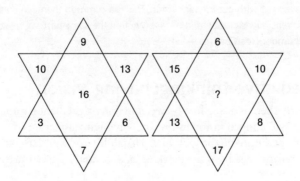

Q2

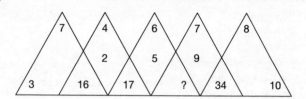

Is beauty in the brain of the beholder?

This was a question that US journalist David Sokol asked of brain scientists in 2007. Unfortunately, at this stage, brain scientists don't know how to answer David's question. Brain science remains humble in relation to the visual arts. Brain scientists have little to teach and everything to learn from artists and art historians and aesthetic philosophers. Professor Zeki, a neurologist at University College London, founded the field of neuroaesthetics in 1994. His colleague, Kawabata, in 2004 scanned the brains of people viewing artwork and discovered that specific regions of the cerebral cortex light up when artwork is pleasing to the viewer, and that other parts of the brain, more commonly associated with fight or flight, are activated when they think the piece is ugly.

This suggests a general human response to beauty that may transcend time, culture and language. After all, whose skin does not tingle before Claude Monet's *Water Lilies*, the Sydney Opera House, or Jayne Torvill and Christopher Dean's *Boléro*? Margaret Livingstone thinks that the brain is tricked into tension by incongruity. For example, Monet's view down Rue Montorgueil is a peripheral vision view that the artist forces us to look at with our forward vision. This is a common theme in creative work: tension, resolution and release. We find the same pattern in jazz and humour (see Chapter 9).

Predictive thinking: having 'vision'

Clearly there is a fine line between making a prediction about what will happen in the future and envisaging a picture of what the future might look like. The ability to have a 'dream' or a 'vision' has been the mark of leaders down the centuries.

In the Bible, Joseph had a dream about famine. Martin Luther King 'had a dream' of an America free for all its people, judged by their character not by the colour of their skin. Predictions can be made by using numbers and statistics (see Chapter 6), by using logic (see Chapter 7), by using hunches or emotional intelligence (see Chapter 2), by recalling past patterns (see Chapter 3), or by using street wisdom (see Chapter 4).

Predictive thinking draws on many contributory thinking skills but probably none more so than visual thinking. Because it is so multi-faceted, problems or puzzles involving visualization and prediction are much sought after by serious brain trainers.

How to use predictive thinking to go to the cinema

We may get information from the internet or a newspaper about what's on at the local cinema. This enables us to estimate the running time of the film and the likely time the film will finish. With an allowance for getting out of the car park (will the film be popular?), we predict what time we will be back home. The newspaper times may be inaccurate, the programme may have changed, there may be advertisements and an interval, the projectionist may arrive late and there may be a temporary powercut. Yet we confidently predict our return time, plus or minus five minutes.

PREDICTIVE THINKING AND WHAT IT MEANS TO BE HUMAN

The ability to predict is one of the defining characteristics of humans. It contributes strongly to the ability to control and to the desire to create and maintain order. Prediction helps to manage the risks associated with change.

Remember this: The leaders and the led

Until work in 2010 that showed that some animals can 'think about the future', the ability to think about the future seemed to distinguish humans from animals. The ability to make good predictions, forecasts and educated guesses about the future still distinguishes effective managers from the managed, and effective leaders from the led.

▶ Weather to go out or not?

We want a better understanding of past weather patterns so that we can make better weather forecasts. We can then adjust our plans accordingly. We make predictions and act on them. Although there is never any guarantee about the future, even that the sun will come up tomorrow, a sound prediction can be founded on past patterns if you can reasonably expect historic conditions to remain unchanged in the future. That is why uncertainties about the effects of global warming are making weather forecasting more difficult now. Predictions can still be made even when you expect the historic conditions to change, provided you know the rate and direction of the change.

▶ 20:20 hindsight

Things will not necessarily continue to increase in the future simply because they did so in the past. The past is not a sound basis for prediction unless you can be sure that past conditions will persist into the future. Simple projections of past trends can be treacherous. For example, past figures for increases in electricity consumption are a misleading basis for predicting next year's consumption unless the effects of such things as the economy, global warming and the popularity of televised sport can be taken into account. An understanding of the forces at work can make it safer to extrapolate an observed trend. Such an understanding comes more from saturation in the situation than from scientific techniques. In this respect, prediction is similar to other generalizations from the known to the unknown: it benefits from age, greater knowledge and wider experience.

How to make predictions

* How far away is the future situation? What do you want to know about it?
* Collect information about the present situation and use it as a benchmark.
* Look backwards from the present over a period equal in length to the period over which you want to make your prediction.
* Determine how much variability there was during the past period.

* Look for pronounced cyclical effects. Check whether there were any sudden discontinuities.
* Find other variables that associate (preferably causally) with the variables you want to predict and look for predictions related to the causally associated variables.

HOW TO GET HELP WITH PREDICTING THE FUTURE

Being 'saturated' with knowledge of the field aids prediction. This favours the use of experts, or older people, to inform predictions. Experts are 'saturated' with knowledge, understanding and experience of their field. Using groups of technical experts, as in the Delphi technique (see below), can intensify this saturation.

The young ones

The people who will be opinion makers and opinion formers in 15 to 20 years' time are teenagers now. If you want to predict the way society's values and interests will change over the next 15 years, talk to young people. Volunteer to help at your local youth club.

When making difficult and dangerous predictions (for example: Will a patient kill himself? Will an arsonist set a fire? Will a paedophile molest a child?), groups of people are called together for a case conference. The case-worker calls together experts from a wide range of disciplines to confer with family, friends and neighbours who have a detailed knowledge of the person, the context, and the history. This has proved a safer method of prediction than relying on one doctor, social worker or probation officer. Bad calls are made of course. We are talking about inductive not deductive logic.

Try it now: 'See' the future – the Delphi technique

When a group needs to predict the future, form as heterogeneous a group as possible. Let every person speak once before anyone speaks twice, then ask each person to write down their predictions anonymously. Feed all the anonymous predictions back to the group. Repeat the process until the overall group prediction is stable.

HOW TO PREDICT YOUR OWN FUTURE

We do not need to reinvent the wheel. There are predictable age-related crises in almost everyone's life. We do not have to wait and see what happens when we do things that affect other people; it is possible to use visual and empathetic thinking to foresee who will resist a change. People who will enjoy a change can also be spotted in advance (Horne and Doherty, 2003).

▶ Prime your intuition

Your brain has a natural and unconscious ability to predict events. It unconsciously processes all kinds of information – much of which it senses at a subliminal level. The more you train yourself to be aware of what you are constantly hearing, seeing, feeling and thinking, the more data you will be transferring into your predictive thinking system and the greater will be the accuracy of your predictions. It will feel like an intuitive sixth sense.

Naisbitt was able to make 20-year predictions about society, technology, economies, institutions, democracy, hierarchies and ways of thinking that have largely proved to be accurate. This was because he had knowledge about changes that had already taken place as he wrote his book. He simply inferred from what he knew had already happened the implications for various aspects of society during the succeeding 20 years. The rate of change in the world is often slower than is claimed by those who can profit from the belief that it is rapid!

Ages and stages: this is your life

Your life will go through certain ages and stages. In westernized cultures, the years 0–10 are for childhood and years 10–25 are for education and training. Then come:

The swapping years (25–35). These will be characterized by swapping homes, swapping jobs and swapping partners, often looking for one with whom to have children.

The dangerous years (35–45). These dangerous years will involve a reassessment of career ambitions and relationships. There may be pressures from teenage children, elderly parents or job promotion. Career change, partner change and sexual panic are likely.

The golden years (45–55). Children will probably be grown up or have left home. Parents may have left a small inheritance. The mortgage may be paid. Work priorities can be readjusted. Less fatigue can rekindle a relationship. Former hobbies and spiritual values may be rediscovered. Reflective thinking can draw on extensive life experience to make this a golden age.

The vintage years (55+). The vintage years might be about retirement, so contingency planning is required. You can use research on thinking and the brain to make these truly vintage years. It will be a good time to consider self-employment – perhaps as a consultant, an artisan, a part-time governor, a non-executive director or the owner of a small business. It is a good time to offer voluntary service abroad or to move to a warmer climate. Do not retire to a nice quiet place. You will die earlier. The brain thrives on stimulation.

THE NEUROSCIENCE OF PREDICTION

Your habit of prediction is not reserved for special situations like hitting a tennis ball. Because most of your thinking has already been done on the basis of your predictions, then most of your daily actions can be carried out on automatic pilot, leaving your brain to deal with what is surprising, curious or novel. For example, when you reach for the handle on a door, your brain will be predicting the moment of contact, the correct angle at which to hold your hand and how the handle will feel when you touch it.

Desimone's work has showed that intention fires neurons. Neurons are always firing. Billions of neurons in your head pop off at least once or twice each second. Friston concludes that this continual firing of your individual neurons reflects your brain's preparedness to act in the event that any one of your constant predictions comes true.

Reflective thinking: how to do better in the future

How can you make your future profit from your past? You can do it by using reflective thinking. This involves thinking about past experiences, yours and those of other people, in such a way that you can come to a present conclusion that strongly implies a future change. Reflective thinking pulls you out of the past, through the present and propels you into the future. The way that reflective thinking relies on combinations of other basic thinking skills is shown in Appendix C.

CAN YOU THINK REFLECTIVELY?

When you consider Appendix C and the complexity of what is involved in reflective thinking, and the extent of its dependence on other supportive modes of thinking, it becomes clearer why many people find it difficult. If the contributory thinking skills have not been trained, you simply won't be able to reflect. Maybe that is why some people are described as reflective and others as unreflective, as though it were an aspect of personality. But it is not; the skills can be developed with training.

One way you can enhance your reflective thinking is to use visual thinking to replay your experience as a video tape in your mind. Try to imagine the tactile sensations as well as tastes and smells as you see and hear the tape. Better still, recount the experience to someone who is free to ask questions about what you remember. Focus first on positive feelings about the event, then express any negative feelings. The following questions might help:

▶ **Recollecting what happened then**

▶ Why did I act as I did?

▶ What were the key issues?

▶ What was I trying to achieve?

▶ How did other people feel about it?

▶ How do I know how they felt about it?

- How did I feel at different points during this experience?

- What were the consequences of my action for others?

- What influenced my decision making and actions?

- What else should have influenced me?

▶ **Thinking about it now**

- How do I feel about it now?

- What other choices might I have had?

- Could I have dealt better with the situation?

▶ **Looking forward to similar situations in the future**

- How might I support others better in the future?

- What might I do differently as a result of what I think now?

Source: Horne and Doherty, 2003

REFLECTIVE THINKING: FOUR USEFUL STEPS

Step 1. If you hope to learn from an experience later, during the experience you should check how you are feeling, as well as what opinions you are forming. If you notice that you have strong feelings about what is happening, mentally 'photograph' what you can see and try to remember the exact words that people are using. Notice *how* people are talking, as well as *what* they are saying. Try to guess how people are feeling. Check out your guesses, if it is appropriate. Use your recollective thinking skills to memorize this information or create a visual map.

Step 2. Later, refer to your memorized or mapped information about what was happening, during the experience. If possible, write down what you recall was happening. You should be using the past tense – 'I noticed that …', 'I saw …', 'I heard X say …' and 'I felt … (single words for emotions)' and 'I thought … (opinions – these are whole sentences)'. Try to label the feelings and emotions before recalling the thoughts. Use your visual thinking skills to recreate a rich mental video of the experience. When you have recorded your information, take a break, preferably a walk.

Step 3. Later, return to your written information and observe it from your new standpoint in the present. Try to ensure that in your internal dialogue, you *now* have a real present-tense reflection on what happened *then*. As you talk to yourself, or your thinking companion, force yourself to begin all your sentences with 'Right here and now I am noticing that ...' and 'Right here and now I am feeling ...' (single words describing emotions)' and 'Right now I am thinking that ... (whole sentences outlining opinions)'. To help yourself to form present-tense inferences, ask yourself questions like 'What pattern can I see now?'; 'What does this remind me of?'; 'What associations, what insights and what realizations do I have *now*, as a result of what I am reading about what happened *then*?'. When you have inferred all the present-tense reflections and lessons that you can, take a break, preferably a walk.

Step 4. Later, try and imagine some future time when you will be in a situation that has something in common with the experience on which you are reflecting. Visual thinking skills and predictive thinking skills will help you. The future situation might involve a similar task, or a similar problem, or a similar mix of people, or a similar process, or a similar incident to the one being reflected upon. In order to help turn the inferences into implications for action, see yourself in this future situation behaving differently from the way you would have behaved normally. How might it be useful to vary your normal behaviour in the light of your new learning? What changes does your new learning imply? Imagine how you are going to feel when you behave in this different way. What will you think? Picture the expressions on the faces of the other people in the scene. Hear any applause or approval. Repeat and intensify your expected experience of it. Notice how you experience it in your body.

Visual, predictive and reflective thinking

LEARNING FROM EXPERIENCE

You have the same brain as Einstein. You are often judged by others to be intelligent when you learn quickly and well. Einstein was a 'slow' child, a late developer. He did not talk until he was three years old. He did poorly in school. Yet he revolutionized the world of physics. After he died, scientists were not able to find any remarkable differences between Einstein's brain and yours or mine. Appearing intelligent by being seen to learn quickly is not determined by the structure of your brain, but by how you use your brain to think. It may be possible to think without learning, but it is not possible to learn without thinking. You cannot turn information into useful action without thinking. Applied thinking turns information into knowledge on which useful action can be based. This kind of thinking is particularly useful in vocational subjects.

THE CHINESE CHAIN OF LEARNING
The Chinese character for learning is made up of two symbols: one means studying; the other means constant repetition. The Chinese character for thinking involves the character for 'head' and the character for 'heart'. The Chinese characters suggest that, when you want to learn, you should first study some relevant information, then use your 'head' to make sense of it, and your 'heart' as a source of emotional energy, so that you can act on what you have learned. Your inner world is a mental laboratory in which you can rehearse proposed actions so that you can anticipate undesirable consequences for others.

▶ **The university of life**
Learning has three purposes:

1 To develop concepts.

2 To develop skills that enable you to apply concepts.

3 To develop the attributes, attitudes and dispositions expected of a 'learned' person.

Traditional universities often neglect 2. Modern universities often neglect 3. You can pay attention to all three points by learning to think for yourself as yourself, and to think for yourself as another.

Some common myths about learning:

Meditation	▶ There is no evidence that soldiers can be taught saintly super skills.
Learning in your sleep	▶ There is no evidence that learn-in-your-sleep audio tapes work.
	▶ Disturbed sleep impairs thinking and learning the next day (see Chapter 1).
Music while you learn	▶ This actually impairs performance for the 20 per cent of students who can only think in silence. The result is negative to indifferent for the rest, unless the music is specifically matched to the type of thinking required for the learning task (see Chapter 5).
Relaxation learning	▶ Only works if it lowers stress or anxiety that would otherwise impair thinking. Otherwise relaxation lowers performance. This is because learning requires thinking and a certain minimum level of arousal is necessary to think. If relaxation takes you below that level you won't learn.
Accelerated learning	▶ Most elements of accelerated learning are present in traditional teaching by effective teachers, so there is no research basis for claims of a 50 times improvement compared to traditional methods.
Left brain, right brain	▶ Techniques such as Hemi-Sync, which are aimed at stimulating one side of the brain or the other, for particular subjects, do not enhance learning. Warming up the whole brain does (see Chapter 9).
NLP (Neuro-Linguistic Programming)	▶ It is difficult to isolate independent variables. For example, use of eye movement data requires paying close individual attention to learners – this is known to be effective with or without NLP.
Parapsychology	▶ There is no evidence that this works.

LEARNING FOR EXAMS

Since learning involves thinking, and a half decent exam paper does too, then whatever helps you think will help your learning and performance in exams. Things that help when preparing for tests in IQ, numeric, visual and verbal thinking (see Chapters 5, 8 and 9) will also help you on the day of your exam. In addition, here are 12 specific top tips.

1 Sweat it out – exercise oxygenates your brain and rejuvenates your hippocampus which is central to memory and learning.

2 Food for thought – eat fish, like sardines and tuna, or a plant-based omega-3 source and plenty of fruit. Avoid sugar, biscuits, bread, refined flour, processed food, chemical additives and chips.

3 Drink the water – drink two to four pints of water a day. Do not drink sweetened, coloured or caffeinated drinks.

4 Come up smelling – not of chemical aftershave or body odour. Try lavender.

5 Warm up before revising and before the exam. Use the mental arithmetic or Sudoku warm-ups (see Chapter 6).

6 Take a break – after 40 minutes' revision, take a 15-minute break. Start and re-start your revision promptly on the hour.

7 Chew gum – it improves brain blood flow by 25 per cent during exams.

8 Avoid T – T for texts, T for technology and T for TV – they all lower IQ scores.

9 Hit the wagon – alcohol, in even small quantities, lowers mental and physical performance not only that night, but for several days thereafter.

10 Eat dark chocolate – dark chocolate (not dairy, never white) stimulates your brain and raises your mood, motivation and performance.

11 Have sex – sex boosts your brain, especially if you're a woman. Prolactin release increases brain cells.

12 Power nap – go to sleep and set a 20-minute alarm. Do not work unusually late at night. Sleep normally. Disturbed sleep lowers IQ. It takes several days to recover from a late night (see Chapter 1).

Can't remember what you learned? The eyes have it!

In May 2007, Andrew Parker reported the results of memory recall of 102 of his students. When he asked them to switch their eyes from side to side, they could remember 10 per cent more. They also made 15 per cent fewer recall errors. Maybe you should add a 30-second morning eye jiggle to your revision warm-up and try it again in the exams if you get stuck and can't remember what you've learned. Maybe your eyes will have it!

Try it now: Where did you get that fact?

Since learning involves thinking about information, inferring your own opinion, and implying useful actions based on those opinions, then the quality of your learning will be limited by the quality of the information you have to think about (garbage in – garbage out!). The quality of your information depends on where you got it.

Complete the following questionnaire about where you get your information as you look and learn your way through life. Consider each topic in turn and faintly tick where you have gained most of your information on that topic. You can tick more than one (or none if you have no information on that topic). Enter the value against each tick, using values from the column on the right.

Sources	Topics	Religion	Science	Politics	Careers	Sex	Cultures	Relationships	Morals	Art	Music	Value	Score
Specialist journals												12	
Books												11	
Courses												10	
Magazines												7	
Newspapers												5	
Friends/peers												5	
Family members												4	
Church												4	
Internet												3	
Radio												2	
Television												1	
Total score													

So how did you get on?

A score of	Indicates that ...
0–50	You are in a dire situation requiring remedial action.
51–200	Your information sources are weak and unexamined.
201–250	You take some interest in the information you are being fed.
251–300	You gather information deliberately.
301–400	You are concerned about credibility.
401–500	You try to protect against 'garbage in'.
501+	An eclectic intellectual.

THE CHEMICAL JOY OF LEARNING

Joyfulness is associated with increased levels of endorphins in the brain. These peptide molecules make us feel good. Levinthal found higher levels of endorphins in people who were strong problem solvers and good learners. High levels of excitement and expectancy about the potential usefulness of new information are key determinants of learning (see Chapter 2). There are many links to explore in your Chinese chain of learning. Vocational learning involves a change in your ability to do something. For you to change what you do, you must not only acquire new information that you understand and think is important and that you want to apply but, in addition, you must have the skills and confidence needed to apply the knowledge and a high enough self-esteem to risk failure.

Whatever new information you acquire, whatever new insights you infer, or whatever new implications you test, your past experience can only inform your future action if you are able to recall accurately what you saw, heard, thought, felt and discovered. Recall is aided by movement, so it is not surprising that people learn better when they are moving – either emotionally or physically.

'LEARNING STYLES' AND OTHER MYTHS

Brain research brings into question some long-running ideas about 'preferred learning styles'. Edelman found that, irrespective of a student's preferred learning style, it was possible to help them to involve those parts of their brains that they normally preferred not to use. Restak reported that the brain made a better job of processing sensory input when several of its systems were working simultaneously. In short, brain research does not appear to support the idea that quality, persistence, extent or depth of learning are achieved by allowing the learner to use only their preferred learning style. What does seem to be important is that learning activities should stimulate several parts of the brain simultaneously since this promotes the increased neural interconnectedness associated with the development of increased cognitive capacity. Repetition and practice also seem to be important since they bequeath thickening of the myelin insulation on the axons of the neurons and this favours future thinking speed and accuracy.

Learning styles and other myths

The (UK) espouses theories of learning styles with scant regard for the evidence.

Phil Revell, *The Times*, 31 May 2005

If your child comes home from school and says 'I'm a visual [or auditory or kinaesthetic] learner' be concerned. Be very concerned. There is little evidence that approaches based on learning styles and learning cycles are valid. Professor Coffield led a team which reported, in 2005, on the validity of the 13 most widely used theories of learning style and learning cycle. This included VAK (visual, auditory and kinaesthetic) learning styles which are the theories most widely used in the UK. Coffield's recommendation was that their use be discontinued. This recommendation has not yet been implemented in many schools and colleges. Similarly, the GSD (Gregorc's style delineator of four learning styles) was found to be 'theoretically and psychometrically flawed'.

WHY GROUP WORKING ISN'T WORKING

Since learning involves thinking and thinking is difficult in groups (see Chapter 5), learning programmes or training courses that are heavily dependent on group work should be avoided. Paired learning, on the other hand, greatly aids thinking. Some employment situations require people to work in groups and teams, in which case very specific techniques are required to enable sufficient thinking to take place to support learning, decision making and problem solving. You should avoid, if at all possible, being drawn into models of work-based learning that are based on experiential cycles attributed to Kolb, Mumford and others. These are deeply flawed and assume that you have particular thinking skills which you may in fact need to develop *before* these models of learning can work for you.

Learning through thinking

* Favour total immersion in multi-faceted, multi-level problem solving.
* Seek out experiences that are emotionally involving.
* Have the kinds of critical conversations that develop your capacity for internal dialogue. Rehearse the application of your ideas in your 'mental laboratory' (Chapter 7).
* Where possible, avoid working on your own. Involve someone else.
* Avoid groups except for information gathering or feeding back inferences and implications.
* Paired working is the most effective. Develop mentoring, appraising, coaching and counselling relationships. Find a critical friend (see Chapter 10).
* Avoid learning experiences or training schemes that claim to be based on Kolb or Mumford style learning cycles, unless or until you have developed and practised your ability to observe (thinking visually);

Visual thinking is not only helpful when predicting and learning but, because it involves at least 23 separate areas of your brain, it is a great warm-up and a good way to expand the connectedness and overall cognitive capacity of your brain. Try the visual thinking workout.

The visual thinking workout

INTRODUCTION

There have been visual and spatial puzzles and mazes for at least 4,000 years. Puzzles were often used to protect tombs and treasure. They are the stuff of pharaohs and Greek legends. It is not surprising that visual puzzles have been with us for a long time because they mirror the way your brain works by piecing together fragments and perspectives until a meaningful pattern is recognized.

The Greeks, great early thinkers and philosophers, developed a passion for puzzles, dilemma and lateral thinking around 500–300 BC. At the same time, the Chinese were keen on spatial and visual patterning games like Go and solitaire. Spatial crosswords did not appear until early in the last century, and Sudoku is more recent even than that!

Brain scan research now enables us to understand the importance of puzzles as brain trainers. The 'chemical' brain is very 'plastic', not rigid like a computer. It develops and reorganizes itself throughout your life and into old age. Depending on what you ask it to do, it can even re-route itself around physical damage caused by accident or disease.

Training and stretching your brain is not only important as a child, but also throughout adulthood. It is one of the strongest predictors of longevity and mental and physical health. There is little difference between a 25-year-old brain and a 75-year-old brain that has been regularly trained and kept active (see *Keep Your Brain Sharp*, Horne and Wootton, 2010).

In this workout we have designed visual thinking puzzles that often involve memory (hypothalamus plus myriad connections), some numerical thinking and some critical thinking (frontal cerebral cortex). Add in the amygdala, which will be busy trying to keep your impatience, frustration and competitive anxiety at bay, and you have got the basis of a good brain training workout.

WARM-UP

1 Rapidly alternate your eye focus, 20 times, between your fingerprint (see the detail) and a distant object (preferably out of the window).

2 Chin back and without moving your head or eyes see as far round to your sides as you can, using your peripheral vision. Complete the 360^0 scan using your imagination, three times.

3 Move your eyes, 30 times, rapidly from left to right.

Now do a Sudoku puzzle. Here are a couple to choose from.

A

8	1	9			5			4
		2		8		7	5	
	3	7	1		4		6	
4			5	9		1		
7			3		8			2
		3		6	2			7
	5		7		9	2	1	
2	6	4		3		9		
						4	3	8

B

	3	6		9	2	5	7	
1			7	8		6		9
9		2	6	1		4		3
4			3		1	8	5	
	1			2		9	4	6
	6	8	5		9			7
7		9			8	2		
3				5	6			4
	2		9			3	1	

MAIN WORKOUT

Q1 What the hex?

Put the seven hexagons i to vii into spaces A–G so that where any hexagon touches another, the numbers on either side of the boundary line are identical. (Hint: Do not rotate the hexagons!)

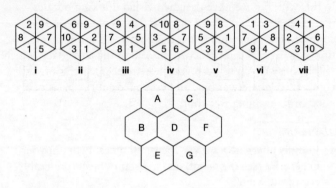

Q2 Which kite will fly?

Which of these box kites will fly?

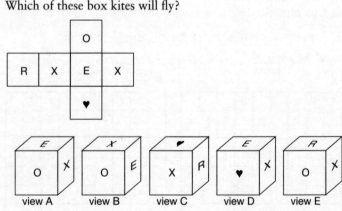

Q3 Which one is too right?

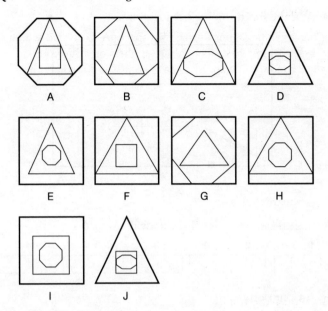

A   B   C   D

E   F   G   H

I   J

Q4 Pack it in

Without using a calculator, how many boxes of size 3 × 3 × 6 can you pack into these containers?

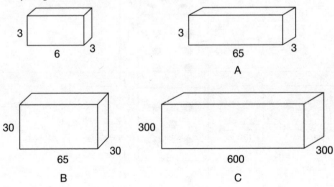

Q5   Which way?

What is the shortest route from A to B?

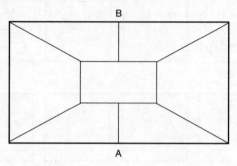

Q6   Square things up

Arrange these pieces into a square with no spaces.

| 1 | 1 | 2 | 2 | 3 | 3 | 4 |

1 ☐ ☐ ☐ ☐ ☐ ☐ ☐

Q7   Gone dotty

How many dots would you see altogether as you walked right around this stack of giant dice? What is the total of the concealed faces?

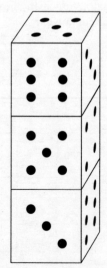

Q8 Drawing on experience

Mr B knows he has only four socks tucked away at the back of his drawer. He only owns black or grey socks. His chances of pulling out two black ones is 50:50. What are his chances of pulling out two grey socks?

Q9 Bottoms up!

Would the flat pack below make the cube?

And if so, what would you see if you turned it over, bottom up?

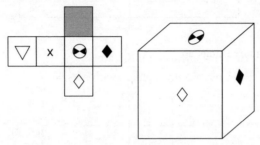

Q10 Site security

You are in charge on a building site where prefabricated buildings are being assembled. This is the bathroom module below. If you remove one block and roll the unit twice anticlockwise (180⁰), it will turn into a tiled bathroom with a slipper bath in the back left-hand corner. But if you as much as even blink, someone will steal the bath. Which block do you need to remove? Rehearse it and work out how you can always get the bath back.

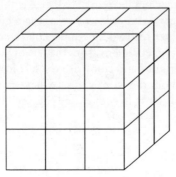

Q11   Perchance to dream

Is this a real dice?

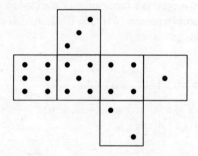

If not, draw a real one using this template:

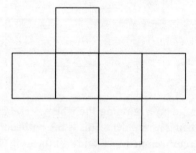

Q12   Waking the dead heads (thoughtfully)

Without using real coins, imagine six 'brain dead' coins in a row, all with their heads down and refusing to give you eye contact. Your teaching/learning challenge is to get them into a state of thought, with at least two of them giving you eye contact. Turn over the two innermost coins and exchange them with the two end coins from the left of your imaginary row. Swap the right-hand coin with the left-hand coin. As best you can, sound out the word you now have in your mind's eye. It sounds as close to thought as you are likely to get with this lot!

Q13 Out of line

The matchstick men A, B and C are waiting in line to be screened on the way in to the Annual Matchstick Ball. What do you predict will happen to Mr C?

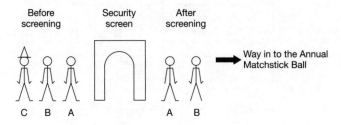

Q14 Learner drivers

These L drivers have a mind of their own. What's on their mind? They have driven from A to B to C. Where next?

Q15 The mutant mouse

Can you spot the mutating mouse?

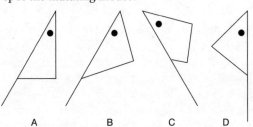

Q16 Sealed with a loving kiss

Where will the next seal go?

Q17   To be 'B' or not to be 'B'

Is there something special about being 'B' or not?

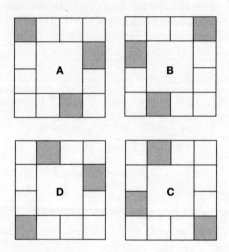

Q18   Rising or falling?

Will the load (L), rise or fall, when the 'driver' star turns anticlockwise about its central axis?

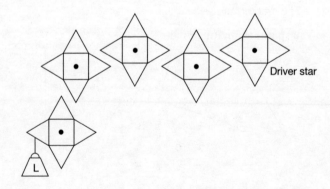

Q19   Pen this!

At a police dog pound, they keep up to nine stray dogs in a square enclosure. The animal inspector insists they be kept separately. Pen in two more squares that will enable you to keep nine dogs separately inside the same enclosure.

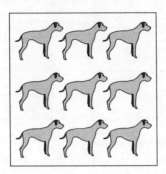

Q20   A shocking solution

Ten lively rams need to be separated temporarily. You have four loops of electric fencing and plenty of stakes. How can you stake out four circular (more or less) pens that will keep the ten rams separated?

Q21   Joining the dots

For a warm-up, join 16 regular spaced dots using six straight lines without taking your pen from the paper and without going over the same line twice.

Then try joining the nine dots with only four lines. Finally, try joining nine dots with one continuous line!

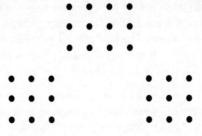

Q22   Divide to conquer

To conquer this puzzle, simply divide each of these shapes into 4 equal parts, each of the same size and shape as the shape you are dividing.

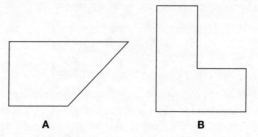

A   B

▶ **How did you get on?**

Check your answers at the back of the book. Don't be surprised if you found some puzzles very difficult. Some are like the ones in a MENSA entrance exam. Remember it's the struggle that trains your brain. The churning is the learning!

Visual IQs are rising

IS TV ALL THAT BAD?

Reporting on the two-year decline in numerical and mathematical ability (see Chapter 6), Michael Shayer and others questioned the impact of childhood TV watching, especially as an alternative to active play in which concepts like size, shape and density are normally developed. As more data emerged, connecting childhood TV with attention deficit hyperactivity disorder (ADHD), and perhaps autism, in August 2007, the American Academy of Paediatrics recommended a total ban on TV before two years old, and a one-hour maximum per day after that. Care will need to be taken with teenagers who may seek out the forbidden. The best plan, if possible, is to keep children too busy with sport, social and extra-mural learning activities for TV time to be an issue.

The picture is less clear with computers and computer games. Visual and spatial IQs are rising, perhaps as a consequence of more children playing computer games. The more worrying effect of computer games is the lack of empathetic thinking and the desensitization to violence that results from active participation in the wounding, torturing and killing of other people in the games. The early development of empathetic thinking and emotional intelligence may help to counter this (see Chapter 2), while ethical thinking may help with older children (see Final thoughts).

Remember this: Children's IQ scores

The numerical and verbal IQs of many children are declining, through changes in the curriculum at school and through a more screen-based lifestyle at home, and this must be reversed. However, there has been a rise in visual IQ, and this can be exploited through imaginative changes in learning plans in schools and colleges.

Focus points

✳ You can use visual thinking to help you predict and learn.

✳ You can use reflective thinking to help you learn from experiences.

✳ You can improve your performance on tests of visual and spatial reasoning.

✳ Visual thinking involves at least 23 separate areas of your brain and so helps to improve connectedness.

✳ You can use visual thinking puzzles to develop visual intelligence and cognitive capacity.

✳ Not everyone can think reflectively. Reflective thinking involves a combination of basic thinking skills that must be developed and practised before you can think reflectively.

✳ Learning on which people are prepared to act is called deep learning. Deep learning involves thought and emotion.

✳ Group work often does not produce deep learning.

✳ Paired learning produces deeper learning and development.

✳ Many models of experiential learning are seriously flawed, because most wrongly assume that everyone can think reflectively; consequently much time and money has been wasted on 'work-based learning'.

Dig deeper

Blakemore, S., *The Learning Brain* (Oxford: Blackwell, 2007).

Bransford, J., *How Students Learn* (Washington DC: National Academies Press, 2000).

Horne, T. and Doherty, A., *Managing Public Services – Implementing Changes: A Thoughtful Approach to the Practice of Management* (London: Routledge, 2003).

Next steps

* Reflective thinking helps you to turn experiences and past events into lessons or ideas that you believe to be true today, and which can indicate how you should behave tomorrow.
* Employers often use visual thinking tests at interviews, so make sure you practise before you attend, using the exercises in this chapter.
* Train yourself to think reflectively using the questions in this chapter.

9

Creative thinking

In this chapter you will learn:

- ► *how to assess your present level of creativity*
- ► *how to be more creative*
- ► *how to use humour and lateral thinking*
- ► *how to train your whole brain to be creative by ignoring myths about 'left brain', 'right brain' and by doing a creative thinking workout.*

> Great wits are sure to madness near allied.
>
> John Dryden

Introduction

It is not necessary either to be born a genius or to drive yourself 'mad' in order to think creatively. Professor Martindale studied the brain scans of people writing creatively and, in *Psychology*, in August 2007, he reported that the most creative writing was done by people who could deliberately shift their brain activity from their rear brain parietal sensory cortex to the front brain lobes of their cerebral cortex. Although it was true that the right-hand sides of their brains were involved, so were the left-hand sides of their brains. The myth that creative people are those who are naturally 'right brained' is mistaken. You can train your brain to shift from back to front, and from left to right.

How creative are you now?

Artists and creative people in general have always had a bohemian reputation. Creative people are often seen as being on the fringe of mainstream society and therefore less subject to rules about what is 'respectable' behaviour, e.g. creative people are more likely to 'live in sin'.

Remember this: Creativity can be developed

There is no evidence that you are either born creative or you're not. Creative thinking can be developed through training. It is important to begin by assessing what kind of creative disposition you have, i.e. how sinful are you?

Try it now: Does creative thinking play a sinful role in your life?

Tick any of the statements that apply to you. Tick as many as you like. Give double ticks if you feel especially strongly about a statement. Then count the number of Ss, Is and Ns you have ticked and read the interpretation.

I would enjoy shredding creative work once it was finished.		S
I would enjoy writing about my life and opinions.		I
I would enjoy talking about my creative work at a conference.		N

If my work was badly reviewed, I wouldn't mind.		S
If my work was badly reviewed, then it's their loss if they don't understand it.		I
If my work was badly reviewed, I would feel low and deflated.		N

In creative work, the most important thing is to look inside yourself.		S
In creative work, the most important thing is to bring different ideas together.		I
In creative work, the most important thing is to make other people think and feel.		N

The best part of creative thinking is finding ways to express feelings.		S
The best part of creative thinking is self-discovery.		I
The best part of creative thinking is publishing or displaying my work.		N

If I could choose, I would prefer to be either a painter or a sculptor.		S
If I could choose, I would prefer to be either a poet or a writer.		I
If I could choose, I would prefer to be either a dancer or a singer.		N

If I were a musician, the best bit would be expressing my emotions.		S
If I were a musician, the best bit would be extending the scope of my instrument.		I
If I were a musician, the best bit would be giving live performances.		N

To be creative, the most important thing is to feel an overwhelming force.		S
To be creative, the most important thing is to love your art for its own sake.		I
To be creative, the most important thing is to want to move others.		N

Your 'S' score reflects the relative importance to you of Self-expression, Self-knowledge, Self-esteem, Self-possession, the Self.

Your 'I' score reflects the relative importance to you of creative thinking as a source of Insight and Intensity and Inspiration, i.e. Introspection and Involvement (see Chapter 2).

Your 'N' score reflects the relative importance to you of your Need for applause, approval, attention and admiration – your Neediness generally.

A dominant 'S' score would suggest that your creative work might enable you to access, or find, an outlet for your strong emotions. For you, creative work can be a catharsis. You may be attracted to an art form that permits power, spontaneity, movement and physical expression.

A dominant 'I' score suggests that you would grow, develop and be enriched by doing creative work. Your creativity is often on the quiet side of life. You can be gentle, harmonious, subtle and patient. Your creativity often requires planning and solitary reflective thinking (see Chapter 8).

A dominant 'N' score suggests that you would use your creativity, if you could, to reach out to communicate with, or perform for, an audience. You want their attention and approval. You hate negative criticism of your work. Although some people may think that you are attention-seeking, they may not realize that it is important to you that others see the good in you and love you for it. This can make you very vulnerable and dependent on continued applause (see Chapter 2).

Right brain versus left brain myths

During the last century, the need to be able to assess rapidly the intelligence (and therefore likely performance) of large numbers of people was driven by the urgencies of war. Even as a battery of their intellectual aptitudes was being labelled 'g' factor, people like Spearman were aware of another set of personal aptitudes that he labelled 's' factor, which at the time seemed less relevant to the killing of other people. Spearman's 's' factors included factors like emotional, lateral, divergent and creative thinking. At the time, there was a widespread belief that these more creative factors were the work of the right side of the brain and this was how myths about right brain (divergent) versus left brain (convergent) thinkers began to arise.

Brain scan work shows that during creative thinking, both hemispheres of your brain are equally involved. Aaron Copland's view of how his brain worked when he composed music is that one half dictated (emotionally), while the other half notated (logically). Ludwig van Beethoven had subsequently to write and re-write the notated dictations of his creative mind to get them to communicate accurately what he was feeling. In doing that, Beethoven is more like most creative thinkers than, say, Wolfgang Mozart, of whom it was said, he composed it in bed, and wrote it out after, straight out of his head!

> **Remember this:** Left, right, front, back, top, bottom
>
> Neuroscience has dispelled many myths about genetic limitations on your mental performance. You have more than either a left brain or a right brain; you have a left and right, front and back, lower and upper brain. The task is to connect them together and then insulate the connections. Brain training makes this possible.

Useful and useless creativity

While creativity includes the ability to think unusual and original thoughts, for applied thinkers, the thoughts have to be useful. Creative inferences need to imply practical applications. People in psychotic states, through drugs or disease, frequently produce original ideas, but these are often divorced from reality and of little practical benefit. While Friedrich Nietzsche argued that 'one must harbour chaos' in the mind 'in order to give birth to a star', applied thinkers are largely concerned to make things better on this planet!

Having said that, one of the strongest arguments, if others were needed, against sterilizing people who carry genes for mental illnesses like schizophrenia or manic depression would be the risk of impoverishing the world by removing a source of artistry and creativity. Artists are ten times more likely than average people to suffer at least one psychotic episode in their lives and, according to Professor Stein, the children of manic depressives have exceptionally high scores for creative thinking.

CREATIVE CHILDREN

Creative children commonly suffer at least one serious illness as a child. They are more likely to be introverted, sometimes antisocial and to have high IQs. They are more likely to develop obsessive preoccupations. This can lead to childhood loneliness, unpopularity and sometimes bullying – although a high IQ, combined with inventiveness, often enables creative children to side-step the worst consequences of their social 'difference'.

The stages of the creative process

In applied thinking, it is useful to view the creative process as having four phases:

1 Immersion.

2 Incubation.

3 Inspiration.

4 Implementation.

Immersion can start with provocative questions and propositions – thoughts of the unthinkable. Do not restrain your investigation, follow your interest, intuition or your instinct. Your right frontal cortex will need to be very active during this stage, so do unusual things – use your left hand if you are right-handed, wear clothes differently, talk to 'odd' people, go to a new library or book shop, take a trip out. Then put the whole topic, issue, project on the back burner. Do something else.

Give your imaginings time to **incubate** – to interweave and interact – especially while you sleep or dream or muse or, if in a lonely or pensive mood, walk up a hill and feel the gift of solitude.

The **inspiration** stage is further replete with 'i's – like insight and illumination. Sometimes, inspiration involves a lot of perspiration – sometimes a lot of breathing in through one nostril, and out through the mouth (see Chapters 1 and 5).

For the fourth, **implementation**, stage, you will definitely need your left front cerebral cortex because you will need to objectively edit, prune and reject those ideas that do not bear upon your creative endeavour. You will be using rational criteria, logically evaluating the feasibility, affordability, practicality and the ethics of your creative ideas.

Barriers to creative thinking

* Aversion to risk.
* Inability to relax.
* Obsessive tidiness.
* Prevalent pessimism.
* A tendency to be cynical.
* A preoccupation with control.
* A tendency to be judgemental.
* Fear of reverie or daydreaming.
* Excessive need for quick success.
* A fear of failure or of making mistakes.
* A limited capacity for delayed gratification.
* An inability to tolerate uncertainty or ambiguity.
* A strong preference for reality rather than fantasy.
* Unwillingness to deal with hypothesis or conjecture.
* A propensity to be 'laid back', unexcited by challenge.

Source: Horne and Wootton, 2003, after Adam

You can break down your creative process into these four stages, all beginning with the same initial i, in order to initiate your creative thinking. Yet the creative thinking itself involves combinations of other thinking skills (see Appendix B).

Remember this: Practical inventions

There are many manifestations of creative thinking. Creative thinkers are concerned with ideas that can be implemented – inventions that work. That's why you need to separate the four 'I's: Immersion, Incubation, Inspiration and Implementation so that the creative flow can work effectively.

Creative thinking

ACTION TIPS FOR CREATIVE THINKING

I'm always trying to do things I can't do
That's how I get to do them!

Pablo Picasso

▶ 1 Don't forget

Keep pocket dictaphones or pads and pencils at desks, by phones, in cars, by beds. Jot down key words. You will forget them quickly, especially after waking or getting involved in an activity (see Chapter 2).

▶ 2 A move with a view

Move your chair, your desk, your room, your house or your country periodically – anything to gain a new perspective.

▶ 3 Make a date

Julia Cameron suggests that you make a 'date' with your creative self once a week. Take time out to meet your creative self for at least a couple of hours at a bookshop, art shop, a fabric shop, a gallery, a café or just a coffee bar where you can be alone with a magazine or a notepad.

▶ 4 Catch the worm (before it turns)

The early bird can catch the creative worm. If it's fiction you want to write, start straight out of bed – some writers do not even turn on the light. Write in longhand, double-line spaced. Edit and re-edit until it is no longer decipherable. Write it out again. Keep going for your allotted time, 30 minutes or an hour at the most. Then stop and clean your teeth. Surprisingly, fixed deadlines seem to aid creativity in the morning, perhaps raising anxiety just enough to sharpen your waking mind (see Chapter 5).

If you are writing non-fiction, or designing something, your routine will be different. You need lots of light to switch off your pineal gland (see Chapter 5). Clean your teeth using minty toothpaste and the hand you do not normally use. Do the head in hand exercises (see Chapter 1). You will then be well oxygenated for a dawn raid on your neurons.

▶ 5 Signal your creative intent

Creative thinking requires a deliberate shift to a new zone. Sometimes it helps to signal your intent to others and to yourself. Victor Hugo signalled his intent by taking off all his clothes. Alexandre Dumas ate an apple every day at 7:00 a.m. under the Arc de Triomphe and then wrote for an hour at a streetside café. Mark Twain lay on the floor. Ernest Hemingway sharpened pencils. Thomas Huxley wrote with his nose.

▶ 6 The long march

Like William Wordsworth, go for a walk! Professor Clayton recommends at least 20 minutes a day. Down the long march of history, Aborigines have gone 'walkabout', Native Americans went on 'vision quests', Christians on pilgrimages and Muslims on the hadj. All of these were very long walks! But 20 minutes a day seems to help!

▶ 7 Become a private eye

In your total immersion phase, you may need to become a private investigator. What style of undercover detective will you become? Hercule Poirot collects all the 'facts' and then sits down and thinks about them. Miss Marple often just sits behind her net curtain and watches the world; she has a great eye for detail – she doesn't miss a thing. Columbo acts dumb but asks good questions. Sherlock Holmes thinks aloud with Watson. Which can be your role model when you become a private eye?

▶ 8 Time's up

Surprisingly, tight deadlines often produce creative solutions, especially in the last ten minutes. Set and stick to deadlines for each of the four stages of your creative process.

▶ 9 Bin the best and keep the rest

The exhortation to 'bin the best' recognizes the blocking effect on your creativity when you become so attached to the good bits of your work that you are reluctant to surrender space to new ideas.

▶ 10 First the good news

Know your creative style before you invite others to comment on your work. Otherwise, problems can arise, especially if your style is predominantly 'N' for needy. You need approval, admiration, attention and applause, so always say 'Okay, give me the good news first', and ask 'What do you like about my work?' Next 'What do you find interesting about my work?', 'What are its potential growth points?', 'What would you like to see less of?' (steel yourself) and finally, 'What would you like to see more of?', 'What is the thing you liked most about my work?' Start and finish with the good news.

▶ 11 Girls and boys come out to play

On an 'I-need-to-be-creative' day, think of life as a game (even if you don't know the rules). Adopt a playful disposition in meetings and encourage it in others. Ignore put-downs like 'Don't be facetious' or 'Don't be childish'. As a child, you probably had no problem thinking creatively.

▶ 12 Get a brainwave

Before a task that requires creative thinking, do relaxation exercises (Chapters 1 and 5). These slow down the electrical activity in your brain and literally produce bigger brainwaves. Favour deep breathing exercises that involve visualizing objects, colours, stories or good memories.

▶ 13 Pass it on

To get up to 80 ideas from eight people, give them each a blank sheet of paper and ask them to write down three ideas working alone. They pass their sheets to the right. Each person reads the ideas on the sheet in front of them and adds one more and again passes the sheet to the person on their right.

▶ 14 Love me, love my dog

If you get stuck, try using analogies to help you become unstuck. Ask yourself what connection this situation has with the problems facing a particular animal such as a dog, an owl, an elephant, etc. Alternatively, try comparing the situation with, for example, using a photocopier, learning to drive, cooking a meal, etc.

▶ 15 Travel is in the telling

Reading, travelling and talking are proactive unlike television, which is passive. Find bantering partners who do not evaluate or judge what you say. The greater the variety of subjects you talk about, the better. Never miss a chance to talk to anyone who is an expert on anything. Try to take holidays in a culture that is very different from your own.

▶ 16 Surprise, surprise!

If you are looking for inspiration from a group of people, do something surprising. Meet them at a theme park, a zoo or on a beach, and then give them the situation about which you want them to think creatively. Then play rounders, five-a-side football or go bowling. Collect and record as many ideas as possible as you mingle with individuals but do not comment, even positively, on any of the ideas. Quantity of ideas is more important than the quality of ideas at this stage.

▶ 17 Make piles

Piles not files – if you file information away in filing cabinets or, even worse, boxes, you will rapidly forget it exists and so you will be unable to combine it with any information in a nearby pile. By making piles, preferably on a horizontal surface like a large table, you are creating a three-dimensional map of information that might be relevant to this or your next creative project. Extract all the creative tension and creative connections you can from the information in competing piles, and then remove yourself to a large empty table somewhere you can do your writing, painting, building or designing without further distraction. Immersion profits from piles, but Incubation,

Insight and Implementation excel in empty spaces. Interruption is the enemy of Inspiration.

▶ 18 Talk to yourself – put on your thinking cap

By all means talk to other people as well – the more perspectives you can get on the situation the better for your Immersion and also for checking your Implementation plans make sense. But if they won't listen to you, let alone talk to you, you can always talk to yourself. Edward de Bono has some good ways of orchestrating conversations between different aspects of yourself:

- ▶ optimist ('What's good about this is…')

- ▶ grower ('We could extend this by…')

- ▶ cardinal ('Ethically, we need to be concerned that…')

- ▶ pessimist ('The problem might be…')

- ▶ logician ('Let's just check if that necessarily follows…')

- ▶ factual ('What do we know and how can we find…')

- ▶ emotional ('This is exciting, passionate, frightening…').

▶ 19 Do it to music

If you can think with music playing, find out which music most favours your creative thinking (see Chapter 5).

▶ 20 A storm in a tea group

We favour the deployment of individual thinking skills rather than group thinking whenever this is possible. However, if you are forced to think creatively as a group, the group size should be at least six, up to around 16. Record every idea that people shout out in a way that everyone can see. Someone will need to keep track of any suggestions that get missed and feed them back to the writer in a steady stream, each time there is a lull. Encourage zany ideas. Respond positively to jokes or humour. Gently squash negativity or cynicism. Fill pauses by reading back the growing list of ideas – the crazier the better.

▶ **21 Madness in the method**

Creative solutions can sometimes be found by borrowing method acting techniques. List the key roles or objects. Take it in turn to be each of the key roles or objects. In each role, imagine what you would feel and what you would think. Record it. If you have a partner you can work with, ask them to interview you about your experience in each role and make the notes for you.

Unblocking blocks to creative thinking

If the block is...

1	Habit	Do one different thing every day.
2	Firm beliefs	Ask 'If I didn't believe this, what might happen?'
3	Familiarity	Ask 'How will I feel when I have solved this problem?'
4	Adult behaviour	Indulge in one piece of 'child-like' behaviour each day.
5	Lack of language	Mix with creative people. Join an art or drama group.
6	Not my area	Say 'Good, most breakthroughs come from non-specialists.'
7	Fear of mistakes	Ask 'What's the worst thing that could happen?'
8	Existing models	Ask 'What if you had arrived from Mars?'
9	I'm too old	Realize that creative thinking involves bringing lots of knowledge and experience together and that the older you are the more you have.
10	Lack of time	Accept that you have all the time there is. (Deadlines aid creativity so long as you don't get anxious.)

HUMOUR AND CREATIVE THINKING

A psychologist was giving a lecture on the effect of regular sex on one's sense of well-being. He took one of his research students with him. To illustrate to his student his thesis that 'more sex produces more well-being', he invited anyone in the audience who had sex every day to stand up. The people who stood up were grinning and animated, despite being a little self-conscious. Next the psychologist invited people who had sex about once a week to stand up. These people were calmer but looked content enough – the odd one smiling nervously. 'What about less than once a month?' As though reluctant to admit it, people shuffled to their feet, but generally looked at their shoes, did not give eye contact and were very subdued. 'Do you see my point?' the psychologist asked his research student, who nodded sagely.

'Just out of interest is there anyone here who admits to having sex only about once a year?' A man jumped to his feet in the centre of the audience. He was waving and grinning all over his face and punching the air. The psychologist checked that he had heard correctly, 'I said only once a year.' 'Yes' the man shouted back, 'I heard you, and tonight's the night!'

Humour and creativity build up tension as the audience is immersed in more and more puzzling or irreconcilable data. The audience are led along one particular path, and then suddenly shown the situation from a different perspective. The release of the tension produces enkephalin flow in the brain. Enkephalin flow is associated with relief, pleasure and a feeling of well-being. It is like a mini-orgasm. Small wonder that comedy shows are so popular and that Casanova claimed that the best way to seduce a woman is to make her laugh (see Chapter 10).

Creating humour, or enjoying humour, predisposes your brain to be open to sudden mental shifts, to the sudden 'Aha!' as you see things from a new and unexpected perspective. It raises your tolerance for surprises. The side-effects of the laughter – relaxation and distraction – help to change your brainwave pattern from high frequency, shorter beta waves, to the slower, longer alpha waves that Bagely has strongly correlated with creative thinking and invention.

Not everyone is a natural humorist, but you can choose to mix with people that are. They will raise your mental energy and maybe your creativity. Children are great; they laugh an average of 450 times a day (compared to about 15 times a day for the average adult).

CREATIVE PLACES: SOMEWHERE A PLACE FOR ME

Winnicott discovered that creative thinking was more likely to take place in some places than in others. He found that creative ideas flowed better in places where the questioning of authority and the challenging of received wisdom were welcomed and where people were encouraged to joke and be playful. Kanter argued for the creation of autonomous 'play areas'. She recognized the close relationship between playfulness, humour and creativity. Hurst reported that people were more likely to produce new ideas when they laughed, felt comfortable and trusted the people around them.

CREATIVITY AND LATERAL THINKING

The term 'lateral thinking' was coined by de Bono. It was an early attempt to systematically codify procedures that would enable you to look at a problem or a situation anew, from a different lateral or sideways perspective – to step out of the thinking pattern you were in and look back at the pattern in which you may be stuck and to become unstuck. It was not originally intended for people who were seeking to be creative in an artistic, aesthetic, imaginative or fictional sense. De Bono's lateral thinking was intended for the real world and in that sense is of great interest to applied thinkers.

A 'creative' artist may have such a different view or 'take' on the world that the work they produce is very 'different', 'unusual' or 'original'. Yet the artist may be as rigid in their perspective or pattern of thinking as the manager who can't see a way around his or her delivery problem. Lateral thinking is about being able to shift sideways to break a pattern, whether or not other people see that pattern as 'rigid' or 'artistic'. Lateral thinking enables you to change your perception at will and not to have to wait on the whim of the muse. Some people are creative thinkers and some people are lateral thinkers; some people are neither, and some lucky people are both. However, you can train your brain to think laterally and that would certainly help with your creative thinking. As you can see from Appendix B, creative thinking for the applied thinker involves much more than lateral thinking. Nevertheless, de Bono has extended the scope of his lateral thinking into the artistically creative domain – he has worked with two national UK theatre groups.

In the meantime, try these lateral thinking exercises.

LATERAL THINKING

Q1   There's a man at the door

You see a man approaching your front door. The man knocks and asks for a drink of water. You whip out a knife and hold it to his throat. After a few moments, his face breaks into a smile. He says 'Thank you' and leaves looking pleased. You feel good. What might have happened?

Q2   Coining it again

Move one coin to make a letter L that has four coins in each stroke of the letter.

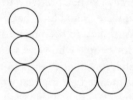

The creative workout

INTRODUCTION

In some workouts, for example numerical, the idea is to do a lot of simple exercises as quickly as you can. In a creative thinking workout, it is different. You need to do a warm-up and then pick one problem. Resist looking up the solution. Immerse, then incubate, and wait. Then try it again. Discuss it with friends. Never reject suggestions. People are not stupid. They will not make a suggestion that is entirely without merit; there's always something in it – your job is to find it. Just look. You may see something in their suggestion that they didn't even know was there. Take these three black lines for example:

Look again and see something in it that's not even there.

WARM-UP

▶ **Your memory**

Remember:

▶ how you recall the number of days in February

▶ how to get from your house to the post office or to work

▶ how to change a nappy.

▶ **Your imagination**

Speak out loud about how the following could apply to your life:

▶ You discover oceans only when you sail out of sight of land.

▶ Turtles only make progress by sticking their necks out.

▶ The small and the fast eat the large and the slow.

▶ Treat others the way you like to be treated.

▶ Don't just sit, do something!

MAIN WORKOUT

Q1   The shy boy is my boy

A shy boy has never touched a girl. Not even for a friendly hug. He wouldn't know where to start. Browsing in his favourite second-hand bookshop he spots just the thing – HOW TO HUG. When he gets home he realizes he has bought far more than he bargained for. Why?

Q2   Pale at Christmas

Some dark winter mornings she wakes up feeling grumpy. What is her name?

Q3   10 cm short: is size an issue?

After a medical examination, I often conclude I am 10 cm under height. Why?

Q4   You've heard this one before

Add your own lines to complete the following rhyme:

Mary had a little lamb

You've heard this one before...

Q5   Something with your coffee, sir?

When the customer put sugar in his coffee, something floated to the surface! Naturally, he asked the waiter for a fresh coffee. As soon as he sipped his replacement coffee, the customer knew that the waiter had simply removed the floating debris and given him back the original coffee. How did the customer know that?

Q6   His last words...

The body had a gunshot wound near the temple. There was a gun near his right hand and a dictaphone near his left. Pressing 'play', the policeman heard 'I can't go on' followed by a gun shot. The policeman immediately called his station to report a murder. Why?

Q7   Ups and downs

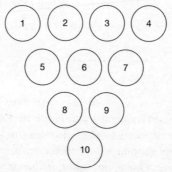

Make the triangle point upwards by moving only three coins.

Q8 Grow up, Grandad

'Grow up, Grandad.' The five-year-old granddaughter is teasing her grandfather. She needs to wait a while because it will be five years before her Grandad is as old as her dad – how can this be?

Q9 Any two for tennis?

A man and his wife went out to play tennis. They agreed to play singles, the best of three sets. On their return their son asked: 'Who won?' Simultaneously both parents said, 'I did!' Which one was lying?

Q10 Deal or no deal

You are dealing clockwise. You lose your place. Without counting cards, how can you still make sure that everyone gets the cards they would have got?

Q11 A neurobic cube

Practise viewing this cube from the top and then from the bottom. Make your view alternate as quickly as you can. Try to make it move 20 times in 20 seconds. (Hint: try getting the line AB to come towards you, then move away again.)

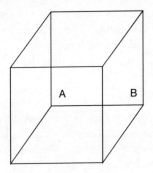

Q12 Don't do it, don't... too late!

You are pleased with your new twentieth-floor high-rise city apartment with a river view. It is good to have light and the view across the city without the noise and smell of the city below you. Your apartment has a balcony, but the apartments below you do not. One night, standing out on your balcony, you are horrified to look down and see a neighbour from the floor below standing on the window ledge. You nearly vomit with vertigo and before you can call 'Don't...!' she jumps. She lands, pitches, and is still. Shortly afterwards, she gets up, straightens her skirt, fluffs her hair and does not appear to be even grazed or marked in any way. How did she do that? (She doesn't have a parachute.)

Q13   Believe it or knot?

How can you take hold of each end of a tie in separate hands and tie a knot in it, without letting go of either end of the tie?

Q14   Time you knew

If a clock takes two seconds to chime at 2 o'clock, how long will it take to chime at 3 o'clock?

Q15   Laterally speaking

If TSIHIMM are the first letters in the series I have in my mind, what comes next in the series you have in your mind?

Q16   Slow cars and fast birds

Two cars heading towards each other (not on the same side of the road!) are averaging 50 km/ph. When they are exactly 100 km apart a bird leaves one and flies towards the other at an average speed of 76.5 km/ph. When it arrives at the other car it immediately turns and flies back to the first car and so on. How far will the bird have flown by the time the cars pass each other?

▶ How did you get on?

If you found the workout difficult, discuss the questions with other people and do more. Creative thinking is 99 per cent perspiration and only 1 per cent inspiration! You can check your answers at the back of the book.

Applied thinking: creativity, society and education

In the twentieth century, science, technology and raw economics resulted in rapid and, in many cases, beneficial change. In the twenty-first century, this has left us with a legacy of difficult problems to solve, including climate change, relative poverty, economic migration, terrorism and nuclear proliferation.

These problems require creative solutions. We can pin our hopes on science, but good science has always relied heavily on creativity and imagination. It is important, therefore, that our schools foster and develop creative thinking.

Creative thinking depends on the development of basic thinking skills and, crucially, on the development of a well-connected brain.

The easiest way to produce a well-connected brain is through a tripartite curriculum that should include a wide variety of subjects; repetitive stimulation of the senses; and explicit training of the brain to think.

This tripartite curriculum should be offered from primary school onwards and supported at home by parents.

Remember this: Creative from the start

The startling scientific and economic advances of the twentieth century have left a legacy of problems for our young people that will require very creative solutions: climate change, poverty, terrorism and nuclear proliferation, are a few examples. Fortunately, children are very creative when they are born. We need to parent them and teach them so that they do not lose their ability to think creatively.

Focus points

* You can train your whole brain to be creative by ignoring myths about 'left brain' and 'right brain', and by doing a creative thinking workout.
* Creative ideas result from persistence, repetition and hard work.
* Changing your location, culture or dress code helps creativity.
* Humour favours creative output.
* Sleeping, napping or doing something different increases creativity.
* Asking lots of questions increases your chances of having creative ideas.
* Positive feedback and constructive criticism aid creative thinking.

* Drawing maps, tables, diagrams and pictures helps creative thinking.
* Immersion, Incubation, Insight and Implementation should be distinct to allow for effective creative thinking.
* The preservation and development of creativity in children is imperative for parents and teachers. The world in which our children will grow up is threatened by complex problems that will require creative solutions.

Dig deeper

O'Keefe, J., *Mind Opening* (London: HarperCollins, 1994).

Sternberg, R. J., *The Nature of Insight* (Boston: Massachusetts Institute of Technology, 1995).

Next steps

Creativity can be developed!

* Identify first how creative you are – complete and score the section 'does creative thinking play a sinful role in your life?' at the start of this chapter.
* Check you are not putting barriers up to when you need to think creatively by reading the section 'barriers to creative thinking' in this chapter.
* Review the tips for creative thinking given in this chapter – use them, try them, reflect on what works for you.
* Remember, creative thinking is 99 per cent perspiration and only 1 per cent inspiration – you have to work at becoming creative!

10

Thinking aloud

In this chapter you will learn:

▶ *how to improve your performance on tests of verbal thinking, verbal IQ and verbal reasoning*

▶ *how to use internal dialogue and dialogue with 'thoughtful companions'*

▶ *how to use thoughtful conversations to develop intimacy through the 'meeting of minds'*

▶ *about differences between typical male brains and typical female brains, and about the brain chemistry of friendship, love and sex*

▶ *how to use verbal puzzles and crosswords to train your brain and expand its cognitive capacity.*

Speaking and listening help to develop your brain. If you can't speak and listen properly, it is harder to think properly. If you cannot think properly, it is harder to write properly. Speaking and listening help you to think and write.

Terry Horne, 2006

Introduction

HUMAN GROOMING

Spiteful... admiring... romantic... Words have the power to alter the chemical balance of your brain and the physical state of your body. 'Grooming' words hold groups together. Gangs develop 'pass words'. Robin Dunbar compared the size of the cerebral cortex in animals, with the average size of the groups that they could maintain. On this basis, a human could maintain a network of about 150.

WORDS AND THE 'BIG PICTURE'

Most of the verbal action takes place on the left-hand side of the brain, which is the side that is active when you are cheerful or optimistic. Perhaps that's why having a chat can cheer you up (see Chapter 2). The areas of the brain that handle speech and meaning are on the opposite side of the brain to the parts that handle visual images (see Chapter 8), which is why you stand a better chance of getting and keeping the whole brain attention of an audience if you can use words to tell a graphic story that conjures up a 'big picture' in the mind of the listener.

The linguistic left-hand side of the brain functions better when levels of oestrogen are higher. Levels of oestrogen are generally higher in typical female brains. Typical female brains (TFBs) display a superior command and use of language than typical male brains (TMBs) (see Appendix D).

TALK AND THOUGHT

The ability to use words and language seems to be definingly human. Chimps, it appears, do not talk after all.

The importance of verbal thinking to critical, creative and reflective thinking can be seen in Chapter 4 (Figure 4.1) and Appendices A, B and C. The importance of language to the development of intelligence and general cognitive capacity might be inferred from a correlation between the mental abilities of three-year-olds and the extent to which their parents have talked to them. According to Hart, mentally able three-year-olds have heard, on average, 600 words an hour more from their parents, than the least able three-year-olds. (However, remember that a correlation is not always a cause, and there are likely to be many socio-economic and genetic co-correlates with parental verbosity!)

Verbal thinking and brain training

Levelt discovered that you use three distinct areas of your brain when you talk to someone else, i.e. you are already connecting many of your neural pathways even before you get to the content of what you want to say. As you search for the next word you need in your spoken sentence, your brain accesses the smell, colour and sounds that are associated with the word you are seeking, thereby calling up even more neural connections. That is why a word can be on the 'tip of your tongue', before you finally say it.

In the meantime, your brain will be finding back-up synonyms and holding them in reserve in case you cannot find the exact word you are looking for. All this happens, word by word, throughout your conversation. Small wonder that thoughtful conversations are such a good workout and that paired learning is the method of choice (see Chapter 8).

Your brain can generally find and provide sounds for between 120–180 words a minute, i.e. up to 10,000 words an hour. It is a myth that this slows down when you get older. True, the older you get, the more possible words you have to choose between, but this can be worked around. It is an asset for verbal thinking and for thinking tasks involving creative and reflective thinking.

Reading is important, but...

Reading can play an important part in training your brain. Reading is a useful source of new information that your brain must struggle to map, connect and cross-check and then integrate with information already dispersed in your memory. Yet reading is not as good at developing your brain as talking and listening. Thoughtful conversations about old and new information involves more of your brain than just reading and so increases your general cognitive capacity as well as helping you to consolidate new information in your memory.

In the UK, under the government's literacy scheme, valuable brain development time is lost teaching children to read too many words. The government literacy scheme requires children to read 158 prescribed words by the age of seven. In 2005, Jonathan Solity from Warwick University, UK, analysed over 900,000 words used in adults' and children's books and discovered that only 100 words are needed before you can read most books in English. (The extra 50 per cent of time needed to learn the extra 58 words added only 2 per cent to children's understanding and this time could be better spent developing a love of reading by giving them as wide a range of stories and topics as possible.)

Remember this: Talk to me!

Your brain develops through activities that require many parts of your brain to interact. Such activities rehearse connections that remain in place to help you with your next thinking task. Brain scans show that book- and screen-based activities, like reading or watching videos or TV, do not involve many areas of your brain, whereas activities that involve thinking aloud, especially with another person, cause many different parts of your brain to interact, thereby increasing your cognitive capacity.

Verbal thinking, verbal IQ and verbal reasoning tests

In 2007, the National Association of Graduate Recruiters in the UK reported that it had failed to fill one-third of its vacancies for graduates because of a lack of suitable applicants. Facing a general decline in literacy standards and a decline in the ability of graduates to think clearly and to express clearly what they think, employers have been forced to employ recruitment consultants to pre-screen graduates by using psychometric tests.

The advice for what to do on the day of the test is the same as you have been given in Chapters 4 and 6. The specific brain training you need for verbal thinking tests is to practise answering the following nine types of questions.

NINE TYPES OF QUESTIONS USED TO TEST VERBAL THINKING

1 Find the synonyms

2 Find the antonyms

3 Double meanings

4 Double uses

5 Missing word pairs

6 Linked words

7 Verbal analogies

8 Redundant words

9 Mistaken use of words

Attempt each type of question before you turn to the back of the book to check your answers. If you do badly on a particular type of question, seek more practice in questions of that sort.

▶ **Type 1: find the synonyms**

Q1   Underline only one word inside the brackets that is closest in meaning to the word outside the brackets.

   changeable (visionary, unpredictable, fickle, indecisive)

Q2   Underline the two words closest in meaning.

   glance, close, proximity, though, commonly, nevertheless

▶ **Type 2: find the antonyms**

Underline one word only inside the brackets that is most opposite in meaning to the word outside the brackets.

Q1 Interesting (asexual, amoral, dreary, uninspiring)

Q2 Underline the two words most opposed in meaning:

> *invariable, inevitable, promiscuous, flexible, valid.*

▶ Type 3: double meanings

Fill in the blanks with a word that simultaneously relates to the words or phrases on either side of the blanks.

Q1 mobile show, or exhibition _ _ _ _ equitable.

Q2 argument _ _ _ _ luggage

▶ Type 4: double uses

Fill in the missing words so that the word completes both the preceding word and the following word.

Q1 flash _ _ _ _ _ _ weight

Q2 buffer _ _ _ _ _ broker

▶ Type 5: two missing words

Decide which pairs of words best and most accurately complete the sentence.

Q1 Three different senior officers _____ required for three separate _____.

Was	were	was	were
Inquiries	courts martial	enquiries	courts martials
A	B	C	D

Q2 The emergency staff must ____ acted very _____.

Of	of	have	have
profesionally	professionally	profesionally	professionally
A	B	C	D

▶ **Type 6: mistaken use of words**

In each sentence, underline the two words that, if swapped with each other, would allow the sentence to make sense.

Q1   Heart transplant procedures must be suspended until safe operations can be followed.

Q2   A settlement has been agreed demanding that both sides make an early statement.

▶ **Type 7: linked words**

Find a pair of words, from top and bottom left, that are linked to each other in a similar way as two words from top and bottom right. Underline the four words. (Linking words are used to show relationships between ideas. Linking words can be used to add ideas together, contrast them, or show the reason for something.)

Q1   writing   reading
Speaking   learning   analysis   maps   glasses   listening

Q2   idealism   realism
acceptance   perfectionism   beauty   flows   ugliness   Persecution

▶ **Type 8: verbal analogies**

Underline the correct answer within the brackets.

Q1   Bark is to tree as shell is to (fruit, nut, root, branch).

Q2   Australia is to Tasmania as India is to (Sri Lanka, China, EU, Malaga).

▶ **Type 9: redundant words**

Cross out the redundant words to reveal a sentence made up of the number of words shown in brackets.

Q1   Many present-day employers have high flying expectations of all the thinking and writing skills of applicants who would have them. (13)

Q2   When they this product is redundant using manufactured by from 100 per cent recycled paper writing and uses wood pulp fiction. (10)

Remember this: The word at work

The battery of psychometric tests used during employee selection and recruitment always include tests of verbal aptitude. Effectiveness at work is determined by your ability to instruct or to guide others, or to communicate with suppliers and customers. Verbal aptitude also reflects memory, and both contribute to overall IQ and general cognitive capacity. Performance on tests of verbal aptitude, or verbal IQ, can be enhanced by practising the kinds of questions used in such tests.

PLAY THE GAME

▶ The association game

One person starts with a word. The next must follow without hesitation with an associated word. The first person to stumble breaks the round and starts a new round with a new word. Any player can challenge any association offered by another player. If the explanation is not satisfactory, the successful challenger starts a new round. If someone uses a word that has already been used earlier in the game, they can be challenged for repetition. This game develops quick thinking, creativity, imagination, concentration and memory.

▶ The adverb game

This is good with children or as an icebreaker at adult parties. Person A and person B leave the room. A gives B a mystery adverb – a word that describes how something is done, for example, quickly, thoughtfully, confusingly, seductively. A and B return to the room and B's task is to get the audience to guess the mystery adverb. The audience guesses the adverb by taking turns to ask person B to carry out various actions in a way that would be described by the mystery adverb, 'Open an envelope, this way.' Person B would then have to demonstrate how they would open an envelope, for instance, quickly or thoughtfully or seductively. The person who first guesses becomes A in the next round and gives another B person a new mystery adverb.

► The dictionary game

You need a dictionary, preferably two, and writing materials. Create two teams. Each member of the team chooses an obscure word and writes its meaning on a piece of paper. The dictionaries are then put away. The rest of their team writes out false definitions. Teams take it in turns to read out a word and a set of possible meanings including the one that is correct. If a nominated member of the opposite team spots which is the correct definition and guesses right first time, they score ten points. If the team confer they can still score six points, provided they guess correctly the second time. A third guess that is correct scores two points. Anyone whose false definition is selected scores four points.

Thinking as an internal dialogue

To think is to talk, if only to yourself!

Simon Wootton, 2003

An internal dialogue is a conversation you have with yourself in your head. Up to and during the 1980s, references to intra-personal conversations were rare. Since the 1990s, the idea of thinking as an internal dialogue has been widely discussed. Key among the implications of this idea is the importance of vocabulary and of brain training exercises, puzzles and games that develop your vocabulary. Clearly you cannot think using an internal dialogue about things for which you have no vocabulary. Neither can you manipulate mental concepts for which you have no labels. Learning to talk clearly will aid clear thinking, and clear thinking will aid clear writing.

Remember this: Talk to yourself

If you cannot find another person with whom to have a thoughtful or thinking aloud type of conversation, at least talk to yourself! Applied internal dialogue is one of the most effective means of orchestrating your thinking process. The precision of your thinking is limited by your vocabulary. The speed of your thinking is limited by your fluency. There are ways to improve both.

INTERNAL DIALOGUE: PHYSICAL FITNESS AND PSYCHOLOGICAL WELL-BEING

Since the 1990s, doctors and sports scientists have shown a lot of interest in the mind–body connection, especially with relation to survival rates for major surgery and cancer (see Chapter 2). Internal dialogues have been found to co-ordinate and connect the work of different parts of the brain, such as the sensory cortex and the motor control functions. The conversations you have with yourself can determine the view you have of your own body, the importance you attach to it, the respect with which you treat it, and whether or not you allow other people to abuse it.

Mind your knee

Sports scientists have been puzzling over why so many super-fit sportspeople in contact sports like rugby and football are injured when there is no contact. In July 2007, Professor Charles Swarick reported on a study of 1,500 [sports] people whose history of injury proneness he had been following. He gave them a battery of neuro-cognitive tests and found that low scores on visual or verbal thinking and memory and information processing were the best predictors of a likely serious non-contact injury, such as an injury to the knee. This sort of injury kept the footballer Michael Owen (and now TV Commentator) out of the World Cup in 2006 and out of the game for nearly a year. Professor Swarick thinks his injured clients were short of training – brain training!

Don't worry, it won't drive you 'mad'

Positron emission tomography (PET) scanning has been used to test the hypothesis that a predisposition to hear voices, in schizophrenia, is associated with abnormal activity in the area of the brain normally involved in your internal dialogue. Patients with schizophrenia were divided into two groups – those who heard voices and those who did not hear voices. They were given thinking tasks that involved the use of internal dialogue and their PET brain scans were observed. The investigators concluded that schizophrenia might be associated with not having enough internal dialogue!

THINKING ALOUD

John Steiner observed that people often introduce their internal dialogues into their conversations with other people. They 'fly kites' or 'float ideas'. Consciously or unconsciously, these people are seeking reactions: 'Will it fly?' or 'Will it sink like a lead balloon?'

While it is clear that thinking aloud, with or without others present, exercises much of the brain (see Chapter 6), it is less clear that all thought necessarily involves the use of language. With or without language, the brain can manipulate more complex symbols than words. Images, metaphors, schema and symbols, as in systems thinking for example, can all be used to aid complex thinking.

Caruthers concluded that normal spoken and written language is definitely involved in thinking processes such as believing, desiring and reasoning. Thus words join images and sounds as symbols that can be manipulated during the thinking process.

Frederiska used an NMR (nuclear magnetic resonance) scanner to compare the brains of otherwise matched men and women and discovered that the parts of the brain that handled verbal thinking were larger and more widely distributed in the brains of women. A typical female brain does think differently from a typical male brain (see Appendix D).

Keep your head, when all about you are losing theirs

If your vocabulary is more sophisticated you can think about more complex things more precisely. If you learn to talk more fluently you will be able to think more quickly. You will be able to think more quickly under pressure and talk more calmly under duress. You will be able to 'keep your head, when all about you are losing theirs' (Kipling, 1910).

How to have a 'thoughtful conversation'

Thoughtful conversations simultaneously improve the quality of your present thinking and develop your subsequent ability to think quickly and accurately, provided that you:

▶ convey non-verbally that you are listening to the other person and taking them seriously

▶ look out for things that puzzle you rather than for things with which to disagree

▶ respect the other person, even if you disagree with them

▶ give good reasons for any opinions you express

▶ ask for clarification of what is puzzling you

▶ ask others for reasons and examples

▶ avoid intimidating language like 'It's obvious that…' or 'nobody in their right mind'

▶ use ideas as temporary 'sky hooks' to hoist up the level of the discussion

▶ stay open to the possibility that you may be wrong, or misinformed

▶ remain tenacious in your desire to get to the bottom of things

▶ avoid disguising statements as questions

▶ connect what you say to what has been said earlier

▶ realize that people need help to understand how practical future actions flow from reasonable opinions and how these, in turn, need to be based on justifiably believable information

▶ delay as long as possible coming to firm conclusions about what is being discussed (when there is time – and there nearly always is – float ideas tentatively. Agree to come back to the matter in ten minutes, or later that day, or that week)

- remain tolerant of the opinions of other people (people do not enter 'thoughtful conversations' expecting to be judged). Try not to interrupt their train of thought, however exasperating you find it. At a minimum let them finish their sentences

- remember that a conversation is not a competition.

Remember this: Conversations clear your mind

It is one thing to show that thoughtful conversations will improve your thinking and intelligence; it is another to know how to make your conversations more thoughtful. The kinds of questions and statements that will enable you to have thoughtful conversations are listed and reviewed in this chapter. Closer and more intimate relationships often result. This is a bonus since it will favour a chemical balance in your brain that will be suited to clearer and more creative thinking.

30 useful things to say in 'thoughtful conversations'

1 My concern is...
2 Why do you say that?
3 What do you mean by...?
4 How would that affect...?
5 What can we agree on?
6 How is this different from...?
7 How is ... consistent with...?
8 What leads you to think that?
9 How are you able to prove that?
10 How can you be sure about that?
11 I'm sorry I didn't quite follow that.
12 Can you explain the relevance of...?
13 What assumptions are we making here?
14 Okay, so where does that take us next?
15 Can you just take me through that again?
16 Have you considered the possibility that...?
17 Do you have any evidence to support that?

18 So am I correct that what you are saying is...?

19 We appear to have two or three separate ideas here.

20 Is it possible to check any of these things out, if so how?

21 Can we agree again what we know to be the case?

22 While I can accept..., what does not seem to follow is...

23 How is that connected with what you just said about...?

24 When you said..., you seemed ... (label the emotion).

25 You seem certain of that, can you help me understand why?

26 You seem to be making some assumptions; what are they?

27 Can you give me a concrete example of how it might work?

28 You might be right, but I don't quite follow how you got there.

29 What would have to happen before you would reconsider?

30 I have lost the thread, how does that connect with what you were just saying?

THINKING COMPANIONS

▶ **Should you choose a man or a woman?**

One of the best ways to improve your verbal thinking, and to expand your overall cognitive capacity, is by choosing carefully those with whom you have 'thoughtful conversations'. Favour constructive, challenging, tentative, non-judgemental, 'thoughtful' companions who are interested in exploring ideas as well as facts. Avoid cynics and people who complain all the time. They will drain your spirit as well as your energy. Avoid people who only want to preach rehearsed statements.

When choosing your 'thoughtful companion', or 'critical friend', should you choose a man or a woman? The answer is that it all depends on what sort of brain you have and what sort of brain your potential partner has. While typical male brains (TMBs) do think differently from typical female brains (TFBs), very few men are 100 per cent TMB and very few women are 100 per cent TFB. (You can gain an indication of the male:female balance in your brain by answering the questions in Appendix D.)

£80 billion: the UK pink pound

There are 3.7 million gay people in Britain who are worth £70–80 billion to the economy. That's a large market to ignore.

Appendix D shows that men with a high score and women with a low score on our test of male/female brain type were more likely to self-report being gay or lesbian. Since these brain scores are likely to indicate that they have more to bring to the party, especially when it comes to work involving other people, it is not surprising that the survey of gay and lesbian incomes reported in *The Guardian* in 2000 showed that gay men earn 40 per cent more than the average for all men and that lesbian women earn 30 per cent more than the average for all women. Based on UK government figures, 6 per cent of the population are gay or lesbian, and that values the UK pink pound at about £80 billion a year. No surprise that companies are asking how they can focus their marketing to attract gay and lesbian customers.

BUILDING CLOSE RELATIONSHIPS

▶ Intimacy and a 'meeting of minds'

When conversations between two people are thoughtful, not only does the thinking benefit, so does the relationship. Research with Steven Duck and Anne Giradot replicated in 2003 with Tony Doherty found that relationships between work colleagues, friends or sexual partners became closer the greater the extent of the disclosure between them. When the disclosure moved from information to thoughtful opinion, the relationship intensified. When empathetic thinking and shared 'visions' of the future were added, intimacy often resulted. Humour, creative thinking, and possibly dark chocolate, sometimes completed the route to bed!

In a virtuous circle, some thinking skills, especially creative thinking, often profit from the relationship becoming closer and more secure, and creative thinkers in turn have been found in other research to be more sexually attractive (see Chapter 9). The exception to the virtue seemed to be affairs – especially affairs at work. These were rarely found to last more than six months and they seemed to adversely affect the ability to concentrate. The end of the affair was often stressful, making it difficult for either partner to think clearly (see Chapter 2).

Making thoughtful relationships closer

* Make disclosures relate to your partner, and the present time and place.
* Keep disclosures in balance with your partner, not under- or over-disclosing.
* Add opinions to the information you disclose.
* Add feelings to the opinions you disclose.
* Begin more sentences with 'I... (notice, think, feel)'?
* Build trust by aligning your actions with your opinions.
* Try to match intimate self-disclosures by your partner.
* Avoid having 'secrets' and 'no-go' areas.
* Are you sufficiently self-aware, honest and courageous?

Source: Horne and Doherty, 2003

YES, BUT WHAT DO YOU TALK ABOUT?

If you are trying to be a **critical friend** try the following:

▶ How is X consistent with Y?

▶ How might you be able to prove that?

▶ How is X relevant to…?

▶ Do we have any evidence that…?

▶ How does that bear on the issue of…?

▶ I have lost the thread, can you recap…?

▶ Accepting X, what does not seem to follow is…

▶ Is there another way that might be interpreted?

▶ Can you give me a concrete example of that…?

▶ What would it take for you to reconsider your opinion?

If you were trying to improve your **reflective thinking**, you might try the following:

▶ This is how I am trying to think about it…

▶ What do you think about what I have said so far?

▶ Is there anything wrong with my interpretation?

- What other possibilities could you see or add?

- There is one particular aspect that I would like you to help me think about.

DON'T ARGUE!

- **A thoughtful conversation is an exploration not an argument**

This is important, but for some people, it is difficult. Some people are so competitive that nearly every discussion becomes an argument, and an argument that they must win. You can keep winning the arguments but losing the friends. It is easier to pick arguments than friends.

Try it now: How argumentative are you?

Consider the 20 statements overleaf and put a number in the untinted box next to the statement as follows.

If the statement is:
* rarely true, score 2
* occasionally true, score 3
* often true, score 4
* always true, score 5.

	Y	X
I try to avoid arguments if at all possible.		
In the middle of an argument, I feel excited.		
I generally come out best in an argument.		
A good argument clears the air.		
I can only think of what I should have said after wards.		
An argument is an intellectual challenge.		
I don't like people who are argumentative.		
I don't like to let things go or take them lying down.		
It takes skill to avoid getting into an argument.		
I will always stand up for myself and defend my corner.		
I feel sick if I sense an argument brewing.		
There's nothing like a good cut and thrust debate.		
Arguments leave me shaking and upset.		
It's nice to get a point over and have a counter-discussion		

(Continued)

	Y	X
Arguments create problems and never settle things.		
Each time it happens, I say 'never again'.		
I feel very energetic and fired up when I argue.		
I avoid arguments at all cost.		
Arguments are good mental exercises.		
If I argue all the time, people won't like me.		
Total score		

How did you do?

Calculate the difference between X and Y. People who can make good use of verbal thinking in thoughtful conversations, or who make good 'critical friends' or 'thinking coaches', generally score between two and six. Below two and they are usually too timid, too 'nice' or too 'polite' to challenge. Sometimes they are students from Asian cultures in which any kind of confrontation is to be avoided. They have to learn that it is not only okay, but that it is expected behaviour in the West. People who score above six are often too adversarial, too competitive, too abrasive and often lack the confidence to concede – fearing that others will see it as a weakness, instead of the intellectual strength that it is.

I'M TOO COMPETITIVE, TOO ADVERSARIAL, TOO ARGUMENTATIVE, SO WHAT?

If you win arguments and lose friends you will be the loser. Having close friendships is strongly correlated with good health, creative thinking and real world achievement. The connection with physical health is not well understood other than there is perhaps an association with the by-product of reduced stress and increased endorphin and serotonin release experienced by friends and enhancements in your immune system (see Chapter 2).

Close friendships form a safe haven from which creative excursions can be made, especially when your creative intent is 'needy', and creative thinking is strongly correlated with worldly reward in professions like science, engineering, medicine and management.

Clearly there is more to forming close, thoughtful relationships than balancing excessive compliance and excessive argumentativeness. For example, everyone would prefer partners (and neighbours and work colleagues) who are reasonable. It is unreasonable to expect your behaviour to be reasonable if you cannot reason!

It's how you row that matters!

In a 2006 yougov.com survey of couples where one or both partners were thinking of splitting up, the number one reason for dissatisfaction with the relationship, perhaps predictably, was disagreements over money. The second reason, way ahead even of disagreements over sex, children, drinking, coming home late, the in-laws etc., was dislike of the way the other person spoke or argued. People disliked the way their partners argued, more than what they argued about. Linda Waite, who has been tracking slow rumbling relationships since 2000, says about half the couples end by splitting up altogether. Yet half the couples improve and describe their relationship as 'happy'. You can learn to argue better! The prognosis is not good if you don't.

The neurochemistry of lust, love and attachment

Here we are talking only about romantic love. Romantic love, lust and attachment all have separate neurochemical systems in the brain. All can occur without the other, but lust, love, followed by attachment, is a common sequence. Lust is a temporary urge for sexual gratification. Romantic love is a sense of elation in the presence of, or at the thought of, one particular person. Attachment is a sense of peace and security. It is conducive to having children.

Remember this: Deeper conversations lead to closer relationships

When you increase the number of thoughtful conversations you have, you will increase your opportunities to form closer relationships. You can learn to have more control over the depth of the conversations you have and the nature of the closeness that develops in your relationships. Lust, love and attachment are each associated with different chemical regimes in your brain and each, in different ways, affects your ability to think.

ONE-NIGHT STANDS

Lust is associated with increased testosterone in the brain. In men, this occurs daily in the morning and is more noticeable in autumn. In pre-menopausal women, it occurs monthly at the time of ovulation. However, testosterone levels can be increased at other times. Testosterone release can be stimulated in men by the sight of cleavage, the flash of leg, by pornography, the opportunity or just an offer. In women, it can be stimulated by affection, words, deeds or humour and in both sexes by danger, novelty and dark chocolate. You should be aware of the risk that 'lust only' sex can lead to romantic love and attachment.

▶ Myths about male and female orgasm

In 2005, Professor Holstep in the Netherlands investigated what happens in your brain when you have an orgasm. He asked couples to have sex while their brains were scanned.

Contrary to myths that the parts of the brain involved in verbal and emotional thinking need to stay engaged for women to have good sex, both male and female brains experienced major neurological shutdown as orgasm approached. The orgasms released endorphins that help creative thinking and reduce depression and anxiety, thereby enhancing speed and accuracy of thinking.

INTERCOURSE: VERBAL AND PHYSICAL

It may be no coincidence that the word for physical and verbal communication is the same – intercourse. Physical communication patterns in bed mirror verbal communication patterns elsewhere. For example, sulking can mirror withholding sex; controlling can mirror dominating sex; anger will turn up as punitive or humiliating sex; teasing can mirror sexual teasing; and so on. Think about it.

The verbal thinking workout

INTRODUCTION

In most societies, playing with words is popular and word puzzles are widely enjoyed. For brain training purposes, word puzzles need to involve more areas of the brain than are needed just to manipulate the letters. The puzzles in this workout involve imagining and remembering – which is enough to warm up nearly the whole of your brain. Sound out the words in your head (internal dialogue) or, even better, out loud, and your brain will really come alive. It will need to be alive if you want to solve the more difficult puzzles that have a 'twist', perhaps requiring careful logic or a creative insight to complete the solution. If you have the chance to discuss the puzzle with another like-minded person, seize it – it might be the start of a thoughtful relationship, 'a meeting of minds', or even a beautiful friendship!

Q1 Climb the ladder oh!

Climb to the top of the ladder by changing one letter at a time, starting from the word at the bottom.

TACT		YEAR		SPAR
DISH		BOON		QUIT

a   b   c

Q2 What a pain!

Use every letter to fit ten words into this 5 × 5 square.

G	N	G	E	D
R	L	D	S	E
A	O	A	N	D
D	V	M	R	I
E	E	O	A	E

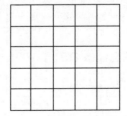

Q3 A(maze)ing letters are misleading

What 15-letter word can you make from letters you can retrieve from the maze? (You may only enter each room once).

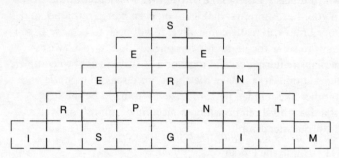

Q4 Pyr(amid): what is the central word at issue in this pyramid?

1 *The disrepair for which a leaving tenant is liable.*

2 *Will make it go faster if you can find the vehicle.*

3 *You can keep it if you take a cold hard view of preservation.*

4 *The first step to creativity.*

5 *Uncoil a rope to hear the singing.*

6 *Confused relatives make a mark.*

7 *Reptilian sibilant.*

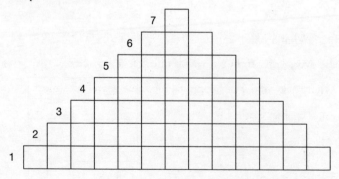

Q5   All the sevens

The following are all clues to seven-letter words.

1   *Propels a sailing ship with nearly a metre start.*

2   *You can wash up in the beginning before moving smartly down the alley.*

3   *First sign of too much fat in a Spanish sailing ship.*

4   *This US state names Mr Jones.*

5   *First signs of becoming a cattle thief.*

6   *Start by floating to the top of the house.*

7   *A vital start to healthy food.*

8   *Initial kernel leads to argument.*

9   *One begins a superb sound chemical.*

10   *Finally then the audition commends.*

11   *The young man starts moving the liquid.*

12   *The stare allows you to lace her up.*

Q6   There were five in a row and...

a   *What is a long-awaited word with four vowels in a row?*

b   *What is a magic word with five consonants in a row?*

Q7   Only the lonely

What's a weird five-letter word with only one consonant?

Q8   Six pack

What rock-solid word contains the same vowel six times?

Q9   Spell checks

1   *Japanese dress: k_____*

2   *Rainbow-coloured: i_____*

3   *To protect from disease: i_____*

4 *To refine, six letters: r*_____

5 *A chemical disliked by moths begins with a small sleep:*
   *n*_____

6 *To see or testify: w*_____

7 *A blushing discomfort: e*_____

8 *Flustered: h*_____

9 *To measure: g*_____

10 *A root vegetable that sort of rhymes with tomato:*
   *p*_____

Q10 Pairs

Which pairs go nicely together?

mince	honey	blackcurrant	scotch	cheese	straw
chocolate	pepper	pie	beef	comb	egg	cake
mint	corn	paper	jelly	dark	berries	rice

Q11 Always a crossed word

For brain training purposes, crosswords are excellent, especially if you talk to yourself or others about what you are doing. Cryptic crosswords are best so, for those of you who are not familiar with the language of cryptic clues, here is an active tutorial. There are eight common categories of cryptic clue.

1 *Anagrams.*

2 *Double meanings.*

3 *Buried words.*

4 *Sounds like.*

5 *Multiple clues.*

6 *Insider clues.*

7 *Backward clues.*

8 *Chop off clues.*

All clues have two parts: *the definition* of the word that you must write in the puzzle plus peripheral *coded words*. Your task is to isolate *the definition* part and decode the *coded words*. The form of the coded words determines the category. Try the following two questions in each category.

▶ 1 anagrams

Look for words like 'scrambled', 'mixed', 'confused', 'wild', – these signal that something in the clue is an anagram of the word required. What are the following?

a *Wild West Soup (4)*

b *Noise of train disturbs slumber (7)*

▶ 2 double meanings

Where the word required has two meanings you may be offered both meanings in the same clue.

a *Keeping an eye on the timepiece (5)*

b *Tidy tree (6)*

▶ 3 buried words

Look for words like 'housed in', 'buried in', 'caught up in', 'part of'. The word required is made up of the letters that are inside the other words.

a *Money to wait in comfort for trial in the Old Bailey (4)*

b *The squat top man hid between two police officers (3)*

▶ 4 sounds like

Look for words like 'sound of', 'we hear', 'said like', 'orally', 'audible'.

a *The roar of a naked mammal (4)*

b *Sounds like reasonable travel offer (4)*

▶ 5 multiple clues

The word required is split and clues are offered for each bit.

a *Living off the land under remote Chinese rule (7)*

b *A military parade is cheap and nasty as well (6)*

▶ 6 insider clues

Look for 'eaten', 'contains', 'in', 'holds', 'grips', 'insider', 'keeps', 'included', etc.

a *The gamble included everything in the dance (6)*

b *He put it in the south east, where the accident happened (4)*

▶ 7 backward clues

Signal words include 'reject', 'back', 'retrospect', 'retro', 'rethink', 'reverse'.

a *Intelligent trams go backwards (5)*

b *Rejected room is high and open to the elements (4)*

▶ 8 chop off clues

Signal words include 'no tail', 'no way', 'without', 'no stand', 'lack of', 'dock'.

a *Without an introduction a beginner has no virtue (6)*

b *You need to dock a fast worker to get a Jewish priest (5)*

Q12   GROAN UP WORDS

Which of the definitions go with which of the groan words?

1 *Abbreviated parent.*

2 *Joint of baby goat.*

3 *An even chance of a sell-out.*

4 *A weapon for recycling.*

5 *American symbol (sic).*

6 *Snug and eye.*

7 *A mynah bird with clipped wings.*

▶ Groan words

a *parole*

b *illegal*

c *kidney*

d *minimum*

e *shotgun*

f *spy*

g *walkie talkie*

Social intelligence – another myth?

The New Science of Human Relationships is the subtitle of *Social Intelligence* by Daniel Goleman. This book is in many ways a much better book than his seminal *Emotional Intelligence* written in the 1990s. The idea of social intelligence is not that new. It was coined in the 1920s by Thorndike, but then booted into oblivion in the 1950s by Wechsler:

> Social intelligence is no more than normal intelligence applied to social situations.

Gardner's idea that there are multiple intelligences (see Chapter 4) breathed new life into the possibility that there was a distinctive social intelligence, but Goleman folded it back into his work on emotional intelligence where it became tainted with techniques and influencing skills that could be used to manipulate people for personal gain. In his work, Goleman re-balances this impoverishment of his ideas, re-emphasizing the role of empathetic thinking and empathy (see Chapter 2), by valuing human capacities for compassion, altruism and concern for others. In this he is prompted by neuroscience. For example:

▶ Neuroscientists have discovered a type of neuron called a 'spindle cell', which is one of the fastest acting neurons on record. The spindle cell helps you to make snap social decisions about liking, lying and trusting others. Spindle cells are more plentiful in humans than other species.

- Neuroscientists have discovered 'mirror neurons' that sense the moves which other people are about to make and instantaneously prepare you to imitate their movements or 'feel their pain' (or to return their serve, even before they have hit the ball!).

So would *Social Neuroscience* have been a better title for Goleman's book on *The New Science of Human Relationships*, and does it matter?

DOES IT MATTER?

Yes it does. It is not just an academic storm in a tea cup. Economic success tends to follow conventional intelligence i.e. your ability to think clearly and express clearly what you think. Yet as you saw in Chapter 2, this will not necessarily make you happy. According to a 2006 survey by David Kuhneman, 'yacht envy' occurs even among billionaires. True, the rich do experience more pleasure than the poor, but they appear to need ever more pleasure before they experience satisfaction (let alone full-blown BLISS – see Chapter 2).

One way to step off this hedonistic treadmill is to develop your social intelligence. You are more likely to experience BLISS, if not happiness, through a life full of rewarding and nourishing relationships than you are through economic and career success alone. As you saw in Chapter 2, the most powerful influence on perceived human happiness is not money (above a minimum level) or even work. Consistently, the top voted pleasures in life are friendships, social activities and sex. Since 1987, we have been arguing for the primacy of close intimate friendships and close relationships with spouses, family and children as a source of BLISS, if not happiness.

Applied thinking includes the turning of thoughts into actions. In the case of the socially intelligent, these actions will be empathetic, altruistic, compassionate and socially concerned. Given the problems we face in the twenty-first century, as a result of raw economic thinking in the twentieth century, interest in social intelligence may be timely.

Remember this: Empathetic thinking

To be free and self-reliant you need to be able to think for yourself. To get others to trust and believe you, and to act on your ideas, you need to be able to think for yourself as another. We call this empathetic thinking. Empathetic thinking skills – social intelligence – are going to prove vital in tackling twenty-first-century problems.

Focus points

* Develop your capacity for internal dialogue through external dialogue with 'thoughtful companions'.
* Your internal dialogue is limited by your command of language.
* Internal dialogues can have a direct impact on physical health.
* Some women may have a greater potential than some men to develop thinking power based on language and dialogue.
* You can improve your score on selection tests based on verbal IQ, verbal thinking and verbal reasoning.
* You can improve your thinking through thoughtful conversations.
* You can deepen your relationships and achieve intimacy through thoughtful conversations and a 'meeting of minds'.
* 'Chemistry' matters in relationships, love and sex.
* Social intelligence, based on verbal and empathetic thinking, needs to be given parity of esteem alongside other forms of intelligence.
* Verbal thinking puzzles, especially cryptic crosswords, can train your brain and develop its capacity for internal and external dialogue.

Dig deeper

Bryon, M., *How to Pass Graduate Psychometric Tests* (London: Kogan Page, 2001).

Bryon, M., *How to Pass Civil Service Tests* (London: Kogan Page, 2003).

Bryon, M., *How to Pass the Firefighter Selection Process* (London: Kogan Page, 2004).

Carter, P., *IQ and Psychometric Tests* (London: Kogan Page, 2005).

Cox, E. and Rathvon, H., *Mensa Cryptic Crosswords* (New York: Stirling, 2007).

Fisher, H., *Why We Love: The Brain Chemistry of Love* (New York: Henry Holt, 2004).

Horne, T. and Doherty, A., *Managing Public Services – Implementing Changes: A Thoughtful Approach to the Practice of Management* (London: Routledge, 2003).

Howard, P. J., *The Owner's Manual for the Brain: Everyday Applications from Mind and Brain Research* (3rd edn, Austin, Texas: Bard Press, 2006).

Tolley, H. and Thomas, K., *How to Pass Police Selection Tests* (London: Kogan Page, 2004).

Tolley, H. and Thomas, K., *How to Pass Verbal Reasoning Tests* (London: Kogan Page, 2006).

Next steps

Thoughtful conversations are great for your brain:

* Try the 30 useful things to say in conversations at the start of this chapter and see how 'thoughtful' they become!

* Thinking aloud – don't be embarrassed, it's been shown to improve people's performance (they use it a lot in sport and before people present).

* Conversation is crucial in relationships – it creates intimacy and the 'meeting of minds'.

* Check how argmentative you are by doing the test in this chapter – conversations are explorations not arguments!

Final thoughts

When I do good things, I feel good.
When I do bad things, I feel bad.
That is my religion.

Abraham Lincoln

Introduction

MAD, BAD OR EVIL?

How can we begin to think about what goes on in the minds of people who would kill, torture or abuse innocent people? Are these people mad? Or are they bad? Or are they just like you and me? Can a child really be evil? This debate is ancient. Does neuroscience have anything to contribute? Yes, it does.

In First thoughts we discovered that chemical activity in the dendrite gaps between your neurons chemically constructs your thoughts and chemically expresses your feelings:

A belief = A thought + A feeling

In Chapter 7, we found that decisions, plans and actions were determined by beliefs. Nowhere did we find antennae pointed towards a devil (or a deity). However, in Chapter 7, we discovered that your brain could make mistakes in what it perceived, so that thoughts based on these perceptions could be mistaken. In Chapter 2, we discovered that you have little control over some primitive feelings, like jealousy, lust and fear. Unless you learn to intervene rapidly, these emotions often bypass your cerebral cortex.

FEAR OF FACES

In 2005, Lieberman reported in *Nature Neuroscience* that when two-thirds of us are shown a photograph of a threatening face our amygdala immediately activates like a panic button. An amygdala panic readies your muscles to fight (or run). Your next action will depend on your belief, which will be based on this instant feeling plus your immediate thought. Unless the thought is quick, or pre-rehearsed to counter the emotion, your belief-based reaction may well be damaging – to you and others. But could such reactions be said to be immoral if they are not premeditated?

MAD, BAD OR JUST MISTAKEN?

In Chapter 7 we saw that even mature adults can continue to believe that something is so, long after they have been shown visible or logical evidence that it is not. They are literally unable to trust the evidence of their own eyes. If such people were to act in the genuine (but mistaken) beliefs that, say, the lives of their children were threatened, would they be bad, mad, evil or mistaken?

SHOULD THE PUNISHMENT FIT THE CRIME?

▶ Myths about free will

Should we punish people for acts that are unintended or not premeditated? Who gains when we lock up people who are mistaken or misguided? One justification for making the punishment fit the crime is that people have 'free will' and so could choose not to act on their mistaken or misguided beliefs. Belief in 'free will' can help you to stay optimistic and stop you becoming fatalistic and suicidal. It can help you to stave off the depression that comes with 'learned helplessness' (see Chapter 2). But the findings of neuroscience are that 'free will' is not always present. This weakens the case for retributive justice that is linked only to the severity of the crime.

Try it now: How good are you?

To be 'good' is more than being 'not bad' or 'not evil'. Are you 'good'?

For each of the following 20 statements put a score in the untinted box:

Score 4 if you believe the statement is nearly always true

Score 3 if you believe the statement is often true

Score 2 if you believe the statement is sometimes true

Score 1 if you believe the statement is rarely true.

How good are you?	A	B
1 We need to resist the power of supermarkets.		
2 When I can, I buy organic food.		
3 I look first to find fairtrade items to buy.		
4 Freetrade, or equitrade, is better than aid.		
5 Genetic modification (GM) of crops is not a good thing.		
6 I only use a car when I can't walk, cycle or use public transport.		
7 I check labels for country of origin and buy local or lowest air miles.		
8 I actively seek reassurances that cheap clothes have not used child labour.		
9 Increased economic growth should not be at the expense of the environment.		
10 Every country should sign up to international action against carbon emissions.		
11 I would eat non-GM foods treated with pesticides rather than GM food.		
12 In the last two years, I have not flown anywhere unless for work.		
13 I use low-energy bulbs, low-energy appliances and avoid using 'standby'.		
14 You should boycott firms whose goods are made by children.		
15 Countries are only entitled to overthrow tyrants as part of United Nations (UN) action.		
16 It is always better to buy local produce, not stuff with thousands of air miles.		
17 I would vote against non-UN action to close a foreign concentration camp.		
18 I always check to make sure my food, or flowers, have not been imported.		
19 Air passengers who buy carbon dioxide offsets are as moral as non-fliers.		
20 Buying organic food is best for people and best for the planet.		
TOTAL A		
TOTAL B		

Mark your A and B score on the axes below and mark the intersection position with an 'X'.

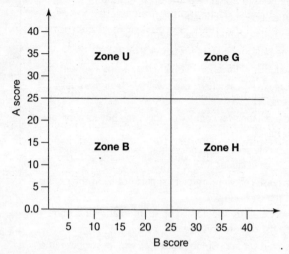

If your X is in Zone U it is unusual to find people behaving ethically who reject the ethical beliefs that can be inferred from their behaviour!

If your X is in Zone B you appear to reject current fashionable Western ideas about what is 'good' and your behaviour reflects this.

If your X is in Zone H you claim liberal values, but your actions contradict your espoused beliefs.

If your X is in Zone G in thought and action, deed and word, you consistently testify to currently ascendant moral values.

HE'S ALL HEART!

As Baggini (2006) points out, there was nothing wrong with Abraham Lincoln's ethical thinking, just because he felt good when he did good. It doesn't have to hurt to be ethical. Altruism need not involve self-sacrifice. In Chapter 8, you saw that the Chinese character meaning 'to think' included the Chinese character for 'heart' as well as the Chinese character for 'head'. The heart reminds you to rethink the issue 'empathetically' from the point of view of the intended beneficiaries, or potential victims.

Ethical thinking and philosophy

Ethical thinking is a branch of philosophy. Philosophy is to 'thinking skills' what circuit training is to sport. To explore philosophical questions, especially ethical questions, is to enter a mental gymnasium. We often leave exhausted, having made little progress, but we can expect to lose some flabby thinking and gain some intellectual muscle to help us confront the next question. In many disciplines – yoga, ballet and martial arts – the physical discipline is associated with values and beliefs. The same is true of the mental training involved in doing philosophy. In philosophy, there are certain philosophical dispositions, or intellectual virtues, that should be reflected in the way you set about thinking. Philosophy helps you to develop good habits of mind. Good habits of mind include the habit of giving good reasons for statements you make, or for the questions you ask. Typical questions that philosophers explore are: What do we know? What is true? What is beautiful? What is good?

This last question is the basis of the branch of philosophy called 'Ethics'. In scientific thinking, it is helpful to have a large sample of data enabling us to analyse a lot of instances, examples or events. If our sample size is large enough, we can analyse and categorize and possibly even formulate a hypothesis. We can then devise experiments to test our hypothesis. If the data we collect is always consistent with our hypothesis, the hypothesis may become accepted as a theory.

In many situations we cannot afford the time, the cost or the risk of waiting until we have enough data to analyse scientifically. Ideally we would like to postulate a theory based on a single example of something very wrong, or something very right. This is the basis of 'Socratic Dialogue'. More recently, Terry Horne (1998) introduced the idea of 'thoughtful conversations', which he used to develop the capacity of his students to think critically, creatively, reflectively and ethically. Questions about effectiveness can be subdivided into questions about economy, efficiency and ethics, and questions about ethics can be subdivided into questions about equity, empathy and ecology. Philosophers love questions!

ETHICAL THINKING, CORRUPTION AND DISHONESTY: WHO CAN YOU TRUST?

In the absence of ethical thinking, individuals tend to maximize personal gain, and the depressing finding is that most adults can only be prevented from acting in their own interests by legal or regulatory restraint. Silverman believes that high principles and high earnings are incompatible. Pauline Vaillancourt Rosenau wrote in 'The Competition Paradigm: America's Romance with Conflict, Contest, and Commerce' that 43 per cent of executives have admitted that they resort to practices they consider 'shady'.

Try it now: Who do you trust?

Rank the following professions as trustworthy. Give 10 to the one you would trust most and 1 to the least trustworthy. Rank the others between 1 and 10.

Clergy	☐
Pharmacists	☐
Doctors	☐
Dentists	☐
Teachers	☐
Police officers	☐
Bankers	☐
TV journalists	☐
Lawyers	☐
Managers	☐

How did you get on?

The order in which the professions were listed, from clergy at the top to managers at the bottom, was the ranking produced in a US Gallup Poll in 1985. How does yours compare? How have the rankings of clergy, doctors and teachers changed in the last 20 years? Why do you think that has happened? Why do you think the ranking of lawyers and managers is so low? Surveys show that we distrust estate agents, solicitors, drug companies, banks, stock markets, mortgage brokers, pension advisers, the police, politicians, TV presenters and even the medical profession. Who can you trust to think ethically? Yourself?

GROWING UP

Attempts have been made to discover how, as young people, we develop our ethical thinking and moral reasoning. Piaget's ideas have been influential. In Piaget's stage of moral realism, children believe that rules are absolute and can't be changed. Gradually as the child matures, he or she learns that people make the rules and that people can change them. This is the beginning of Piaget's stage of moral co-operation. But in Piaget's world, children learn these things experimentally through social interaction and play. In a world of TV, texts and computer games, ethical thinking and moral reasoning may have to be taught explicitly.

TRAINING YOUR BRAIN TO BE 'GOOD'

Moral development depends on exposure to situations and on practice in different types of reasoning. People are unlikely to behave reasonably if they cannot reason. You need to engage in discussions that allow you to surface your deeply-held beliefs so that you can recognize some of your deeply-held beliefs as personal values. Such discussions can be with yourself, but 'thoughtful conversations' are better (see Chapter 10). Discussing moral dilemmas and puzzles involves surfacing, balancing and prioritizing personal values. By repeatedly doing brain training exercises that involve moral dilemmas, a ranking of personal values can emerge. Particular rankings of personal values may then become your moral principles. You can use these moral principles to take ethical decisions quickly, before you are swept along by your amygdala panic button.

Try it now: How ethical are you?

Consider the 15 questions below and circle:

4 if you can answer 'nearly always'

3 if you can answer 'often'

2 if you can answer 'sometimes'

1 if you can answer 'rarely'

−1 if your answer is 'I don't know'.

	Do you...	Circle either...
1	Declare conflicts of interest?	4 3 2 1 −1
2	Interact with other people respectfully?	4 3 2 1 −1
3	Give honest, constructive, timely feedback ?	4 3 2 1 −1
4	Avoid compromising gifts or hospitality?	4 3 2 1 −1
5	Acknowledge the contribution of others?	4 3 2 1 −1
6	Distance yourself from cynicism or defamation of others?	4 3 2 1 −1
7	Have a well-founded reputation for fair dealing?	4 3 2 1 −1
8	Ensure that what you say is complete and not misleading?	4 3 2 1 −1
9	Recognize the capabilities and individuality of other people?	4 3 2 1 −1
10	Help to develop a friendly and satisfying working environment?	4 3 2 1 −1
11	Give priority to the safety, health and well-being of other people?	4 3 2 1 −1
12	Listen to the ideas and views of other people in a kindly manner?	4 3 2 1 −1
13	Pursue your personal and career ambitions without prejudicing others?	4 3 2 1 −1
14	Respect the confidentiality of any information given in confidence?	4 3 2 1 −1
15	Ask, what is it essential that I know?	4 3 2 1 −1
Total score		

How did you do?

40–60   Are you a saint?

30–39   This is hard to believe!

20–29   This is the most frequent score (but still self-deluded?).

15–19   This seems realistic.

0–14   An infrequent score (perhaps not many people are this honest?).

Can you become more ethical? How good are your intentions?

THE NEUROSCIENCE OF GOOD INTENTIONS

J. D. Haynes of the Max Planck Institute has been using brain scanning to detect people's intentions before they act on them. More advanced techniques will eventually allow neuroscientists to become aware of what a person will do even before the person is conscious of it. This may enable the brain to control an artificial limb, but it might also enable a neuroscientist to decide if it is safe to release a particular criminal from custody. In effect, this could punish prisoners by extending their imprisonment for crimes they have not yet committed. Is this ethical?

Haynes extended work that was carried out at University College London and at Oxford University, on identifying tell-tale patterns in the medial prefrontal cortex to reveal when you are lying or harbouring racial prejudice. Since 'bad' behaviour that is premeditated or intended, generally attracts harsher punishment than that which is judged to be misadventure, mistake or accident, neuroscientists could become more prominent deciders of right and wrong than prosecutors, cross-examiners, judges or even juries. Is this desirable?

Should we rely more on our own intuitive sense of right and wrong? How far can we trust ourselves to do the 'right' thing?

THE INNOCENCE OF CHILDREN

If babes and sucklings are so innocent, what do we do to them that appears to turn them into two-year-old tyrants for whom all they see is theirs, and for whom the only truth is their truth! The average two-year-old appears to have no capacity for sharing, reciprocation, negotiation, compromise, fairness or moderation. According to Cordelia Fine, a two-year-old, or at least her two-year-old son, Isaac, takes almost nothing extraneous into account before screeching out a moral judgement! Yet in Chapter 9, you saw how your creative thinking benefits if you pay attention to the two-year-old that hopefully lurks within you. Unfortunately, at a reflex level, this same two-year-old will also dispatch two-year-old justice unless you learn quickly to override your two-year-old self with explicitly trained ways of thinking. Unless trained to look to the circumstances of others, to think empathetically, we will applaud or condemn as when we were two years old.

ETHICAL TAILS WAGGING EMOTIONAL DOGS

According to Haidt (2001), unless you make strenuous efforts to the contrary, your rational tail will struggle to wag your emotionally judgemental dog. If your cerebral cortex is not put into gear very quickly, it may have little to do with your 'ethical' decision, save to find a rational explanation for it after the event. Students who claimed that their guiding moral principle concerning sex was: 'all is permitted that does not harm others', instantly condemned a man who, they were told, regularly engaged in sexual behaviour with his dog. Disgust instantly wiped out even their pre-thought-out moral principles, and left the students floundering to find rational reasons for their moral condemnation.

BLINDED BY RAGE: HOT HEARTS AND WRONG HEADS

Your brain can be prey to emotions that do not even belong to the ethical decision that your brain is trying to make. For example, students angered by scenes of a student being attacked were quicker to hand out stiffer sentences to perpetrators of an unrelated crime. Students blinded by rage literally could not 'see' many mitigating factors in the unrelated case they were subsequently shown.

Hot hearts often result in wrong heads. Yet this is not inevitable. For example, if students know that they may be asked to give good reasons for their verdicts, they are more able to park their feelings to one side while they think about the circumstances and details of the matter in hand.

INTELLECTUAL VIRTUES AND ETHICAL HABITS OF MIND

By training your brain using the workouts in this book and practising thinking about moral dilemmas, you can develop ethical habits of mind. You can engender intellectual virtues, like the giving and expecting of good reasons, and this can help you to park your feelings where you can take them into account without them clouding your ethical judgements.

Try it now: How virtuous are you?

For each of the following, quickly allocate A, B or C:

* where A is definitely a strong point in you
* where C is a definite weakness (or absence) in you
* where B is neither A nor C.

I appreciate beauty
I can express gratitude
I am optimistic
I am playful
I can laugh
I am spiritual
I am loving
I am a good citizen
I am kind
I am diligent
I am genuine
I am open-minded
I am a critical thinker
I am a creative thinker
I am streetwise
I am self-controlled
I am prudent (or discreet)
I am humble (or modest)
I can forgive others
I am loyal
I am fair
I am intelligent
I am a good leader
I have zest
I am brave
I have integrity
I love learning
I am curious
I have practical solutions
I am an applied thinker

If you have more than five As, for each A, allocate X, Y, or Z:

* where X = I did not make use of this strength last week
* where Y = I used this strength many times last week
* where Z = neither X or Y.

For each of your five As (or your top five As), work out how you could make use of this strength every day. You only have to become what you are already. By your deeds shall they know you!

The search for social justice

At some level, many of us harbour fairytale learning (and yearning) that white knights always win and the bad guys always get caught. A series of mock electrocution experiments, reported by Cordelia Fine (2007), showed that so strong can be our desire to believe that we all get what we deserve, that even when people in experiments are innocent victims of unfairness, injustice or misfortune, we search for reasons why it might be their own fault. They should have known better! Sometimes we compound the misfortunes of the poor, and the victims of gun and knife crime, by censure that is commensurate with their misfortune. They shouldn't be there at the time. They shouldn't mix with those sorts of people. They shouldn't take drugs. How else could we sleep at night, our heads filled with harrowing images of Auschwitz, Africa and the aftermath of Hurricane Katrina? Surely the people involved contributed in some way to their own demise? Surely victims of domestic violence are complicit, after all, 'it takes two to tango'? Surely victims of rape 'ask for it'? These are unhelpful starting points for ethical thinking.

IT'S NOT MY FAULT

According to Buehler, when you are late, ratty, rude or inconsiderate, it is rarely your fault. 'Troubling circumstances' are usually responsible for your failings but you rarely see these same 'troubling circumstances' as an excuse for others. Your life is paved with good intentions; theirs is blighted with disasters of their own making. We apply double standards to others unless they are part of our own family.

It's not our Jimmy's fault

We are remarkably understanding of the difficulties facing our own families, compared to street gangs of youths, for example. We readily find excuses for the behaviour of our wives and husbands. Perhaps it would reflect badly on us to have to admit that we had chosen (or had settled for) an imperfect partner. Yet this protectiveness of our partners goes into sharp reverse once separation, or divorce, is contemplated.

YOU STARTED IT!

Schultz (1999) found that a formidable self-serving bias pervades our accounts of the behaviour of 'about to be separated' partners. For example, people commonly dismiss undeniable acts of generosity, kindness and consideration as aberrant attempts to look good in the eyes of others. People blatantly rewrite the history of their relationships. The pain of 'rubbishing' what has been shared is often worse than the pain of losing the partner.

DILEMMAS

As adults, can you really be relied upon to be truthful? To be fair? To think ethically?

Try thinking about the following three dilemmas and then read the comments that follow.

▶ Dilemma 1: sexual honesty

You are happily married and you and your partner have a pact to be faithful and a pact to be honest with each other. One night you are a long way from home at a conference. You spend the night sleeping with one of your work colleagues. Would you confess to your partner?

▶ Dilemma 2: kiss and tell?

A manager in the agricultural department has been badly treated by her lover who is a prominent local politician. Soon after the politician ends the relationship, he is elected to the national assembly. A newspaper offers her £50,000 for her story. Should she sell?

▶ Dilemma 3: whistle blowing

You discover that one of your colleagues responsible for purchasing office furniture and fittings has been requisitioning small items of equipment for personal use. Your two families are very close. You often visit him at his house. During one visit, the door of his study was left open. You noticed that his study is furnished with items that he has requisitioned from work. You often depend on him for a lift. He often takes work home at evenings and weekends. What would you say or do?

DISCUSSION

▶ Sexual honesty, dilemma 1

For this dilemma, nearly all our students say that they would not confess. The men more so than the women. Most agreed that there is everything to be lost and little to be gained for the sake of feeling 'honest' about it. Their partners would lose the good feelings associated with their prior honesty pact knowing that it had now been broken; and lack of trust would further corrode the relationship. Not confessing was not seen as the same as directly lying, or even as deception; the damage of confessing could be extensive, involving innocent parties and perhaps children.

▶ Kiss and tell, dilemma 2

The majority of our students say take the money. Women more so than men. Just deserts and come-uppance feature strongly in the reasons given. Considerations used in the first dilemma are not consistently transferred to this dilemma. Inconsistent judgement and double standards are common.

▶ Whistle blowing, dilemma 3

This case produces very few whistle blowers ('Why rock the boat?' 'None of my business.'). When does silence become complicit? When does collusion become co-operation and co-operation become conspiracy to defraud? And does it really matter? Isn't it okay to vary one's standards?

Are there no absolute rights and wrongs in human behaviour?

▶ Where will it all end?

Where will it all end if we allow deception in the first dilemma, betrayal in the second, and do not blow the whistle in the third? Does it matter if we don't speak out? In a series of studies, Milgram showed that it ends not just in tears, but in Srebrenica, Auschwitz, Abu Ghraib and Guantanamo Bay. In landmark experiments on the consequences of compliance and obedience, Milgram took a cross-section of 40 decent citizens, including professional people and engineers, and showed that they would administer 450 volt electric shocks to fellow subjects when 375 volts was marked 'severe' and 425 volts was marked 'dangerous'. The 'good citizens' were given demonstration mild shocks at the 45 volt level to show them that the officially inscribed shock generator was working properly.

These experiments were done at a time when the world was asking what went on in the minds of ordinary German citizens – adults – who tortured and killed Jewish people. Milgram shocked our complacent view of ourselves. In the absence of trained ethical thinking, would we do the same? At 315 volts, our representative good citizens could hear their subjects screaming and banging on the walls. Yet 90 per cent of us continued to raise the voltage even after the subjects began banging on the walls. Two-thirds went beyond 'severe' shock to the maximum 450 volt 'dangerous' level. Yet the experimenters had no power. They did not threaten or coerce the adults controlling the selective shock machines. The controllers had 'free will' and they chose to electrocute their fellow citizens.

WHAT ABOUT FAITH SCHOOLS – WOULD RELIGIOUS TEACHING HELP?

One answer to the problem of moral development that has been suggested is to send children to 'faith' schools. Would religious teaching help?

Not according to James Darley, who got religious scholars to walk from one studio to another, in order to give a televised talk on the Good Samaritan (the one who went out of his way to help a stranger in distress). Half way between the buildings, Darley had planted a stooge, acting as though he had suddenly been taken ill. He told the students they were already late and that the studio was waiting for them. The distressed man, an actor, was told to cough twice and groan as the students approached. In a pre-questionnaire, Darley ascertained the extent to which each student was familiar with religious teachings on helping one's neighbour, caring for the sick and the poor, and, in particular, with the story of the Good Samaritan.

Darley was interested to see if knowledge of religious teachings increased the likelihood that students would stop to help the distressed man. It did not! If he told the theology students that they had plenty of time to stroll over to the studio, then some would stop and show concern for the distressed stranger. But if he told them they were late, they showed no compassion, often stepping over the stranger as they rehearsed their presentation on the teachings of the Good Samaritan! Religion and religious teaching do not seem necessarily to lead to moral development. They do not necessarily teach ethical thinking or moral behaviour.

What is the answer?

In the absence of any training or intervention, neuroscience predicts that we will be easy prey to prejudice and easily swept along by emotions that are not mediated by our cerebral cortex. We are slaves to self-serving bias. Our capacity to find excuses for ourselves, to explain behaviour that does not meet our exacting double standards will remain breathtaking. Where we cannot explain away our behaviour, we will continue to adjust our standards. As Groucho Marx said:

> 'These are my principles. If you don't like them…
> I have others.'

The answer is to learn to think ethically by developing and combining other basic thinking skills (see Figure 11.1).

Ethical thinking seeks to stop flight into judgement. It involves the systematic use of the thinking skills that can be developed. Ethical thinking involves verbal thinking. This usually takes the form of an internal dialogue with yourself, the skills for which can be practised as described in Chapter 10. Visual thinking (see Chapter 8) is required to envisage the future situation and foresee the possible consequences. Ethical thinking is dependent on your memory (see Chapter 3) and your capacity for empathy (see Chapter 2). The brain's capacity to combine these thinking skills can be expanded by thinking about moral dilemmas, problems and paradoxes.

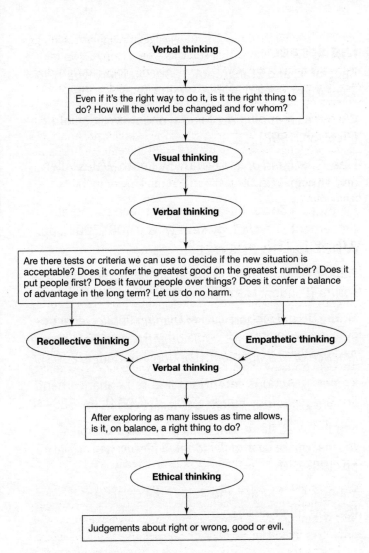

Figure 11.1 Thinking ethically.

Dig deeper

Baggini, J., and Stangroom, J., *Do You Think What You Think You Think?* (London: Granta Books, 2006).

Carter, R., *Mapping the Mind* (London: Weidenfeld & Nicolson, 1998).

Fine, C., *A Mind of its Own* (New South Wales: Allen and Unwin, 2007).

Haidt, J., 'A Social Intuitionist Approach to Moral Judgement', *Psychology Review*, vol. 108 (2001), pp. 810–40.

Handy, C., *The Empty Raincoat: Making Sense of the Future* (London: Hutchinson Business, 2003).

Horne, T. and Doherty, A., *Managing Public Services – Implementing Changes: A Thoughtful Approach to the Practice of Management* (London: Routledge, 2003).

Kruger, J., 'Actions, intentions and self enhancement', *Social Psychology Bulletin*, vol. 30 (2004), pp. 320–40.

Schultz, A., 'Self-serving Bias in Married Couples', *Journal of Social and Personal Relations*, vol. 16 (1999), pp. 190–210.

Younge, G., 'Murder and Rape', *The Guardian* (6 September 2005).

→ Next steps

Ethical thinking is to 'thinking skills' what circuit training is to sport.

✶ Find our how ethical you are by trying the 'how ethical are you?' quiz in this chapter.

✶ Try all the workouts in this book as by practising thinking you can develop ethical habits of mind.

Appendices

Appendix A: Critical thinking

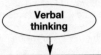

Verbal thinking

What does this assume? Do I accept this? Is it reasonable? Is it fair? Is it logical? Is it consistent? Under what conditions is it valid? Is it useful or reliable? Is it flawed – partially or fatally? By what criteria and who says? Who is trying to achieve what and why? What are the key questions here? What do we actually know? Are the options reasonable?

Recollective thinking

What principles might be helpful? Is it economic? Is it the best use of these resources? Is it efficient? What are we trying to achieve? Does this make a worthwhile contribution? What will be the consequences for others affected? Is it equitable? Is it ecological? Is it ethical?

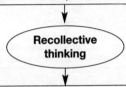

Numerical thinking	**Ethical thinking**	**Empathetic thinking**
Is it economic? Is it efficient? Is it effective?	Is it the greatest benefit for the greatest number? Does it do the least harm? Does it waste the least resources?	What are the likely thoughts and feelings of beneficiaries unintended victims, participants, observers?

Critical thinking

Critique, judgement, opinion, view, evaluation, scepticism.

Appendix B: Creative thinking

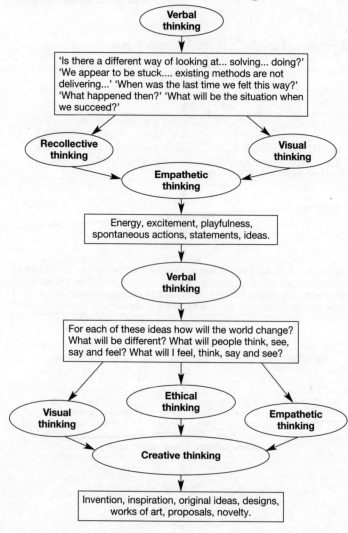

Appendix C: Reflective thinking

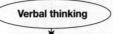

Verbal thinking

↓

'I wonder what that was all about?' 'What does it mean?' 'What really happened and so what?' 'What can we learn from this and where do we go from here?'

↓

Recollective thinking

↓

What was seen, heard and by whom? Who felt and thought what? What actually was said at the time and in what sequence? What else do we know? What was the picture?

↓

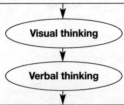

Visual thinking

↓

Verbal thinking

↓

'Remembering all that, here and now, what do I feel and think?' 'What feelings, thoughts and associations occur?' 'Is there a pattern here?' 'Has this happened before?' 'What insights are there?' 'What might I infer?'

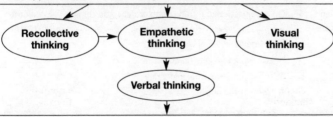

Recollective thinking → **Empathetic thinking** ← **Visual thinking**

↓

Verbal thinking

↓

'What are the implications for some future situations: how might this cause me to feel, think, behave differently?' 'What could I do to ensure this?'

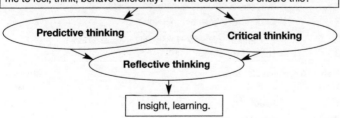

Predictive thinking   **Critical thinking**

Reflective thinking

↓

Insight, learning.

Appendix D: Do you think like a man or a woman?

Men score			Women score
	1	At the end of a hard day you prefer to:	
3		▶ talk to someone about your day	4
2		▶ listen to other people talking	2
0		▶ not talk at all	0
2		▶ None of the above	2
Men score	**2**	Thinking about your spelling and writing:	**Women score**
3		▶ You find both easy	4
2		▶ One is okay but not the other	2
0		▶ Both are weak	0
2		▶ None of the above	2
Men score	**3**	In arguments you are most upset by:	**Women score**
3		▶ a lack of response, silence or sulks	4
2		▶ a refusal to agree with you	2
0		▶ being contradicted or questioned	0
2		▶ None of the above	2
Men score	**4**	On the question of routines, you prefer to do things:	**Women score**
3		▶ whenever you feel like it	4
2		▶ according to a general but flexible plan	2
0		▶ about the same time every day	0
2		▶ None of the above	2
Men score	**5**	When shopping you tend to:	**Women score**
3		▶ buy special offers, frequently on impulse	4
2		▶ sometimes buy, sometimes don't	2
0		▶ purchase only what you went for	0
2		▶ None of the above	2
Men score	**6**	You prefer to read:	**Women score**
3		▶ fiction	4
2		▶ newspapers or general magazines	2
0		▶ specialist magazines or non-fictional information	0
2		▶ None of the above	2

Men score	7	You prefer to work:	Women score
3		▶ with a group of people you like	4
2		▶ on your own task but in the company of others	2
0		▶ in solitude	0
2		▶ None of the above	2

Men score	8	A friend has a personal problem:	Women score
3		▶ You can generally understand and sympathize	4
2		▶ You can usually explain why it's not so bad after all	2
0		▶ You usually give advice or suggestions on how to solve the problem	0
2		▶ None of the above	2

Men score	9	Today you meet more than seven new people. Tomorrow:	Women score
3		▶ you can picture at least seven of the new faces	4
2		▶ you could put some names to some faces	2
0		▶ you could remember names but not many faces	0
2		▶ None of the above	2

Men score	10	You cannot find your keys:	Women score
3		▶ You do something else until they turn up	4
2		▶ You try to do something else, but you're distracted by the loss	2
0		▶ You keep retracing your movements until you find them	0
2		▶ None of the above	2

Men score	11	When predicting what is going to happen:	Women score
3		▶ you use your intuition	4
2		▶ you rely on gut feelings to interpret relevant information	2
0		▶ you use trends based on historical statistics or other data	0
2		▶ None of the above	2

Men score	12	When you have heard a song:	Women score
3		▶ you can sing some of the words next time you hear the tune	4
2		▶ you can remember the tune but not the words	2

| 0 | ▶ you can vaguely remember the tune | 0 |
| 2 | ▶ None of the above | 2 |

Men score	13	You are listening to the radio or TV and the phone rings. Do you:	Women score
3		▶ just take the call and talk	4
2		▶ turn down the radio/TV and talk	2
0		▶ turn off the radio/TV, tell others to be quiet and talk	0
2		▶ None of the above	2

Men score	14	You need to reverse a vehicle into a tight spot to park it. Would you:	Women score
3		▶ look for another parking spot	4
2		▶ attempt to park, preferably with assistance	2
0		▶ just try to reverse in	0
2		▶ None of the above	2

Men score	15	In a place you are visiting for the first time:	Women score
3		▶ you would not know which way was north	4
2		▶ you could have a good guess which way was north	2
0		▶ you would know which way was north	0
2		▶ None of the above	2

Men score	16	A child's mechanical toy won't work:	Women score
3		▶ You can sympathize with the child and discuss how they feel about it	4
2		▶ You can find somebody else to fix it	2
0		▶ You will usually try to fix it	0
2		▶ None of the above	2

Men score	17	After a good film you prefer:	Women score
3		▶ to picture the scenes in your own mind	4
2		▶ to describe it to someone else	2
0		▶ to relate ideas or themes or lines from the film	0
2		▶ None of the above	2

Men score	18	When explaining or defining something:	Women score
3		▶ you often use a pencil, pen, paper or gestures	4
2		▶ you rely on verbal and non-verbal communication only	2
0		▶ you could define it clearly without repeating yourself	0
2		▶ None of the above	2

Men score	19	Asked to read a map:	Women score
3		▶ you would prefer some help	4
2		▶ you would have to turn it to face the way you were going	2
0		▶ you find it straightforward	0
2		▶ None of the above	2

Men score	20	When thinking about your forthcoming day:	Women score
3		▶ you often write a list	4
2		▶ you think about what you want to achieve that day	2
0		▶ you run through places and activities in your mind	0
2		▶ None of the above	2

If you are a man, add up your score under the men score column.

If you are a woman, add up your score under the women score column.

Most men we have tested scored less than 44. Most women we have tested scored more than 40.

People with lower scores tended to use typically male brain (TMB) thinking skills. People with low scores were more likely to rely on logic, deduction, analysis and disciplined organization. The closer they were to zero, the more likely it was that they were good at making detailed plans. They tended to be less easily swayed by emotions and more objective when making decisions.

People with high scores tended to make more use of the thinking skills more frequently used by women. People with a higher score were more likely to be creative or artistic. They made greater use of intuition or gut feelings. They could think inductively, recognize patterns and identify and solve problems on the basis of less information. Men who scored closer to zero had great difficulties when in relationships, especially with women who scored nearer 80, and vice versa.

Mid-range scores indicated people who had the ability, under many circumstances, to think either like a TMB man, or like a typically female brain (TFB) woman. Such people seemed to perform well when working in groups, or when working as managers, especially where there were multi-factor problems to be solved and where novel solutions were needed.

Since we began our research in 1982, knowledge about the structure and working of the brain has exploded. This has helped us to infer that brain differences might account for the differences in the thinking and behaviour that we encountered. In turn, this has allowed us to examine some implications for the way we might behave more effectively when talking to, relating to, working with, or working for people of the opposite sex.

Glossary

Alzheimer's disease can produce cognitive deterioration when there is insufficient spare cognitive capacity. Alzheimer's disease is often characterized by progressive cognitive deterioration but this is not inevitable.

Amygdala almond-shaped groups of neurons located deep within the medial temporal lobes of the brain. They perform a primary role in the processing and memory of emotions.

Axons long, slender projections from a neuron. They conduct electrical impulses away from the neuron's soma, the bulbous end of a neuron.

Cerebral cortex so-called grey matter of the brain. The thinking cap, responsible for functions such as language, logic and information processing.

CT or CAT scanner a machine that uses X-rays to take pictures of sections of the body and brain.

Dementia is a progressive decline in cognitive function exacerbated by lack of spare cognitive capacity. It is due to disease not ageing.

Dendrites the antennae of the neurons.

MEG scanner a scanner that allows brain activity to be viewed while a particular task is performed. It measures the tiny magnetic fields generated by brain activity.

MRI scanner a machine that uses a magnetic field and radiowaves to show what is happening inside the body and the brain.

Neurons chemically excitable cells in the nervous system that process and transmit information. Neurons are the core components of the brain.

PET scanner a machine that detects radioactive material which is injected or inhaled to produce an image of the brain.

Serotonin a neurotransmitter.

Synapse a small gap separating neurons. The gap is between the axon of one neuron and the dendrite of the next. The gap contains neurotransmitters such as acetylcholine derivatives.

Answers

Chapter 3

SUDOKU A

2	9	1	3	4	7	8	6	5
8	6	7	1	5	9	2	3	4
4	3	5	2	6	8	7	1	9
7	8	2	6	1	5	4	9	3
6	1	4	7	9	3	5	8	2
3	5	9	4	8	2	1	7	6
1	2	3	9	7	4	6	5	8
5	4	6	8	3	1	9	2	7
9	7	8	5	2	6	3	4	1

MENTAL ARITHMETIC EXERCISE

$18 - 10 = 8$

$6 + 6 = 12$

$2 \times 10 = 20$

$14 - 9 = 5$

$3 \times 7 = 21$

$9 - 6 = 3$

$1 + 7 = 8$

$15 - 8 = 7$

$2 + 8 = 10$

$10 - 4 = 6$

$9 + 9 = 18$

$9 - 4 = 5$

$6 \times 6 = 36$

$7 + 9 = 16$

$8 \times 6 = 48$

$5 - 5 = 0$

$3 + 8 = 11$

$8 + 7 = 15$

$13 - 8 = 5$

$0 \times 8 = 0$

$8\ 3 = 5$

$3 \times 10 = 30$

$6 + 7 = 13$

$10 - 3 = 7$

$1 + 10 = 11$

$9 \times 9 = 81$

$7 - 3 = 4$

$6 \times 7 = 42$

$6 - 1 = 5$

$4 + 8 = 12$

$7 \times 6 = 42$

$4 \times 5 = 20$

$5 + 4 = 9$

$10 - 8 = 2$

$2 \times 5 = 10$

$4 + 2 = 6$

$12 - 5 = 7$

$7 + 10 = 17$

$5 \times 2 = 10$

$5 \times 4 = 20$

$3 + 6 = 9$

$10 - 9 = 1$

$9 + 5 = 14$

$6 \times 8 = 48$

$6 \times 9 = 54$

$12 - 4 = 8$

$1 + 8 = 9$

$9 \times 10 = 90$

$11 - 8 = 3$

$8 + 9 = 17$

Chapter 4

Q1 12 (a number in the bottom row is half the sum of the two numbers above it)

Q2 Quadruple

Q3 35 minutes after 9 o'clock

Q4 Adulthood

Q5 $\sqrt{-49}$

Q6 Thorough

Q7 With

Q8 Verdi

Q9 23

Q10 9/22. The first figure is the number of letters in the composer's name; the second figure is always 17 plus the gain in number of letters from the first name (i.e. Brahms has 2 more letters than Bach, hence 6/19)

A MORE MODERN IQ TEST

Q1 Women

Q2 Present

Q3 Intersect

Q4 Full English

Q5 Timber

Q6 Religion

Q7 Water

Q8 Synonymous

NEUROCHEMISTRY OF INTELLIGENCE

Q1 2 (the relationship between numbers from one diagram to the next remains the same)

Q2 The snowman has melted

Q3 Cut it into quarters using two slices. Then make the third cut halfway down parallel to the base of the cake.

THE IQ WORKOUT

▶ **Puzzles**

Q1 Take one coin from the box labelled 'copper and silver'. (Hint: remember each label is incorrect)

Q2 40 m

Q3 Invert one triangle on another. Plant one tree at each apex plus one at each intersection

Q4 ? = zero. The poles must be touching back to back, because the 12 m rope is hanging 6 m (8 m – 2 m) vertically.

Q5 Yes

Q6 He realized he must have a black mark (otherwise the other two candidates would have known straight away that they were black)

Q7 Take one coin from bag 1, two coins from bag 2, three from bag 3 and so on. Weigh the coins you have removed together. The number of grams short is the number of the bag with the shaved coins.

Q8 The car was seven years old when the new engine was fitted: the car is now 28 years old and the engine is 21, so when the car was 21 the engine was 14, and twice 14 is 28.

Q9

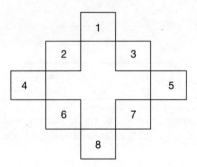

Q10 B (hour hand moving 15 minutes clockwise, minute hand moving 15 minutes anticlockwise)

Q11

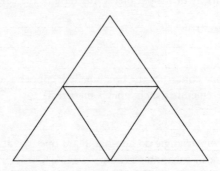

Q12

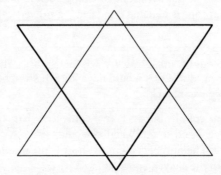

Q13

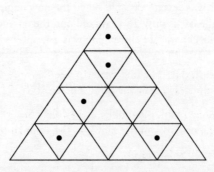

Count each triangle from left to right, starting with the first • in the top triangle. Count 2 for the next •, then 3, then 4, and so on.

Q14   Applied thinking

A	N	T
P	I	E
P	L	Y
L	I	E
I	N	K
E	Y	E
D	O	N
T	W	O
H	A	T
I	R	E
N	A	P
K	I	P
I	C	E
N	O	T
G	A	Y

Q15   Move one match from the equals sign and place it
        parallel to the minus sign

Q16   Rotate the pool through 45° so that the trees are at the
        centre of the new elongated sides

Q17   Tip the contents of glass three into glass six

Q18   Pour two half bottles into two other half bottles

Q19   The 29th day. The lilies will double their area overnight
        to completely cover the pond on the 30th

Q20   Place one plank diagonally across the corner of the moat
        and the other from the plank to the steps of the castle

Q21   Water (H to O) (H$_2$O)

Q22   One owes nothing for one ate nothing to owe for

Q23   3 chances in 4, i.e. the reverse of his chance of picking
        two whites (1 in 4). As there are 2 boxes, with 4 black

balls and 4 white balls in, the man is blindfolded, the chance of picking one black is 1 minus picking 2 whites. So 1 – 1 in 4 (chance of picking 2 whites), hence 3 in 4 chance of picking a black.

Q24   32 (total number of chests less one)

Q25   £2.00

Q26   40,320 (1st knight can go in 8 places, 2nd knight can go in 7 places, 3rd knight can go in 6 places, etc., hence 8 × 7 × 6 × 5 × 4 × 3 × 2 × 1)

POST-TEST

Q1   Paper

Q2   Source

Q3   Burger

Q4   Simple

Q5   F

Q6   Water

Q7   NEAT DAM

Q8   127 ((because the difference between successive numbers is a value to the power of 2 . 1–3 (2), 3–7 (4), 7–15 (8), 15–31 (16), 31 – 63 (32), 63 + 64 = 127

Q9   24

Q10   Correct

Chapter 6

CAN YOU DO THE NUMBERS?

18 – 8 = 10	8 + 7 = 15	2 × 3 = 6
6 + 6 = 12	13 – 3 = 10	4 + 0 = 4
2 × 10 = 20	0 × 6 = 0	12 – 3 = 9
14 – 7 = 7	8 – 1 = 7	7 + 8 = 15

3 × 5 = 15	3 × 8 = 24	5 × 0 = 0
3 + 6 = 9	6 + 5 = 11	5 × 2 = 10
9 − 4 = 5	10 − 1 = 9	3 + 4 = 7
1 + 5 = 6	1 + 8 = 9	10 − 7 = 3
15 − 5 = 10	9 × 7 = 63	9 + 3 = 12
2 + 6 = 8	7 − 1 = 6	6 × 6 = 36
10 − 2 = 8	6 × 5 = 30	6 × 7 = 42
9 + 7 = 16	6 − 0 = 6	12 − 2 = 10
9 − 2 = 7	4 + 7 = 11	1 + 6 = 7
6 × 4 = 24	7 × 4 = 28	9 × 8 = 72
7 + 7 = 14	5 + 2 = 7	11 − 6 = 5
8 × 4 = 32	10 − 7 = 3	8 + 7 = 15
5 − 3 = 2	4 × 3 = 12	

TESTS ON NUMERICAL THINKING

Q1

1/2	0.5	50%
3/4	0.75	75%
3/5	0.60	60%
1/3	0.33	33%
1/4	0.25	25%

Q2 The middle number

Q3 $66 \div 6 = 11$

Q4 T = 36

Q5 1 in 12. $P_{(A+B)} = P_A \times P_B = 1/2 \times 1/6 = 1/12$ where P = Probability

Q6 $243 = 3 \times 3 \times 3 \times 3 \times 3$

Q7   6 metres

Q8 $3.142 = \pi \,(\text{Pi}) = 22/7$

Q9   6 (1, 2, 4, 8, 16, 32)

Q10   A prime number has only itself (and 1) as a factor

Q11   Circumference = $2 \times 22 \div 7 \times 6377 = 40{,}084$ km
(Circumference = $2 \times \text{Pi} \times \text{R}$)

Q12 $85 \times 1.15 = 97.75$

Q13   £5; 25 per cent (or 1/4) of 20 = £5

Q14   £300 = 100 + 20 = 120% ... 100% = £250 (i.e. 300 less 1/6)

Q15   3:6 = 1:2 i.e. three parts 1/3 = 21 and 2/3 = 42. Ratio 3:6 = 21:42

Q16 $X = 9$

Q17 $Y = X$

Q18   £6,620

Q19   6 sides $\times 20 \times 20 = 2{,}400$ sq cm

Q20 $(10 \times 10 \times 10) + 1/2\,(10 \times 10 \times 10) = 1{,}500$ cubic metres

Q21   3 in 4: one minus the probability that you will get two tails = $1 - (1/2 \times 1/2) = 3/4$

Q22   1 in 8 ($1/2 \times 1/2 \times 1/2 = 1/8$)

Q23   **a** 3 (see Team E)

        b 11 (Total wins, losses and draws ÷ 2)

        c 4 (Total to be played = $6 \times 5 \div 2 = 15 - 11$ played = 4)

        d 2; E + F (A + B cannot catch F. If F loses last match and E wins, E could overtake F. If F wins, F wins

        e 44 (4 games remain which could be $4 \times$ (3 for a win) = 12 to be added to 32 already scored)

Q24 **a** Subscription TV gained 5 per cent share (10 – 5)

b Public access TV lost 25 per cent (9 ÷ 36 × 100)

c Internet with 400 per cent (from 1 per cent to 5 per cent gain = 4 (4 ÷ 1 × 100))

d 25 per cent (five-fold increase in last ten years. Same in next ten years would give 5 × 5 per cent = 25 per cent)

HOW TO SCORE ON A BLIND DATE

Q1 Going late. It has a net value of 2 – 2 – 1 = –1

Q2 Going on time. It has a net value of –1 + 1 + 3 = 3

Q3 Going on time (The likelihood of you being on time, if you choose this strategy, is only 2 out of 10 … likely benefit is 2 ÷ 10 (–1 + 1 + 3) = 0.6 (and it turns into 8 ÷ 10 of being late, i.e. 8 ÷ 10 (+2 – 2 – 1) = –0.8, so net score is –0.2)

Q4 Going early (This would give you 1 ÷ 10 (–2 + 2 + 1) = 0.1 and as long as you are not catastrophically late, you would still have a 9 out of 10 chance of being on time 9 ÷ 10 (–1 + 1 + 3) = 2.7, so a net score of 2.8). So, your best chance tonight is to decide to go early (try to actually do it this time). You could always loiter out of sight until you see your date and then engineer a simultaneous rendezvous. Of course, we do not know what your date's pay-off table looks like, but at least you will have maximized your main chances of getting the outcome you want.

THE NUMERICAL THINKING WORKOUT

Q1 5 metres; 9 metres; 165 blocks (81 + 49 + 25 + 9 + 1 = 165). Also 165 = 2 × 100 × 1000 kg ÷ 1212!

Q2 Four triangles

Q3

5	1	8	7	8	9
9	4	7	1	7	4
7	2	6	3	6	9
8	3	5	2	9	8
6	5	4	3	2	1
4	6	3	5	1	2

Q4 Vowel = 20 km, consonant = 10 km; London = 80 km

Q5 Top row 9, 1, 4; Middle row 7, 2, 6; Bottom row 3, 8, 5

Q6

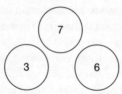

i.e. add 222 to 514 and place first number of the answer on top of last two

Q7 5.35; the minute hand is moving forward 1 × 5, 2 × 5, 4 × 5, 8 × 5 and now 16 × 5 and the hour hand is moving forward 1 × 2, 2 × 2, 4 × 2, 8 × 2 and now 16 × 2

Q8 Tilt the barrel towards you so that the liquid just comes to the edge without spilling. Shine the torch into the barrel. If you can see the bottom of the barrel, it is less than half full.

Q9 Start both sand glasses. Your time starts when the seven-minute glass is empty. Turn the 11-minute glass again when it is empty 4 + 11 = 15 minutes.

Q10 146 (Opposite sides of dice always add up to 7, so 4 sides always add up to 14, 10 dice = 140, plus 6 you can see on top!)

Q11 Wrap it as a rectangular package, 30 cm × 40 cm and lay it along the diagonal of the package, which will be 50 cms

Q12 0, 1, 4

Q13 All routes score more than 300: 4 × (−27) = −108, and all routes involve +108 at the final NE corner, so the 108s and the −27s can always be ignored. All routes start with 114 and involve collecting a further three positive numbers, so if the route has three further numbers totalling more than (300 − 114), i.e. 186, then more than 300 will be collected. Trial and error involves lots of mental arithmetic, which is good for your brain!

Chapter 7

HOW LOGICAL ARE YOU?

Q1 A and D

Q2 Cards A and C (it doesn't matter if card D or B has blue or a triangle on it, as only concerned with red cards

INDUCTIVE LOGIC

Q1

a No

b Try adding 'Most' to the first line. Replace 'Therefore' with 'Probably' in the last line.

c Yes, it is now inductively forceful

Q2

a No

b No, Brazil could have a better chance than others without that chance being greater than the 50:50 necessary to justify 'probably win'

c Therefore they are more likely than Germany, France and Argentina to win, etc.

Q3

a No

b No

c We need a justifiably believable premise, plus a more than 50:50 chance of the outcome. How about: 'English fans will probably cause trouble at the World Cup, because they usually do in matches against foreign teams... And English fans have been warned that trouble at the World Cup will lead to expulsion from the European Cup. So England will probably be banned from playing in the next European Cup.' This seems like an inductively reasonable argument.

d We need a justifiably reasonable premise plus an inescapable conclusion for an argument to be deductively reasonable. How about: 'Some English fans are bound to cause trouble at the next World Cup because some English fans cause trouble at every non-friendly away match. If English fans cause trouble at the next World Cup, then England will automatically be banned from the European Cup. Therefore England will not play in the next European Cup.'

A LOGICAL WORKOUT

A

2	5	3	9	8	7	6	4	1
8	1	6	3	5	4	9	7	2
9	7	4	6	2	1	5	3	8
3	4	2	8	7	5	1	6	9
6	8	5	4	1	9	3	2	7
1	9	7	2	6	3	8	5	4
7	3	8	1	4	6	2	9	5
4	6	1	5	9	2	7	8	3
5	2	9	7	3	8	4	1	6

B

7	3	9	5	2	1	4	8	6
8	4	5	7	6	9	3	1	2
1	6	2	3	8	4	5	9	7
5	8	7	2	1	6	9	4	3
9	2	4	8	5	3	7	6	1
6	1	3	9	4	7	2	5	8
4	5	6	1	3	2	8	7	9
3	7	1	4	9	8	6	2	5
2	9	8	6	7	5	1	3	4

Q1 OCT(OBER) (tri (3) to sex (6), quad (4) to Oct (8))

Q2 Harold (Wilson) and Gordon (Brown)

Q3 Surgeon

Q4 Astronomer

Q5 Audio, Adieu

Q6 Noel (no L)

Q7 Switch 1 on for ten minutes and then switch it off; switch 2 on and enter to find one light on (2), one off (3) and one warm (1)

Q8 £600 and £1,200

Q9 Yes. Take B and send B back with torch. Call for C and D, then take torch back yourself to collect B, with two minutes to spare

Q10 8 (Hint: 4, 6, 5, 2, 7, 1, 3, 8)

Q11 Runner 3

Q12 Larry

Q13 12

Q14 'Do you spell your name with a V?'

Q15 59 brain trains

Q16 We don't think so, but what do you think? How logical are you? And would you stake your life on it? Your first choice you have a 2 in 3 chance of living. Your next choice you have a 1 in 2 chance of living. You should stick with your original choice. Don't follow intuition, follow logic!

Chapter 8

TYPE 1: PATTERN RECOGNITION

Q1 A (all the rest have a 'hole' in the bottom right of their 'boat')

TYPE 2: VISUAL ANALOGY

Q1 External number of sides goes up by one, number of black dots goes up by one, but the number of white dots goes down by one (some breed some die, see title of question)

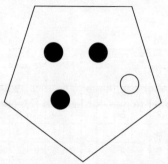

Q2 Only lines that appear twice (exactly) in the three figures are carried forward into the next single figure

TYPE 3: VISUAL SEQUENCE

Q1 Add blacks and whites progressively to vertical and horizontal. Starting with vertical, alternate the colours.

TYPE 4: VISUAL CLASSIFICATION TEST

Q1 D (all small icons common)

TYPE 5: SPATIAL REASONING

Q1 A

Q2 A

TYPE 6: NUMERIC DIAGRAM

Q1 23 (sums of opposite points)

Q2 27 (6 + 5 + 7 + 9)

WARM-UP

A

8	1	9	6	7	5	3	2	4
6	4	2	9	8	3	7	5	1
5	3	7	1	2	4	8	6	9
4	2	6	5	9	7	1	8	3
7	9	5	3	1	8	6	4	2
1	8	3	4	6	2	5	9	7
3	5	8	7	4	9	2	1	6
2	6	4	8	3	1	9	7	5
9	7	1	2	5	6	4	3	8

B

8	3	6	4	9	2	5	7	1
1	5	4	7	8	3	6	2	9
9	7	2	6	1	5	4	8	3
4	9	7	3	6	1	8	5	2
5	1	3	8	2	7	9	4	6
2	6	8	5	4	9	1	3	7
7	4	9	1	3	8	2	6	5
3	8	1	2	5	6	7	9	4
6	2	5	9	7	4	3	1	8

MAIN WORKOUT

Q1 A iii, B iv, C v, D vi, E ii, F i, G vii

Q2 D

Q3 I (the only square in a square)

Q4 A = 10; B = 1050; C = 1,000,000 (using each space you can pack more in)

Q5 There is no one shortest route because the diagram is symmetrical about the AB axis. (Hint: Simpler than geometric or trigonometric calculations, is to lay a piece of thread along possible routes, or to mark the routes off on the edge of a piece of paper.)

Q6

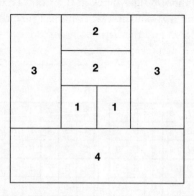

Q7 47; 16 (The opposite face of a dice makes 7 if add opposite faces together. Total face of each dice adds up to 21 (1 +2 + 3 + 4 + 5 + 6). The hidden faces = 3 × 21 – value of visual faces)

Q8 We have to draw out (visualize) the possible scenarios that would give Mr B a 50:50 chance of picking one black sock and then another black sock. Visualize the possible combinations of black socks and/or grey socks. They are:

A 4 grey

B 3 grey; 1 black

C 2 grey; 2 black

D 1 grey; 3 black

E 4 black

If Mr B is to have any chance of a black pair we can eliminate A and B straight away. In case C his chances would be 1/2 × 1/3 = 1/6, so not C. In case E his chances are 100 per cent, so a 50:50 chance of picking two black socks must be case D, in which case, there is no chance of a grey pair! Just look.

Q9 Yes; a triangle

Q10 Remove the top right block at the front. (Prove it by redrawing without the block and just turn the page upside down and the bathroom will appear – but don't blink or it will disappear again:

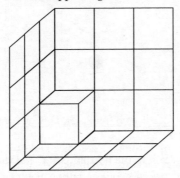

Q11 In your dreams! Real dice have opposite faces totalling seven.

Q12 THTTTH (i.e. sounds like thought)

Q13 He will lose his hat! (Each loses one more line than his predecessor in a different area of the body.)

Q14

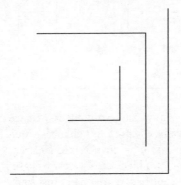

Small L always rotates clockwise by 90°. Middle L never moves. Big L flips.

Q15 C looks more like a Scottish terrier dog!

Q16 Each time the seal is put on the back of the envelope, it moves an extra number of quadrants clockwise

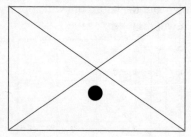

Q17 Yes. To be 'B', is to B 'real'. (A, D, C are only mirror images of B)

Q18 It will first fall, to the bottom point, and then rise as it turns anticlockwise, before falling again – reciprocating motion

Q19

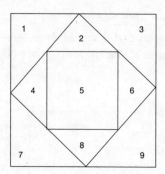

Q20

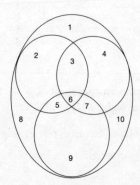

Q21

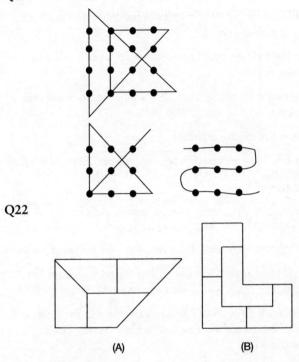

Q22

(A) (B)

Chapter 9

LATERAL THINKING

Q1 The man was a neighbour who often has hiccups. He came for help. The shock you gave him stopped his hiccups.

Q2 Take the end coin from the bottom row and place it on the corner coin

MAIN WORKOUT

Q1 The book is from an encyclopedia set – he has the edition from HOW through to HUG alphabetically

Q2 Snow White

Q3 Because I am overweight for a person of my height

Q4   It's up to you as long as it rhymes and is in rhythm

Q5   The customer again put sugar in his coffee and realized why it was too sweet

Q6   A suicide victim could not rewind the tape (or it was a female voice)

Q7   Move coin 10 to top, then coin 1 adjacent to 8 and coin 4 adjacent to 9

Q8   This is her mother's father!

Q9   Neither. They played different opponents. They didn't play each other

Q10 Deal anticlockwise from the bottom, starting with yourself

Q11 [No solution needed]

Q12 She jumped inwards, back into her own carpeted room

Q13 Fold your arms. Grip one end of the tie with your left hand, the other with your right hand. Unfold your arms

Q14 4 seconds (If it takes 2 seconds to chime 2, the interval between chimes must be 2 seconds when the clock chimes 3.)

Q15 TSYHIYM are the first letters of the series you have in your mind

Q16 76.5 km (Distance = speed (76.5) × time (1 hr)). The bird will be flying until the cars meet, i.e. for one hour (that is, after 100 km ÷ closing speed of cars, which is 100 km/ph)

Chapter 10

TYPE 1: FIND THE SYNONYMS

Q1   fickle

Q2   though, nevertheless

TYPE 2: FIND THE ANTONYMS

Q1   dreary

Q2   Invariable, flexible

TYPE 3: DOUBLE MEANINGS

Q1   fair

Q2   case

TYPE 4: DOUBLE USES

Q1   light

Q2   stock

TYPE 5: TWO MISSING WORDS

Q1   B

Q2   D

TYPE 6: MISTAKEN USE OF WORDS

Q1   Heart transplant <u>procedures</u> must be suspended until safe <u>operations</u> can be followed.

Q2   A <u>settlement</u> has been agreed demanding that both sides make an early <u>statement</u>.

TYPE 7: LINKED WORDS

Q1	<u>writing</u>			<u>reading</u>	
<u>speaking</u>	learning	analysis	maps	glasses	<u>listening</u>

Q2	<u>idealism</u>			<u>realism</u>	
acceptance	perfectionism	<u>beauty</u>	flows	<u>ugliness</u>	persecution

TYPE 8: VERBAL ANALOGIES

Q1   nut

Q2   Sri Lanka

TYPE 9: REDUNDANT WORDS

Q1   Many ~~present-day~~ employers have high ~~flying~~ expectations of ~~all~~ the thinking and writing skills of applicants ~~who would have them~~. (13)

Q2 ~~When they~~ this product is ~~redundant using~~ manufactured ~~by~~ from 100 per cent recycled paper ~~writing and uses wood pulp fiction.~~ (10)

THE VERBAL THINKING WORKOUT

Q1

TACT	YEAR	SPAR
FACT	NEAR	SPAN
FAST	BEAR	SPIN
FIST	BOAR	SPIT
FISH	BOOR	SUIT
DISH	BOON	QUIT
a	**b**	**c**

Q2

G	L	A	R	E
R	O	M	A	N
A	V	O	I	D
D	E	N	S	E
E	D	G	E	D

Words start from the top down and from the left to right.

Q3 MISREPRESENTING

Q4 SNEEZED (Hint: 7 – S; 6 – ink (kin confused); 5 – opera (uncoil a rope) 4 – immerse; 3 – freezable; 2 – accelerator (locate racer); 1 – dilapidations)

Q5

1 Y A R D A R M

2 B O W L I N G

3 G A L L E O N

4 I N D I A N A

5 R U S T L E R

6 R A F T E R S

7 O R G A N I C

8 N U T C A S E

9 A C E T O N E

10 E N D E A R S

11 L A D L I N G

12 E Y E L E T S

Q6 a Queuing b Witchcraft

Q7 Eerie

Q8 Indivisibility

Q9 1 kimono 2 iridescent 3 inoculate 4 rarefy 5 naphthalene
6 witness 7 embarrassment 8 harassed 9 gauge 10 potato

Q10 Mince pie, honeycomb, blackcurrant jelly, scotch egg,
cheesecake, strawberries, dark chocolate, peppermint,
corn beef, rice paper

Q11

▶ **1 Anagrams**

a stew

b rumbles

▶ **2 Double Meanings**

a watch

b spruce

▶ **3 Buried Words**

a bail

b CEO (squat here means shortened abbreviation)

▶ **4 Sounds Like**

a bear (sounds like bare (naked))

b fare

▶ **5 Multiple Clues**

a farming (far + ming)

b tattoo (tat + too)

▶ **6 Insider Clues**

a ballet (b(all)et = dance)

b s(it)e (south east = s e)

▶ **7 Backward Clues**

a smart (trams backwards)

b moor (reject = send back)

▶ **8 Chop Off Clues**

a novice ((no) vice)

b rabbi (dock the 't')

Q12   1D, 2C, 3A, 4E, 5B, 6F, 7G

Taking it further

Further reading

Al-Jajjoka, S., *How to Pass Professional Level Psychometric Tests* (London: Kogan Page, 2004)

Arbib, M. A., (ed.), *Handbook of Brain Theory and Neural Networks* (2nd edn, Boston: MIT Press, 2002)

Baggini, J., and Stangroom, J., *Do You Think What You Think You Think?* (London: Granta Books, 2006)

Barrett, J., *Test Yourself* (London: Kogan Page, 2000)

Bear M., et al., *Neuroscience: Exploring the Brain* (New York: Lippincott, 2002)

Blakemore, S., *The Learning Brain* (Oxford: Blackwell, 2007)

Bransford, J., *How Students Learn* (Washington DC: National Academies Press, 2000)

Bryon, M., *How to Pass Graduate Psychometric Tests* (London Kogan Page, 2001)

Bryon, M., *How to Pass Civil Service Tests* (London: Kogan Page, 2003)

Bryon, M., *How to Pass Advanced Numeracy Tests* (London: Kogan Page, 2004)

Bryon, M., *How to Pass the Firefighter Selection Process* (London: Kogan Page, 2004)

Butterworth, B., *The Mathematical Brain* (London: Macmillan, 1999)

Carter, P., *IQ and Psychometric Tests* (London: Kogan Page, 2005)

Carter, R., *Mapping the Mind* (London: Weidenfeld & Nicolson, 1998)

Cohen, M., *Philosophy Problems* (London: Routledge, 1999)

Covey, S. R., *The 8th Habit: From Effectiveness to Greatness* (London: Simon & Schuster Ltd, 2004)

Cox, E., and Rathvon, H., *Mensa Cryptic Crosswords* (New York: Stirling, 2007)

Dayan, P., and Abbott, L. F., *Theoretical Neuroscience: Computational and Mathematical Modeling of Neural Systems* (Boston: MIT Press, 2001)

Fine, C., *A Mind of its Own* (New South Wales: Allen and Unwin, 2007)

Fisher, H., *Why We Love: The Brain Chemistry of Love* (New York: Henry Holt, 2004)

Fixx, J., *Games for the Super Intelligent* (London: Muller, 1972)

Gardner, H., *Changing Minds* (Boston: Harvard Business School Press, 2004)

Greenfield, S. A., *The Human Brain: A Guided Tour* (London: Weidenfeld & Nicolson, 1997)

Haigh, J., *Taking Chances: Winning with Probability* (Oxford: Oxford University Press, 1999)

Handy, C., *The Empty Raincoat: Making Sense of the Future* (London: Hutchinson Business, 2003)

Holford, P., *Optimum Nutrition for the Mind* (London: Piatkus, 2004)

Horne, T., and Doherty, A., *Managing Public Services – Implementing Changes: A Thoughtful Approach to the Practice of Management* (London: Routledge, 2003)

Horne, T., and Wootton, S., *Keep Your Brain Sharp* (London: Hodder Education, 2010)

Howard, P. J., *The Owner's Manual for the Brain: Everyday Applications from Mind and Brain Research* (3rd edn, Austin, Texas: Bard Press, 2006)

Janda, L., *The Psychologist's Book of Self-tests* (New York: Perigee, 1996)

Kandel, E., et al. (eds), *Principles of Neural Science* (4th edn, New York: McGraw Hill, 2000)

Kawashima, Dr, *Train Your Brain* (London: Penguin, 2007)

Levitan, I. B., and Kaczmarek, L. K., *The Neuron: Cell and Molecular Biology* (3rd edn, Oxford: Oxford University Press, 2001)

Middleton, J., *Upgrade Your Brain* (Oxford: Infinite Ideas, 2006)

Nicholls, J. G., et al., *From Neuron to Brain* (4th edn, New York: Sinauer Associates, 2001)

O'Keefe, J., *Mind Opening* (London: HarperCollins, 1994)

Parkinson, M., *How to Master Psychometric Tests* (London: Kogan Page, 2000)

Quartz, S. R. and Sejnowski, T. J., *Liars, Lovers and Heroes* (New York: HarperCollins, 2002)

Restak, R., *The New Brain: How the Modern Age Is Rewiring Your Mind* (New York: Rodale Press, 2003)

Rupp, R., *Committed to Memory* (London: Aurum Press Limited, 1998)

Schaie, K., *Intellectual Development in Adulthood: The Seattle Longitudinal Study* (Cambridge: Cambridge University Press, 1996)

Sternberg, R. J., *The Nature of Insight* (Boston: Massachusetts Institute of Technology, 1995)

Sternberg, R. J., *Successful Intelligence* (New York: Plume, 1997)

Swanson, L., *Brain Architecture: Understanding the Basic Plan* (Oxford: Oxford University Press, 2002)

Tharp, T., *The Creative Habit* (New York: Simon & Schuster, 2004)

Thompson, A., *Critical Reasoning* (New York: Routledge, 1999)

Tolley, H., *How to Pass Numeracy Tests* (London: Kogan Page, 2000)

Tolley, H., *How to Succeed at an Assessment Centre* (London: Kogan Page, 2001)

Tolley, H., and Thomas, K., *How to Pass Police Selection Tests* (London: Kogan Page, 2004)

Tolley, H., and Thomas, K., *How to Pass Verbal Reasoning Tests* (London: Kogan Page, 2006)

Wiseman, J., *Quirkology* (London: Macmillan, 2007)

Wootton, S., and Horne, T., *Strategic Planning* (London: Kogan Page, 2000)

Wootton, S., and Horne, T., *Strategic Thinking* (London: Kogan Page, 2003)

Index